S0-BCN-226

Letters from a "Modernist"

Letters from a "Modernist"

The Letters of George Tyrrell to Wilfrid Ward
1893–1908

Introduced and Annotated by
MARY JO WEAVER

THE PATMOS PRESS, SHEPHERDSTOWN
SHEED AND WARD, LONDON

Library of Congress Cataloging in Publication Data

Tyrrell, George, 1861–1909.
Letters from a modernist.

Bibliography: p.
Includes index.
1. Modernism—Catholic Church—History—Sources. 2. Tyrrell, George, 1861–1909. 3. Ward, Wilfrid Philip, 1856–1916. 4. Newman, John Henry, Cardinal, 1801–1890. 5. Jesuits—England—Correspondence. 6. Catholics—England—Correspondence. I. Ward, Wilfrid Philip, 1856–1916. II. Title.
BX1396.T83 1981 282'.092'2 80-28372
ISBN 0–915762–12–9

ISBN (UK) 0–7220–4917–X

Manufactured in the United States of America

For ROSEMARY SHEED *with thanks*

Contents

Acknowledgments

A BOOK like this one, which begins with a surprising discovery, is never a single-handed enterprise. Without the friendship and support of Maisie Ward in the last years of her life, I would not have had the opportunity to find this material. Without the generosity of Frank Sheed, Teresa Blundell (1891–1979, Wilfrid Ward's last surviving child), Hester and Brian Whitlock-Blundell, and Ward's grandson, the present Wilfrid Ward, I would not have been able to discover the letters or prepare this book; they were especially generous with their time and resources. Rosemary Sheed, especially, has become a good friend and was invaluable as a source of excellent ideas; it was at her suggestion that I originally went to *Crosby* where I found Tyrrell's letters packed away and forgotten.

After the elation at the discovery passes, one is faced with the challenge of making obscure references meaningful. I was helped in this work by Dorothy Coil, research librarian at the University of Notre Dame, Pat Riesenman, librarian at Indiana University, and by the librarian at the quiet Farm Street library in London; they were kind and inventive searchers without whose help I could not have untangled some of the mysteries.

From the letters and annotations one then hopes to produce a coherent interpretation of the period, to fit the information into its context so that it illuminates rather than obscures understanding. I take responsibility for any mistakes in my introduction, but must acknowledge a clear indebtedness to scholars and friends who have read the manuscript and helped me to sharpen my arguments, refine my definitions and avoid some serious problems. I offer my thanks to Ron Burke, Anne Louis-David, Nicholas Lash, Marvin O'Connell, John Root, David Schultenover and Alec Vidler; I appreciate the great care with which they read my work, corrected my mistakes and led me to see the issues in a more nuanced manner. I would also like to thank my excellent typist, Star Kelley, whose flawless work and attention to detail made everything much easier for me. I am grateful to Beulah Fanguy for helping me through some of the initial proofreading drudgery, and to Danna D'Esopo who helped me with the bibliography.

Besides the libraries at the University of Notre Dame and Farm Street (where I did most of my work), I have enjoyed using the University Library at Cambridge, the University Library at St. Andrew's (where I must thank Mr. Robert Smart for his courteous and speedy help on many occasions), the Center for Research Libraries at the University of Chicago, and the research libraries at the University of Illinois and Indiana University. I was able to go to England in the summer of 1976 because Indiana University honored me with a Grant in Aid of Research; I found the time and space to finish the preliminary annotative work in the summer of 1978 because of the support of my colleagues at Indiana University and the generosity of many friends at the University of Notre Dame; I would especially like to thank Anne Fearing for finding a spacious carrel for me in the Notre Dame library. My colleagues in the Department of Religious Studies read the Introduction in an early form at a faculty colloquium and offered encouragement as well as clear and valuable suggestions for its improvement. I was able to return to England in 1979 to finish the last bit of research because Indiana University again supported my travel and time. For all this help and to all these people (and institutions) I am and remain deeply grateful.

Finally, I am most grateful to Rosemary Sheed for giving me permission to publish this material.

List of Abbreviations

A&L Tyrrell, George and Petre, Maude. *Autobiography and Life of George Tyrrell.* 2 volumes. London: Edward Arnold, 1912.

EFI Tyrrell, George. *Essays on Faith and Immortality*, arranged by M. D. Petre. London: Edward Arnold, 1914.

FM Tyrrell, George. *The Faith of the Millions: A Selection of Past Essays.* London: Longmans, Green & Co., 1901.

LL Ward, Wilfrid. *Last Lectures.* London: Longmans, Green & Co., 1918.

MW I Ward, Maisie. *The Wilfrid Wards and the Transition.* London: Sheed & Ward, 1934.

MW II Ward, Maisie. *Insurrection versus Resurrection.* London: Sheed & Ward, 1937.

PP Ward, Wilfrid. *Problems and Persons.* London: Longmans, Green & Co., 1903.

SAUL St. Andrew's University Library (Scotland).

S&C Tyrrell, George. *Through Scylla and Charybdis; or, The Old Theology and the New.* London: Longmans, Green & Co., 1907.

SSP Balfour, Arthur, comp. *Papers Read Before the Synthetic Society, 1896–1908.* London: Privately printed, 1909.

T George Tyrrell.

W Wilfrid Ward.

WWP The Wilfrid Ward Papers at St. Andrew's University Library (Scotland).

Introduction

Wilfrid Ward (1856–1916) and George Tyrrell (1861–1910) began and ended their friendship with discussion about the ideas of John Henry Cardinal Newman (1801–90). They both changed their style over the years, Ward growing more cautious while Tyrrell grew more daring. Perceiving them in the encapsulated descriptions of historical judgment—Ward as an obscurantist, a biographer rather than a thinker, and Tyrrell as a "modernist," disillusioned and condemned by his church—it is hard to believe that they were ever friends. These letters, though they reflect only one side of a correspondence, show us how close they were for a while and why they became estranged. The demise of their relationship tells us more about the place of Newman's thought in the modernist controversy, and helps us to understand more clearly why late nineteenth century Catholic intellectuals were drawn to one another and to a common dream of a more expansive church.

I. PRINCIPALS OF THE CORRESPONDENCE

Wilfrid Philip Ward was a biographer, essayist and editor of the *Dublin Review* (1906–1916). He was a child of the Oxford Movement and, by virtue of his birth, had intimate connections with most of the traditions and personalities of that movement. His marriage to Josephine Hope, daughter of James Hope-Scott and niece of the Duke of Norfolk, bound Ward to English Catholicism in a wide variety of ways. He studied and patterned himself on Newman and thus differed significantly from his Ultramontanist father, William George Ward (1812–82). By birth and by marriage, Ward was in a position to be a liaison officer between the new Oxford converts and the old Catholic element in English life. At the same time, he felt himself able (perhaps even called) to be a bridge between the Catholic community in England and the non-Catholic but theocentric philosophers of religion who seem to have populated late Victorian drawing rooms and clubs. His participation in the Synthetic Society[1] as well as his friendships with fashionable members of English society, gave him an audience and mobility that he used to further the causes of theism in general and to promote the thought of Newman in particular.[2] His stunning literary success in 1897 with the biography of Nicholas Wiseman (1802–65, first archbishop of Westminster when, in 1850, the Roman Catholic hierarchy was restored in England), and his contacts in the publishing world assured him of a welcome from some of the most prestigious periodicals of the time.

Ward was, no doubt, moved by Newman's description of Roman Catholicism:

> One and all of us can bear witness to the fact of the utter contempt into which Catholicism had fallen by the time that we were born . . . No longer the Catholic Church in the country—nay, no longer, I may say, a Catholic community; but a few adherents of the old religion, moving silently and sorrowfully about, as memorials of what had been. "The Roman Catholics"—not a sect, not even an interest, as men conceived it; not a body however small, representative of the great communion abroad—but a mere handful of individuals, who might be counted like the pebbles and *detritus* of the great deluge, and who, forsooth, merely happened to retain a creed which, in its day, indeed, was the profession of a Church. Here a set of poor Irishmen, coming and going at harvest time, or a colony of them lodged in a miserable quarter of the vast metropolis. There perhaps, an elderly person seen walking through the streets, grave and solitary, and strange, though noble in bearing and said to be of good family and a "Roman Catholic." An old fashioned house of gloomy appearance, closed in with high walls, with an iron gate and yews and the report attaching to it that "Roman Catholics" lived there, but who they were or what they did or what was meant by calling them Roman Catholics, no one could tell—though it had an unpleasant sound, and told of form and superstition . . . Such were Catholics in England, found in corners and alleys, and cellars, and the housetops, or in the recesses of the country; shut off from the populous world around them, and dimly seen as if through a mist, or in a twilight, as ghosts flitting to and fro, by the high Protestant lords of the earth. At length so feeble did they become,

> so utterly contemptible, that contempt gave birth to pity, and the more generous of their tyrants actually began to wish to bestow upon them some favour, under the notion that their opinions were simply too absurd ever to spread again, and that they themselves were they but raised in civil importance, would soon unlearn and be ashamed of them.[3]

Accordingly, he was determined to see that Catholics begin to take a prominent place in English life. The Synthetic Society, whose membership represented "the best in religious and philosophical thought in Edwardian England,"[4] had many Roman Catholic members. Ward was the real founder and promoter of the Synthetic and understood the Society's combined efforts to find "a working philosophy of religious belief" as one way to draw Catholics into an important segment of English life.

Ward was a Victorian intellectual in an age where that kind of intellectuality was being challenged by a new, critical manner. His predilection and training disposed him to preserve and pass on traditional values, not to attempt their replacement with the hasty conclusions of a new method. His devotion to the thought of Newman did not prepare him to support the historical-critical methods of some of the religious thinkers of his time, nor did it suggest to him that he had no place in the regions of the theological expert. Like Newman, Ward's support of free intellectual inquiry was carefully limited by the boundaries of a divinely-established teaching authority. Ward's understanding of Newman and of the infallibility of the Roman Catholic church constrained him, finally, to avoid the paths and conclusions followed by some of his friends.

Still, since many of the Roman Catholics who were most willing and able to enter into the mainstream of a general religious discussion tended to be interested in new, critical methods of approaching texts of Scripture and tradition, Ward tended to join their interest in those issues. Anchoring his thought in Newman, he wrote sympathetic, encouraging articles about men whose work and scholarly desires eventually led them to conclusions Ward could not accept.[5]

As a young man Ward was a budding philosopher of religion. His early essays show a lively mind and an ability to enter sympathetically into the positions of his opponents.[6] His first major writing project—the biography of William George Ward[7]—was motivated by a genuine appreciation of his father as a conspicuously intellectual Roman Catholic. Increasingly, however, he was drawn to the thought and style of Newman; with Newman as a guide, he hoped to enter creatively into the religious dialogues of the late nineteenth century. With the publication of "New Wine in Old Bottles"[8] he moved away from philosophy of religion and into the arena of Catholic apologetics. Ward spent twenty years as an apologist for Catholicism, the first decade moving to the left and the last ten years in retreat back to a more conservative position. It was during his first ten years that he and Tyrrell were friends; they parted company when Tyrrell continued to move in a "liberal" direction and Ward could go no further. The last years of Ward's life were devoted to his impressive biography of Newman and to other modes of Newman scholarship. What would have happened had Ward lived longer no one can guess, but his Lowell Lectures delivered at Harvard in 1914 and the Lectures given at the Royal Institution in London in 1915, augured well for a bright future as a mature Newman scholar.[9]

Ward was, in some ways, hopelessly sanguine about the church and its official policies. In the epilogue to his biography of Wiseman, Ward used Wiseman's name to cover an exposition of his own view. The epilogue was entitled, "The Exclusive Church and the *Zeitgeist*" and aimed to defend official church policies *vis-à-vis* innovators: "if Biblical criticism at a given time tends to destroy the faith of numbers, the exclusive church may, then, in the interests of the many, be hard on Biblical critics."[10] For Ward, faith—both as doctrine and as the posture of an individual believer—was more important than the results of biblical research. For Tyrrell, on the other hand, faith was more important than the misuse of ecclesiastical authority. Both cared to preserve faith and strengthen religious understanding, but they disagreed about the source of the danger. In the *Wiseman* epilogue Ward proposed Newman's thought as a perfect *via media* balancing the tension between old ecclesiastics (guarding ancient truths) and young scholars (discovering new ones), and he concluded by harking back to Roger Bacon's medieval fantasy about a golden age of religion where a wise and holy pope ruled a gratefully obedient people. Ward wondered if it were not now time to renew medieval dreams?

Both Ward and Tyrrell agreed that Catholic devotional life was important, but they understood its place in the church differently. Tyrrell was willing to accept devotional life of believers as an important datum of theology, while Ward thought the gentle spirit of Catholic devotion needed to be guarded by the spiked palisades of anathema and definition, a protective strategy basic to his position as an apologist. The differences between Ward and Tyrrell were not always so obvious; they corresponded from 1893 to 1907, and were in agreement as to aims and strategies from 1893 to 1901.

No letters *from* Ward survive; Tyrrell destroyed most letters written to him. One can get a sense of Ward's personality and his aims by consulting some of his works in conjunction with Tyrrell's letters to him. It was sad but inevitable that they had to part company. By 1905 neither was really able to understand the other and in the next few years the situation in the church so distorted everyone's perspective that old friendships could end quickly and with bitterness. Ward deserves a study of his own to show where the enthusiastic hopes of an 1890's intellectual Catholic went besides down the road of modernism. Tyrrell has attracted and will probably continue to attract more attention. When that attention is given, however, it should be broad enough to include this interlude with Ward as a contributing factor in our efforts to understand late nineteenth century English Catholicism as containing more stories than "modernism."

George Tyrrell was a Jesuit priest, essayist and reviewer for the Jesuit periodical the *Month*, who was condemned as a "modernist" and excommunicated from the Roman Catholic church. He was a convert to Roman Catholicism (1879), five years younger than Ward, and perhaps the most able theologian of the period among Roman Catholics in England. How and why he moved from an adherence to Thomistic philosophy to some of the modernist positions of his later life has been explained in various ways. Maude Petre (1863–1942) argued strongly that Friedrich von Hügel (1852–1925) led Tyrrell astray and that the Jesuits did not understand him.[11] Maisie Ward was relieved to be able to explain some of Tyrrell's opinions and behavior as the result of Bright's disease.[12] Explanations of this kind do not explain so much as they hide, and while they may be helpful as clues, we ought to search Tyrrell himself for an understanding of his development. It is perfectly reasonable to assume that he had a vision of the church which was so clear and strong that he could not deny or forget it. By temperament, Tyrrell was disposed to attack where Ward was wont to retreat and this difference eventually led to the severance of their friendship. It should be remembered, however, that when they became friends in 1893, both dreamed of and worked for a way to move the Catholic church into the twentieth century, and both believed that caution and patience were the order of the day. Tyrrell and Ward knew that in order to move the church forward a new theological method would be required; both believed that Newman was the vessel into which the best of the Catholic tradition could be transferred to the new, demanding situation of the modern period.

Tyrrell's friendship with von Hügel introduced him to the problems and demands of biblical criticism, problems about which Newman was not particularly helpful. Ward, too, was a friend of von Hügel, the recipient of more than 200 of the baron's letters and also introduced by him to some of the urgencies of the biblical situation. Why Tyrrell was moved to take up the cause of criticism and Ward was not is explainable partly in terms of temperament. Ward was cautious, even stodgy in his approach. He was so convinced a Newmanian that what he could not find in Newman did not much interest him; his desire was to be both a faithful disciple of Newman and the guide of the new age. Tyrrell was more eager than Ward to effect change; he was not cautious at all, but often polemical in his thought and writing. If Ward saw what ought to be done and immediately saw why one ought to *wait*, to take a lesson from the slow movements of church history, Tyrrell sensed the urgency of a situation and the obligations one had to make some things happen.

Tyrrell's pastoral inclinations and hopes led him to search for newer methods of religious discourse and more flexible models of religious authority. Disappointed with the Thomistic revival he had at first embraced enthusiastically, he turned to Newman to seek a path to a more attractively modern church. He was comfortable for a time with Ward's brand of Newmanism, but ultimately rejected Newman in favor of new critical methods. He adopted these things with characteristic vigor but often without much discipline. There has been some speculation about what precipitated such a radical shift in attitude—the nefarious influence of von Hügel, the unstable character of Tyrrell himself, the burden of censorship under which he had to labor and which drove him to extremes in an effort to present his views—a change Ward attributed to condemnation of "liberal Catholicism" in the Joint Pastoral Letter (1900).[13] That document set the stage for reactions from both men which were and would remain typical.[14]

Tyrrell hoped for a church polity which was more attuned to the needs and desires of the people; he was interested, finally, in religious synthesis and cooperation. Ward, on the other hand, understood that people's religious spirit ought to be restrained as well as enhanced, that complete freedom (for synthesis, decision, discussion or anything else) was as dangerous as complete repression. On some levels their differences parallel the differences between democracy and oligarchy. Interestingly, both men claimed Newman as godfather. Ward's understanding of Newman may have been too narrow; his identification with him, which served him well as a biographer, tended to make him defensive and led him to the conclusion that there was only one way to interpret Newman. Tyrrell, on the other hand, who had not read widely in Newman, parted company with his ideas at the end of the nineteenth century; he was later led, by friendship or by fatigue, to accept and extol Henri Bremond's interpretation of Newman, which is a travesty.[15]

Ward surely understood Newman better than Tyrrell did, but leaving that issue aside and looking instead at the religious situation as it appeared to each man we find the real differences between them. Ward saw a situation in which Catholicism was finally emerging from "the corners, alleys and cellars" and, more importantly, in a position to abandon the defensiveness left over from the counter-Reformation. Ward's aim, therefore, was to use Newman's ideas to break down the siege mentality but at the same time to call men of good will together in order to combat the modern dangers to theism as presented by modern science and a new critical intellectuality. He was a conservative intellectual who understood the situations of government and church to be God-given and to be tampered with lightly (if at all). He suggested changes in outlook in order to preserve the old traditions and to make them stronger, and took this task upon himself as an *expert*, one of the few qualified men who could speak to the situation. Tyrrell saw the same situation as one which required a new religious synthesis, one in which a more religiously and politically open policy was required, lest the whole church collapse or, worse, be completely destroyed from the inside by authoritarian extremists. His early aim was to use Newman's theory of the development of doctrine and his ideas about consulting the faithful about matters of doctrine to encourage a more inclusive, democratic and more Scriptural ecclesiology. For Tyrrell, the present positions of the church, especially in some of its official pronouncements demanded action of a combative kind. He promoted change to expose and destroy what he understood to be heretical overextensions of church authority issuing from Rome itself.

The letters from Tyrrell speak for themselves. He is witty and perceptive and one can see how his mind and heart operate in an increasingly volatile situation. Tyrrell's development of radical postures is not as interesting as the fact that there was a relationship between him and Ward at all. So long as one considers this in the light of the modernist controversy only, it is incongruous and an aberration. When we set it in the context of "liberal Catholicism" in the 1890's where we can see some of the temptations and directions involved in that enterprise, the friendship makes more sense. One does not need to take sides in any case; Ward is no better or worse for not having been condemned and Tyrrell is no more heroic for marching resolutely to his own internal drummer. Both found themselves in the same situation at the same time, inspired by the same mentor. The interlude of commonality says something about liberal Catholicism and its relation both to the modernist controversy and to the work of John Henry Newman.

II. LIBERAL CATHOLICISM AND THE MODERNIST CONTROVERSY

Scholarly interest in the figures and issues of the modernist controversy, which can be located historically between *Providentissimus Deus* (1893) and *Pascendi* (1907),[16] has obscured the larger context of nineteenth century religious thought. One important part of late nineteenth century Roman Catholic thought was "liberal Catholicism;" but how does that differ from "modernism?" Part of the confusion stems from the use of undefined terms: Meriol Trevor says, "the link between liberal Catholics of the nineteenth century and the general attitude which emerged at the recent council [Vatican II] is clear enough,"[17] and Lawrence Barmann insists that "the modernist crisis in England, as mostly elsewhere too, did not grow out of earlier nineteenth century liberalism."[18] Whatever the merits of their arguments, the reader is left somewhat mystified because neither of them defines liberalism and liberal Catholics. So, too, with the modernist controversy: Thomas Michael Loome called it "a resounding catastrophe for all concerned,"[19] while Nicholas Lash argued that it was "the painful and often tragic beginning of a significant success."[20] Does their argument proceed from commonly understood definitions of the modernist controversy?

Loome's distinctions as to the meanings of modernism are not altogether helpful. He argues that there are four meanings of the word "modernism": one is the "system" condemned by *Pascendi*, a second is the teaching of any condemned modernist writer, a third is the frame of mind or attitude manifest in those writers condemned as modernists, i.e., ("a determination to promote such an intellectual renewal of Catholicism as would equip it for the task of confronting the twentieth century world with a genuine understanding of its needs and problems,") and the fourth is the attempt to come to terms with historical criticism.[21] The first two meanings clearly relate to the ideas and persons condemned by the encyclical. Those meanings raise some problems—who was really condemned? whose ideas were condemned? etc.—but are fairly straightforward as they stand. The last two meanings lead to some confusion because the third meaning also describes the work and aspirations of religious thinkers who were not "modernists" in any other sense of the term. The fourth meaning may come closest to describing what many of the condemned modernists thought they were doing. I would suggest, therefore, that we take the third meaning—the sweeping one which describes a general attitude—to describe liberal Catholicism, and distinguish that from modernism with the fourth meaning. All the thinkers in category four will also be described by category three, but many of those included under the third distinction will not be described by the fourth. We may, therefore, have an initial way to suggest that liberal Catholicism was the larger context of some religious thought in the late nineteenth century while modernism was a specific episode within that context.

One is still left with complex problems of definition. What is meant by "liberal Catholicism"? Liberalism is a tortured word with unclear definitional limits: it has theological roots in the work of Johann Semler (1725–91), a Lutheran theologian and early biblical critic, but that has no apparent connection either to the socio-political liberalism emergent in Spain and France during the nineteenth century, nor to the Catholic brand of liberalism—partly political, partly religious—condemned by Pope Pius IX in the *Syllabus of Errors* (1864). The liberalism which touches upon both the modernist controversy and late nineteenth century liberal Catholicism is related to German Protestant liberalism, which began with Friedrich Schleiermacher (1768–1834) and reached many English Catholic scholars in the work of Adolf von Harnack (1851–1930). That kind of liberalism was both attitudinal (a readiness to welcome new ideas) and specifically theological (anti-dogmatic and informed by a critical approach to Scriptural texts). As such it was attractive to those who favored progress and to those in search of a new, critical theological method.

Late nineteenth century liberal Catholicism was also influenced by earlier Catholic liberals whose works encompassed religious, philosophical and religious issues. No absolutely clear principle links them together: Johann Adam Möhler (1796–1836) confined himself to serious theological issues; Charles Réne Montalembert (1810–70), and Henri Lacordaire (1802–61) are linked to the political liberalism of Félicité de Lamennais (1782–1845) which was condemned by Pope Gregory XVI in *Mirari Vos* (1832), yet they are also remembered for their support of papal (versus state) government of the church; Ignaz von Döllinger (1799–1890) and John Acton (1834–1902), both historians, were united in their opposition to the declaration of papal infallibility; John Henry Newman, leader of the Oxford movement, was associated with political liberals like Acton, and was involved in liberal projects which attempted to stimulate ecclesiastical reform, but did not consider himself to be a liberal.[22] At least one scholar has suggested that liberal Catholicism was something rooted most clearly in the Enlightenment, which flourished in Germany in the 1830's where it attracted papal opprobrium and was effectively destroyed by authoritarian ecclesiastical officials within ten years.[23]

Whether late nineteenth century liberal Catholics can be linked to earlier historical movements is not clear and will not be until scholars establish specific links between individuals or ideas. Nor is it certain that late nineteenth century liberal Catholicism can be adequately described in relation to its opponents; most liberal Catholics found scholasticism to be an inadequate theological method for the problems of their day, and most of them were opposed to what they took to be excessive uses of ecclesiastical authority, but there were some differences among them on these issues. One relationship in which some of these differences emerge is the one between Tyrrell and Ward, and we can learn something about both liberal Catholicism and the modernist controversy by examining their friendship.

Tyrrell and Ward first exchanged letters in 1893; Ward's appreciation of Tyrrell's review of the William George Ward biography received a warm response. Apparently, they did not meet and did not write to each other again until 1898 when Tyrrell was preparing a review of Ward's biography of Cardinal Wiseman. Their friendship began at that time, nurtured by a mutual appreciation of Newman, participation together in the Synthetic Society, and the common cause of a new Catholic apologetics. The letters from Tyrrell show that he and Ward both worked for an end to the siege mentality of the counter-Reformation and hoped the Roman Catholic church would learn to invite rather than compel attention and devotion. Both were drawn to the power of the devotional life of the church, and were at pains to defend the faithful from some of the intemperate statements of more radical liberal Catholics. For a while, at least, they were united in the project of "mediating liberalism."[24]

It is true, as a colleague wrote after Ward's death, that to call Ward "liberal" was ludicrous:

> He could hardly have been a liberal in thought—any more than he could have been a democrat in politics. By temperament he was essentially conservative: it required the full weight of his intellectual ability to make him an open-minded conserv-

ative, that is to say, a conservative who believes the world has a future as well as a past.[25]

And it is true, as Petre argued, that Tyrrell passed beyond a stage of mediating liberalism and left Ward behind.[26] Maisie Ward goes out of her way to say that her father and Tyrrell were never close.[27] Still, these letters show that there was a strong and mutually supportive relationship for a time, a relationship which was nurtured by a common purpose and style. Both men changed and the relationship dissolved, but it may be time to recall it and to see what, if anything, it can tell us about the relationship between liberal Catholicism and modernism.

In 1902 Ward wrote an article contrasting Newman and Ernest Renan (1823–92), and asked: "Whence the difference between the two men? Why did they come to opposite conclusions in respect of Catholic dogma, when their general philosophy of knowledge had so much in common?"[28] The difference, Ward believed, lay in the fact that Newman was a Christian and Renan, finally, was not; in terms of intellectual style, Newman had humility and patience and Renan did not. The difference in style—patience versus anxiety for change—gives us another way to contrast Ward and Tyrrell and makes one wonder if "modernists" were liberal Catholics with "impatient" temperaments?[29] If, in the closing years of the nineteenth century Tyrrell was more sanguine about the possibility of moderation and more apt to support the cautious approach Ward extolled, so was Ward more enthusiastic about the work of many who would later be condemned as modernists. The writings of radicals and the reactions of church authorities tended to make Ward a little more cautious and Tyrrell a little more daring. The letters show the changes in Tyrrell's position and point to the discomfort Ward experienced in his association with liberalism.

Ward's liberalism was always cautious, a renewal of theological arguments in the light of current historical and scientific knowledge. For him, any process of updating had to be carried out in an atmosphere of sure authority, a place where individuals could be protected from hasty and potentially harmful conclusions. His interest in a new apologetic was motivated by his desire to find a compromise between the rigid authoritarianism of earlier Roman Catholicism and the individualism of Protestantism. Still, Ward was a son of the triumphal Catholicism of an earlier generation—he gloried in the Roman Catholic church and its infallible authority—he pointed out that both William George Ward and John Henry Newman had seen the need for an authoritative church and an infallible religious authority. Ward argued that religion needs authority because the deep truths of dogma are sometimes beyond mere reason. Because of his own temperament and acceptance of ecclesiastical authority, Ward did not grasp the difference between the impatience associated with youthful ignorance (which often leads to harmful conclusions) and the impolite questions of a mature and disillusioned thinker. For him, the degree of honesty and public candor about issues was determined by political considerations, i.e., what people were ready for. In that frame of reference, the institutional church, hierarchy, tradition and authority had to be respected and submitted to to prevent dismemberments from the body of Christ.

Tyrrell's liberalism led him, finally, to "modernism" and excommunication from the Roman Catholic church. He was one with Ward in eschewing the work of some radical Catholics he thought were doing more harm than good, and he, too, hoped to protect the faithful and coax the church into less rigid postures. Unlike Ward, however, he never showed a triumphal side; his vision of the church, from very early in his life, was more democratic and flexible. He could also distinguish between naive impatience and studied protest and marshalled his energies to protest what he considered to be heretical excesses in the use of ecclesiastical authority. Ward's criteria leads one to interpret rebellion as impatience coupled with a lack of humility; but, from Tyrrell's perspective, one could say that patience has its limits and that there comes a time for action. The letters show Tyrrell explaining his protests to Ward and finally trying to tease some of Ward's positions out into a more critical atmosphere.

Their real bone of contention, however, lay not so much in different understandings of liberal Catholicism, but in their divergent views on the role and function of Newman's thought within the work of liberal Catholics.

III. NEWMAN AND THE MODERNIST CONTROVERSY

The permanent rupture between Tyrrell and Ward occurred in 1904, in the context of Tyrrell's review of Ward's *Problems and*

Persons (London, 1903). The letters show the significant shift in Tyrrell's understanding of Newman as early as 1899, and suggest some exasperation with Ward's continued hope to use Newman's ideas to promote a progressive apologetic. Ward used a phrase associated with Newman—*via media*[30]—to argue for moderation; he hoped to find a *via media* between the obscurantism of the right and the foolhardiness of the left. Many of Ward's friends had pushed beyond the search for a moderate apologetic and were pursuing the path of critical methodology in religion, a path Ward was little prepared to take. Ward was at home with the aims of liberal Catholics and some modernists to a degree: they all hoped for a more modern Catholicism and understood the inadequacy of the scholastic method as a vehicle for change. Many of them began to forge a new theological method with Newman but went on from there into a more critical methodology; Ward stayed with Newman throughout, convinced that his thought and style was the best approach to the problems of the time. Ward did not understand the urgency of critical methodology as applied to the Bible because Newman did not prepare him to accept anything but a relatively simple view of the authenticity of the Gospels. Newman was dead before the wave of criticism affecting the New Testament was felt in England and was therefore not concerned with some of the issues which were the most burning ones for the modernists. Finally, therefore, Ward was not sympathetic to (or internally aware of) some of the deeper problems of the modernists, nor was he able to understand Newman as inadequate for the tasks at hand.

A more serious argument between Tyrrell and Ward about Newman occurred when *Pascendi* was issued (8 September 1907). Was Newman condemned by the encyclical? The question continues to be important in the face of the claim that Newman was the real inspiration behind the second Vatican council.[31] As Newman's biographer, Ward ignored or refused to mention some of the direct connections between Newman and the modernists, connections he himself helped to clarify in some of his own articles. One obvious connection is with Loisy who published a series of articles under the pseudonym, A. Firmin, in the *Revue du clergé français*. The articles are sketches of the material he eventually reshaped for *L'Évangile et l'Église*,[32] and the first of them had been praised by Ward in an article at the turn of the century.[33]

Ward and Tyrrell differed sharply over the question of Newman's connection with the condemned modernists. In reality, however, they may not have been as far apart as it appears. Ward was clearly troubled by a letter to the editor of *The Times* exonerating Newman;[34] he himself kept Newman's connections with the modernists out of his biography.[35] It is not at all clear, however, that he really believed Newman escaped condemnation. The difference between Tyrrell and Ward on this issue was more one of strategy than of belief—Tyrrell acted quickly and wrote in *The Times* that Newman had certainly been condemned; Ward brooded for a long time before writing anything on *Pascendi* and then adopted a strategy of diverting attention away from Newman to the positions of the modernists themselves.[36]

Tyrrell's position on the matter is clear enough from his public utterances; Ward's has been slightly obscured by his biographers. There is no evidence that the writings of Ward's wife and daughter[37] are deceptive in any way; but neither of them was willing to expose Ward's belief that Newman had been condemned by *Pascendi.* When William J. Williams (1858–1930) wrote to the editor of *The Times* to argue that Newman had been condemned and all his propositions repudiated,[38] Ward was distressed because Williams put the matter into print where it was bound to do damage.[39] On the same day, Ward wrote to his friend and his wife's uncle, the Duke of Norfolk, and said:

> Williams is a friend of mine . . . he is, I suppose, except myself, the Catholic who knows Newman's writings the best. [His] letter is likely to bring to a head what I still think is a most grave crisis. Please look at my letter to you of October 10th and you will see this is no new impression, and please observe what I there said as to the disingenuous quibbling likely to come in the attempt to prove that the Encyclical did not hit Newman. I believe such an attempt may be made seriously by some, *because they do not really know Newman's writings and thought* thoroughly and believe on the face of it that Rome cannot have condemned him.[40]

Ward's only public utterance on the Encyclical, his article in the *Dublin Review,* proceeded from a strategy he began to unfold almost immediately after the Encyclical was published. He thought it useless to try to extricate the Pope from the position or to try to prove that his words did not condemn Newman; the best tactic, he believed, was to argue that the doctrines specified in the Encyclical were condemned only in the sense in which they were to be found in writings of the modernists. He held to the duty of obedience, as his biographers tell us, but it is not clear that he did so with an untroubled conscience.[41]

In a long letter to Norfolk, dated 10 October 1907, Ward put his position clearly and outlined the strategy he later employed in his article about the Encyclical. What he says about Newman's condemnation is clear:

> I don't believe the Pope *meant* to condemn Newman. But he has done so beyond all doubt so far as the words of the Encyclical go—not only on development but on much else. Here is the nemesis Newman foresaw arising from Popes trying to give the Church *intellectual* instructions by Encyclicals—which has never been done before Pius IX's time. It is a piece of "modernism," . . . Its theology is drawn up not by a keen mind alive to the religious controversies of the age (or even to the *established facts* of history), but by a scholastic theologian who may either be an anti-Newmanist, as they often are, or does not know Newman's work and condemned the modernists on certain points in terms which beyond question equally condemn Newman's theories. The situation is, I cannot but think, most serious.[42]

How *much* connection there was between Newman and the modernists, I am not prepared to say. Some of those condemned were hiding behind Newman, but some of the more serious modernists had been nurtured and inspired by Newman. Ward surely thought Loisy's article in *Revue du clergé français* was "remarkable," and praised Loisy as an interpreter of Newman in a review of William's book, *Newman, Pascal, Loisy and the Catholic Church.*[43]

When Tyrrell was almost sure he could not contine to base his thinking on Newman he turned from the *Essay* on the development of doctrine to Newman's sermon on the same topic.[44] From the letters it appears as if Tyrrell had to justify this shift in his interest, yet Ward himself had adopted a similar position.[45] Finally, however, Newman constituted a serious flirtation for Tyrrell and a lifelong devotion for Ward. The letters show the development of Tyrrell's thought, especially in regards to Newman and his theory of development. Read in conjunction with Ward's work on Newman—originally supportive of the work of liberal Catholics and their aims and finally used to vilify some of them[46]—they deepen our understanding of Newman's relationship to some of the figures of the modernist controversy.

IV. THE LETTERS AND DOCUMENTS

This collection contains sixty-eight letters from Tyrrell to Ward. On the basis of the Wilfrid Ward Papers (when they were still in London), scholars have for some time believed that there were five letters from Tyrrell to Ward extant. Clearly, from references in Maisie Ward's biography and from long quotations in Maude Petre's biography of Tyrrell, there once had been others, but they were assumed missing or destroyed. A few letters were copied by Ward and sent to Lord Halifax (1839–1934), but they attracted little attention. No one had any reason to believe that Ward and Tyrrell had been friends or that the correspondence between them still survived. I found them quite by accident on a trip to *Crosby Hall* near Liverpool, the home of a granddaughter of Wilfrid Ward's. It is impossible to say for sure what happened, but I conjecture that Maisie Ward took these letters and some others (probably the letters from von Hügel) to *Crosby* during the war for safekeeping, and left the bulk of the papers in two old trunks in a basement in London. Michael de la Bedoyère used the von Hügel letters in the early 1950's for his biography of the baron,[47] which would account for the return of those letters to the general bulk of the papers. When Loome looked through the papers while writing his dissertation,[48] therefore, everything was there but the Tyrrell letters and manuscript. It seems odd to think that Maisie Ward *forgot* about the Tyrrell papers, but not altogether unlikely. She told me in 1972 that she found it "peculiar" that Jesuits were beginning to get interested in Tyrrell "after the way they treated him while he was alive," but never mentioned the papers. They are published here along with an unpublished manuscript and some other letters, not addressed to Ward. I have published all original letters *from* Tyrrell now in the Ward Family Papers at St. Andrew's. In the case of the other letters, the ones to Mrs. Ward show us something of his relationship to her. One to Charles Devas explains Tyrrell's strategy in his review of *Problems and Persons*, and the ones to Mrs. Bellamy-Storer show us a little of his mind during his dismissal from the Jesuits and eventual excommunication.

In transcribing these letters for publication, I have regularized Tyrrell's spelling, punctuation and dating system. I have written out all numbers and months, supplied proper names when he simply uses initials, italicized titles of books and names of periodicals, and written out those abbreviations—common and uncommon—that appear throughout Victorian letters. In the letters now published one finds: and for &, archbishop for archbp., Christ for Xt., could for cd., development for devel., extreme for e., Father for F. or Fr., His Eminence for H.E., Jesuit for S.J., Liberal for Lib., *Month* for M., *Monthly Register* for M.R., *Weekly Register* for W.R., New Year for NY., part for p., post card for p.c., namely for sc., Saint for S., Synthetic Society for Syn., or SS., should for shd., theology for theol., though for tho., volumes for vols., versus for v., would for wd., etc. Since some of this material has been published before, I have used brackets to indicate where it has appeared. Double brackets have been used for editorial purposes in the correspondence. In the few places where there was not a complete date, I have placed the letters through internal evidence.

Since the Joint Pastoral Letter was such an important turning point document for Tyrrell, it has been reproduced here in full. Published here for the first time is Tyrrell's manuscript, "Who Are the Reactionaries?". Why Tyrrell sent this particular manuscript to Ward, I do not know, nor can I guess why Ward kept it. He shared the manuscript with von Hügel,[49] but apparently did not return it to Tyrrell. It was with the bulk of the Tyrrell letters at *Crosby Hall.* So far as I can determine, it is not only *unpublished*, it is virtually *unknown*. The notes are as complete as possible. Occasionally I could not locate something, but not often. It is hoped that the letters, annotations, and supporting documents present another facet of Tyrrell and also spurs some interest in his one-time friend, Wilfrid Ward.

Notes to Introduction

1. See *MW* I.344–79, 417–20. For an analysis of *T*'s participation in the Synthetic Society and more about its inner workings and *W*'s role see John D. Root,

"George Tyrrell and the Synthetic Society," *Downside Review* 98 (January 1980): 42–59.

2. Ward is best remembered in some circles for his biography of Newman. His devotion to and identification with Newman and the problems involved in being allowed to write the biography tell us a good deal about *W*'s understanding of Newman. That complex story has been interpreted in an excellent article: Sheridan Gilley, "Wilfrid Ward and his Life of Newman," *Journal of Ecclesiastical History* 29 (April 1978): 177–93.

3. Newman described the isolated enclave of Roman Catholics in the early part of the nineteenth century in his sermon, "The Second Spring" preached 13 July 1852 at the First Provincial Synod of Westminster. The text can be found in *Sermons Preached on Various Occasions* (London, 1881), pp. 163–82; quotation from pp. 171–3.

4. Root, p. 43.

5. One of *W*'s more daring articles was "The Ethics of Religious Conformity," *Quarterly Review* 189 (January 1899): 103–36, an article printed anonymously and never anthologized (as most of *W*'s other work was). In it, he talked about the *evolution* of doctrine and was enthusiastic in his praise for Auguste Sabatier (1839–1901), a French Protestant theologian who applied the methods of historical criticism to the New Testament and influenced many Catholic thinkers later condemned as modernists. In his "Unchanging Dogmas and Changeful Man," *Fortnightly Review* 67 (April, 1900):628–48, he analyzed the problem of change and continuity in the church in ways that went beyond Newman. And in "Newman and Sabatier," *Fortnightly Review* 69 (May, 1901):808–22, he compared Newman to Sabatier in glowing terms. In "Liberalism and Intransigence," *Nineteenth Century* 47 (June, 1900):960–73 he made a case for the place of the *expert* in religious dialogue, and he linked Newman's thinking with the work of Sabatier, Harnack and Blondel; and praised the work of *T*, Henri Bremond and Loisy (though he did not mention Loisy by name). Ultimately, *W* found himself at odds with all these people and was at pains to differentiate Newman's thought from theirs.

6. See for example *The Wish to Believe* (London, 1885) and *The Clothes of Religion: A Reply to Popular Positivism in Two Essays and a Postscript* (London, 1886).

7. *William George Ward and the Oxford Movement* (London, 1889) and *William George Ward and the Catholic Revival* (London, 1893).

8. *Nineteenth Century* 27 (June, 1890):942–56; reprinted in *Witnesses to the Unseen* (London, 1893), pp. 68–97.

9. Published in *LL*, pp. 1–149, the Lowell Lectures, "The Genius of Cardinal Newman" and pp. 150–230, "The Methods of Depicting Character in Fiction and Biography." His two-volume *Life of John Henry Cardinal Newman* (London, 1912) must also be mentioned as a *tour de force* of his Newman scholarship.

10. *The Life and Times of Cardinal Wiseman*, 2 volumes, (London, 1897) p. 551. *W* admitted to his son, Leo, that the epilogue had nothing to do with Wiseman at all, that the Cardinal would not even understand most of the ideas put forth there and that the using of his name was "mere Jesuitry;" cf copy of letter (undated, but c. 1915) in *WWP, SAUL.*

11. *A&L*; also *My Way of Faith* (London, 1937), and *Von Hügel and Tyrrell, the Story of a Friendship* (London, 1937).

12. *MW* II, p. 189.

13. The Cardinal Archbishop and the Bishops of the Province of Westminster, "The Church and Liberal Catholicism: A Joint Pastoral Letter," published in the *Tablet* 62 (5, 12 January 1901):8–12, 50–2. *W*'s opinion about the effect of the Joint on Tyrrell can be found in *MW* II, p. 134. The document is published as Appendix B in this volume.

14. See my "George Tyrrell and the Joint Pastoral Letter," forthcoming in the *Downside Review* 99 (January 1981).

15. *The Mystery of Newman* (London, 1907); see Gilley, pp. 177–8.

16. The first, an encyclical by Leo XIII opened Biblical studies to Catholic scholars (albeit very cautiously) the second, an encyclical by Pius X condemned modernism as the "synthesis of all heresies."

17. "Who Were the Modernists," *New Blackfrairs* 49 (August 1968):600–8.

18. Lawrence Barmann, *Baron Friedrich von Hügel and the Modernist Crisis in England* (Cambridge, 1972), p. xi.

19. "The Enigma of Baron Friedrich von Hügel—as a Modernist," *Downside Review* 91 (January, April, June 1973):13–34, 123–40, 204–30; quotation from p. 210.

20. "Modernism, Aggiornamento and the Night Battle" in Adrian Hastings (editor), *Bishops and Writers. Aspects of the Evolution of Modern Catholicism* (London, 1977), pp. 51–79.

21. "The Meaning of Modernism," *Tablet* 255 (1971):544–7.

22. See his letter to Richard Clarke, 20 December 1868: "I am struck from your letter with the difference of senses in which the word 'Liberalism' is used. You consider it designates a course of action, I a set of principles. You would call Gladstone a liberal, I an anti-liberal. You might call me a liberal, because I do not deny that under existing circumstance the abolition of tests is the advisable course; I should call myself an anti-liberal, because in harmony with the Pope's syllabus, I should say that the best thing of all is to have Unity of religion in a country and that so *real* that its Ascendancy is but the expression of the universal mind." *Letters and Diaries* (Oxford, 1973), xxiv, pp. 191–2.

23. Leonard Swidler, "Liberal Catholicism—A Lesson from the Past," in *Cross Currents* 21 (Winter 1971):25–37.

24. The term is suggested by Maude Petre, *A&L* II, pp. 98–112.

25. Father Cuthbert, "Apologist of the Catholic Church," *Dublin Review* 159 (October 1916):1–22, quotation from p. 1.

26. *A&L* II. chapter 4, "Mediating Liberalism" and chapter 9, "Break with Newmanism."

27. *MW* II, p. 165.

28. "Newman and Renan," *Monthly Register* 1 (April 1902):10–4; reprinted in *PP*, pp. 283–300.

29. See my "Wilfrid Ward, George Tyrrell and the Meanings of Modernism, *Downside Review* 96 (January 1978):21–34.

30. *Via media* is a term associated with Newman which originally appeared in Tracts 38 and 40 of *Tracts of the Times* (1834). Newman used it to argue that the genius of the Anglican church was in its *via media* between Protestantism and Romanism. In Tract 41, Newman dismissed the theory as a "paper theory" because, as he saw it, the Church of England refused to accept (in practice) the Tractarian challenge to reformation.

It is not clear what *W* means by continually referring to religious moderation as a *via media*. It could be urged that Newman never considered himself to be a "moderate," and that *W*, in pressing forward his own moderate views as a *via media*, misreads part of Newman's intention. An interesting corollary to this view would be the suggestion that *T*, in pressing premises to their logical (if sometimes difficult) conclusions, was more faithful to the spirit of Newman; which, of course, is what *T* argued all along.

31. Edward Kelly, "Newman, Wilfrid Ward and the Modernist Crisis," *Thought* 48 (Winter 1973):509–19 argues that Newman was one of the heroes of Vatican II and that his theory of doctrinal development was invoked there, but that very little had been done to relate this theory to the work of the modernists.

32. The articles appeared in the following volumes: 1) 17 (1898):5–20; 2) 17 (1899):202–14; 3) 18 (1899):193–209; 4) 21 (1900):250–71; 5) 22 (1900):126–53; 6) 24 (1900):337–63. *L'Évangile et l'Église* was published in 1902.

33. "Liberalism and Intransigence," *Nineteenth Century* 47 (June 1900):960–73. Written to claim that liberalism meant freedom of thought for *experts only*, *W* commended the work of Harnack and Sabatier as being in line with some of the best of Newman's thought, and mentioned the work of *T* and the article in the *Revue du clergé français* as written by one who has inherited the spirit of Newman's philosophy.

34. Letters to the editor of *The Times* in October and November, 1907, argued vociferously about whether or not Newman had been condemned as a heretic. *W* hoped for some authoritative word to the contrary and on November 4, 1907, p. 10b, John Norris wrote from the Oratory in Birmingham to say, "I am enabled to state on information received today from the highest authority that 'the genuine doctrine and spirit of Newman's Catholic teaching are not hit by the Encyclical, but the theories of many who wrongly seek refuge under a great name are obviously censured.' "

35. See Gilley and Kelly. Kelly contends that *W* was so fearful of *any* connection between the condemned modernists and Newman that he refrained from making any connection between them in his biography of Newman.

36. "The Encyclical, *Pascendi*," *Dublin Review* 14 (January 1908): 1–10.

37. *MW* II, pp. 254–95 and Mrs. Wilfrid Ward, "An Introductory Study," to *LL*, pp. v–lxxi, esp. p. xxxviii.

38. November 2, 1907, 10e. Williams said, "the late Encyclical [is] an unprecendented evil that, while one Pope has implied a direct approval of the writings of an English Catholic by making him a Cardinal, his successor should reverse the decision by condemning every characteristic proposition for which that writer made himself responsible."

39. See *MW* II, pp. 270–2 for *W*'s reply to Williams.

40. *WWP, SAUL*, emphasis mine.

41. *MW* II, pp. 254–95. The whole chapter, "The Encyclical *Pascendi*" is an account of *W*'s state of mind and activity when the encyclical came out and is remarkably objective and good, but a little underestimates the real problems *W* had with the encyclical and Newman. The letters to Norfolk were not used. The choice may be accounted for in part by *W*'s own regret at some of the letters he wrote during this time. It is not enough, however, to regret it as if he never believed that Newman was in serious trouble because of the Encyclical; the letters to Norfolk may likely reflect his true mind.

42. *WWP, SAUL*.

43. Reviewed in the *Dublin Review* 140 (January 1907):178–83. In the course of the review he said, "we are quite in accord with Mr. Williams's view as to the place which Abbé Loisy's ostensible aim—namely, a careful analysis of the results of modern criticism—would occupy in the carrying out of the theological development on the lines of Newman's *Essay*."

44. This is Sermon XV in *Fifteen Sermons Preached Before the University of Oxford Between AD 1826 and 1843* (London, 1872), hereafter cited as *Oxford University Sermons*. The sermon, "The Theory of Development in Religious Doctrine," was preached by Newman in 1843, i.e., *before* his conversion to Roman Catholicism. The *Essay* was published in 1845. *T* found Newman more daring and suggestive in the sermon; see his letter to Charles Devas, Appendix C.

45. *W* wrote to von Hügel on February 27, 1900, and said, "The ideas which I am working out are really in Newman's Sermon on Development (not in the Essay so distinctly)." In the von Hügel papers *SAUL*; *MW* II, p. 325.

46. See "The Functions of Prejudice," *Dublin Review* 138 (January 1906):99–118, or his introduction to *The Scope and Nature of the University* (New York, 1915), pp. vii–xxiv.

47. *The Life of Baron von Hügel* (London, 1951).

48. Published as *Liberal Catholicism, Reform Catholicism, Modernism: A Contribution to a New Orientation in Modernist Research* (Mainz, 1979).

49. Von Hügel wrote to *T* 7 July 1900: "Wilfrid Ward has lent me your MS. 'Who are the Reactionaries?', and I have found it, especially in its quotations from yourself, full of deeply stimulating and suggestive writing,—with that enchanting note of spiritual aloofness and pathetic, patient, brave loneliness, which is ever characteristic of one side and aspect of all spontaneous and deep religion."

Letters from a "Modernist"

1

S. Aloysius, Oxford[1]
12 December 1893

[Dear Mr. Ward,

I was delighted to learn through Father Clarke[2] that you were so satisfied with my review of your first volume.[3] To have pleased you ever so little would go some way to repay the very great pleasure and profit I derived from my labour. I confess that as regards the reconciliation of Newman's theory of faith with current theological terminology, the wish is to a great extent father to the thought; but still on re-reading the *Grammar of Assent*[4] in the light of my four years at Saint Beuno's,[5] I felt convinced that a deeper and more patient study would show a fundamental agreement. I was beginning my fourth re-reading when your books were put into my hands, for review.[6] I am most anxious that Newman should not be shelved by our theologians as a mere literary ornament. We are lamentably out of touch with English non-Catholic thought and expression, and I cannot but think that if Newman were studied and assimilated it would tend to unbarbarise us and enable us to pour Catholic truth from the scholastic into the modern mould without losing a drop in the transfer. Much of our want of sympathy with Newman is no doubt due to our training under foreign professors, naturally unversed in Anglican thought and terminology, and suspicious of a convert. I exemplified this in regard to the dictum: 'faith in venture,' which is usually ascribed to Newman in the sense of 'I stretch lame hands of faith and grope, and gather dust and chaff and call to what I feel is Lord of all, and faintly trust the larger hope'; than which nothing could be more unjust to his teaching. Such a blunder comes from assuming that 'faith' in English can only be the *fides* of scholastics. I am afraid you will not be so satisfied with my second article which is already printed. Had I been in communication with you a day sooner I should have submitted it to you for suggestions. I have attempted a summary of Dr. Ward's[7] character which proved to be very much beyond my power; but as the second attempt seemed as much a caricature as the first I gave it up with an apology. I am also afraid that I have, for the sake of clearness, somewhat exaggerated his position as an Ultramontane,[8] in order to bring out more sharply by contrast the true doctrine as I conceive it;

and, if I mistake not, as you conceive it. The point of divergence is that which distinguishes the Pope's mind from the mind of the Church. Of course Dr. Ward did not extend to the Pope's unofficial and private theological cogitation and utterance the prerogative of infallibility, but it seems to me that he invested much that was personal with an official character, so much, as to leave hardly anything private. I have not touched his philosophical controversies at all, though they were to me perhaps the most interesting and satisfactory. Still the readers of the *Month* are not patient as a class with such disquisition, and I had already tried them enough. Your approval and sympathy has encouraged me very much to prosecute my analysis of the *Grammar of Assent.*][9]

I enclose Henry Sidgwick's[10] letter which you kindly sent me. His opinion on the subject is well worth having.

Yours most faithfully,
G. TYRRELL S.J.

Notes to Letter 1

1. *T* "was sent in 1893, for a very short time, to the Jesuit mission house at Oxford, with the idea . . . of giving him the opportunity of writing." (*A&L* II.34)

2. Richard F. Clarke, S.J. (1839–1900), a confrere of *T*'s and author of theological pamphlets for the Catholic Truth Society.

3. The first volume of *W*'s biography of his father, *William George Ward and the Oxford Movement* (London, 1893). *T*'s review, "The Oxford School and Modern Religious Thought" appeared in the *Month* 79 (December 1893):560–8.

4. Published by Newman in 1870, it is a mature theological work on the difference between real and notional assent. He discusses the function of conscience in one's knowledge of God and the role of the "illative sense," i.e., the faculty of judging from the given facts by processes outside the limits of strict logic, in reaching religious certitude. *T* did not read Newman widely, but deeply, and the *Grammar of Assent* was a book he returned to time and again. In a letter to Raoul Gout (26 May 1906) *T* recalled a "profound revolution" in his thinking caused by reading Newman; see *A&L* II.209–10.

5. A Jesuit college in north Wales where *T* studied theology; he did his philosophical work at the Jesuit college at Stonyhurst.

6. *W*'s two-volume biography of his father. *T* was, at this point, preparing the second installment of his review, i.e., the second volume of *W*'s biography, *William George Ward and the Catholic Revival* (London, 1894). *T*'s review was published in the *Month* 80 (January 1894):59–68 as an extension of his review of the earlier volume (note 3).

7. *W*'s father, William George Ward (1812–1882) was a fellow and a mathematics tutor of Balliol when he decided to join the Roman Catholic church. He was deprived of his degrees for publishing *The Ideal of the Christian Church* (London, 1844), a book which purported to demonstrate that an Anglican could hold the full cycle of Roman Catholic doctrines. For the rest of his life he was a strong Ultramontanist and champion of papal infallibility.

8. A position which favors centralization of authority and influence in the papal Curia and Pope as opposed to episcopal or national independence. In the eighteenth and nineteenth centuries it gained popular support as a way to oppose interference in church affairs by national despots. It triumphed in the latter part of the nineteenth century, especially in the declaration of papal infallibility at the first Vatican council (1870). According to Derek Holmes, all the archbishops of Westminster in the nineteenth century were strong Ultramontanists; see *More Roman than Rome* (Shepherdstown, 1978).

9. Bracketed material has been published in *A&L* II.56–8.

10. Henry Sidgwick (1809–1900), a philosopher and ethicist who had known William George Ward later became a friend of *W*'s. He played an interesting part in the "ethics of belief" question; see James C. Livingston, *The Ethics of Belief: An Essay on the Victorian Religious Conscience* (Tallahassee, 1974).

2

Wimbledon College, Wimbledon.[1]
22 September 1898

My dear Mr. Ward,

[The consciousness that I have studied your 'Epilogue'[2] very carefully as well as your volume on the *Catholic Revival*,[3] and that I have been always a devout disciple of Newman, makes me less startled than you are at the coincidence of our conclusions.][4] Still I do not for a moment deny the influence of [[a]] certain ecclesiastical Time-spirit; although I neither regard it as literally atmospheric; nor even as a subsistent Idea of Platonic philosophy; nor as explicable by immediate thought-transfer between mind and mind. I fancy that cattle fed in the same pastures develop like characteristics,—say, a novelty in horns, or tails, or tempers; which no one from mere consideration of their diet would have anticipated; yet there it was, latent,—a horn in a turnip. So people in the same age and country, fed on the same literature, and determined by like surroundings and interests, will naturally and necessarily leap to the same conclusions with an independence which is merely apparent and relative to our ignorance. It is this view that gives me great confidence in the prevalence of the wider spirit now abroad in the Church *Frustra expellas.*[5] Doubtless the opposition it meets with is just as necessary for its confirmation and development; but all who stand against it must eventually be borne down by it. The worst of this optimism and belief in Truth's prevalence is that it makes one lazy. Indeed this faith is answerable for the listlessness of Catholics; they are Calvinists in respect to the Church. She is saved already. ' "Well," said his Lordship, "God mends all." "Aye, but by God, we must help Him to mend it," said the other.' We want more of this. I send you herewith another copy of the article. The A.C.Q.[6] does not give reprints, but sends three copies of its lumbering self which I promptly burn. I shall retain one so I shall not be bankrupt. An excursion to Eastbourne[7] such as you kindly propose would not be comfortably feasible; besides it has been so evidently fated that we are never to meet, that it would be uncanny to take such defiant measures. There would surely be a railway accident.

Ever yours faithfully,
G. TYRRELL S.J.

Notes to Letter 2

1. *T* was staying in the Jesuit house in Wimbledon, Surrey.

2. The epilogue to *W*'s *The Life and Times of Cardinal Wiseman* was entitled "The Exclusive Church and the *Zeitgeist.*" It is not an exposition of Wiseman's thought at all, but a means *W* used to convey his own programme for the Catholic church in the nineteenth century. Nearly twenty years later *W* wrote to his son, Leo, at Oxford to say: "a point to bear in mind is that the introduction of Wiseman's name is mere Jesuitry, the thoughts which fill the bulk of the epilogue are totally outside Wiseman's purview." (Undated letter, c. 1915 in *WWP*, *SAUL*) During the modernist crisis *W* was asked to withdraw the epilogue from further editions of the Wiseman biography; cf. *MW* II.318–29.

3. The second volume of *W*'s biography of his father was entitled *William George Ward and the Catholic Revival* (London, 1894).

4. Bracketed material was published in *A&L* II.99. *T* reviewed the Wiseman biography, "Wiseman: His Aims and Methods" in the *Month* 91 (February 1898); reprinted in *FM* I.22–39. In that review *T* aligned himself with *W*'s liberal apologetic as put forth in the epilogue under Wiseman's name; he can therefore refer to "our conclusions."

5. Literally, "in vain may you expel," i.e., you cannot get rid of it.

6. The *American Catholic Quarterly Review* in which *T* had just published an article, "The Church and Scholasticism" 23 (July 1898):550–61. The article would have interested *W* very much and he apparently had asked for an off-print. *T* undoubtedly means that no off-prints were sent, just three copies of the journal itself. He is correct to describe it as "lumbering"—the July issue runs to 223 pages.

7. *W*'s home in Sussex, nearly 50 miles from Wimbledon. *W* lived there from 1891–1900; cf. *MW* I.228–46.

3 31, Farm Street, London. W.[1]
3 February 1899

Dear Mr. Ward,

[To be very frank and simple with you, my reason for hesitating[2] is that I am not a man of all round general education owing chiefly to my wilful perversity in youth; nor am I easy and expansive in society; nor am I ready of tongue in debate and discussion. Yet I feel these qualifications are very needful in one who should represent the Jesuits among the sort of men whom you have gathered together. I am however altogether in sympathy with the aim and spirit of the Synthetic so far as I understand it; and still more evidently with yourself and Hügel;[3] and therefore if you think my wit sufficient to atone for my ignorance and that I should really strengthen and not weaken the Catholic element, I shall be very glad to join by way of experiment, since I can drop out quietly if I find it doesn't do. I suppose I shall hear later the details as to the rights, duties and payments.][4]

Ever yours faithfully,
G. TYRRELL.

Notes to Letter 3

1. The Jesuit residence and church in London where *T* was sent at the end of August 1896 to join the staff of the *Month*, a Jesuit periodical.

2. *W* invited *T* to join the Synthetic Society, successor to the old Metaphysical Society (1869–1880), which had been founded to foster debate between leading exponents of religion and science. The Synthetic Society was a lineal descendent of the Metaphysical, but founded with clearer religious intentions. The constitution restricts membership to "those who desire to find a working philosophy of religious belief." The name was agreed upon at a meeting of Arthur J. Balfour (1849–1930), philosopher and statesman; Edward Talbot (1844–1934), Anglican bishop of Southwark; Charles Gore (1853–1932), Anglican theologian, editor of the *Lux Mundi* series and later bishop of Oxford; and *W*. The first meeting was held on 28 February 1896. Information about membership, rules and more specific details about meetings can be found in *MW* I.305, 344–79, 417–20.

T was a guest at the Synthetic Society meeting 24 February 1899 and was elected a member 24 March 1899.

3. Baron Friedrich von Hügel (1852–1925), a leading Roman Catholic thinker and writer in England. He was a strong proponent of Biblical criticism and for this support has sometimes been remembered as a leading figure in the modernist movement. In other circles he is remembered as a great spiritual writer whose major work, *The Mystical Element in Religion*, two volumes (London, 1908) is still

something of a classic. He was a friend of *W*'s and of *T*'s and engaged in a long correspondence with each of them. For further information about von Hügel and his relationships with both *W* and *T* see Barmann.

4. Bracketed material appears in *MW* I.361.

4

31, Farm Street. London, W.
Monday.[1]

My dear Ward,

I mean to be at the meeting on Friday—nay, even at the dinner on the faint chance of getting next [[to]] you on my right side, which is my left side.[2] Myers' paper[3] seems very diffuse; it will be hard to keep to any one point. I believe we should appropriate and utilise all the certified results of S.P.R.[4] but though they may confirm, I don't see how they can be substituted for philosophical proofs of theism. Myers I fancy regards all philosophy as 'up-in-a-balloon' work and yet, needing some religion to satisfy another side of his nature, is determined that positivist methods shall yield him all he asks. Hence he hammers out the S.P.R. data with a full-blown religion, on his own anvil without waiting for the tardy process of evolution. What puzzles me in him, and even in this 'synthesis' of his, is the curious 'synthesis' of the poetic temperament and the materialist mind. Perhaps the latter is an accident—a revolt against the absurdities, arrogancies, dissensions of philosophers. But making an allowance for enthusiasm it is rather trying to be asked to consider seriously the stability of so elaborate a structure raised on so slight a foundation in so short a time.

[I confess I enjoyed the last meeting very much, though I was trembling for my seriousness once or twice owing to the haunting thought of the mirth there must be in heaven before the angels of God at the spectacle of a grave assembly of creatures discussing the existence of their Creator, and trying to make out a case for Him—not very successfully. But then there is no humour in heaven—doubtless because heaven is so largely the structure of theologians, a race void of all sense of the ridiculous. The Greek heavens rang with peals of celestial laughter; but then it was the work of men's hands, a most human heaven, with lust as well as laughter. This by the way. But

Haldane's[5] remarks and manner were fascinating in their seriousness. I should like to see an Hegelian at his prayers. A 'colloquy' with the subject-object must be difficult to manage; though a book of devotion to the angels, used here, chats freely with the 'Thrones'—almost as difficult a feat, I should have thought.[6] Yes, I am going to publish the Oxford Catechisms.[7] I had no idea you were there or I should have waited. Had I not been going to Bruges that evening I should have accepted Canon Kennard's[8] kind invitation to meet you.

Ever yours faithfully,
G. TYRRELL, S.J.

Notes to Letter 4

1. The context—Myers' paper—places this letter between 17 and 24 March 1899; his paper was to be delivered on 24 March and the papers were distributed in advance.
2. *T* is referring to his political and religious views, not to some hearing disability.
3. Frederic W. H. Myers (1843–1901), was a writer interested in psychical research. His paper was entitled "A Provisional Sketch of Religious Synthesis."
4. The Society for Psychical Research founded by Myers and Henry Sidgwick in 1882 to undertake scientifically-controlled experiments about psychic matters.
5. Richard Burdon (later Lord) Haldane (1856–1928), statesman and philosopher.
6. Bracketed material was published in *A&L* II.10.
7. *T* sometimes lectured to Roman Catholic undergraduates at Oxford. He did so in 1893 (*A&L* II.34, 192). The lectures here referred to are probably those given during Lent Term 1899, later collected and published as *External Religion: Its Use and Abuse* (London, 1899). The book, a statement of *T*'s ecclesiology aimed at a non-Roman Catholic audience, is compatible with much of *W*'s thought and work at this time. *T* sees the need for a principle of dogmatic authority under which Roman Catholics can think and act with freedom and confidence. Nevertheless, the book caught the negative attention of Rafael Merry del Val (1865–1930), later to serve as Secretary of State to Pope Pius X. For a discussion of Blondel's influence on *T* at this time (and in this book) and Merry del Val's reactions to it, see David G. Schultenover, *George Tyrrell: In Search of Catholicism* (Shepherdstown, 1981).
8. Charles H. Kennard (d. 1921), was a Roman Catholic chaplain at the University Catholic Oratory (St. Aldate's) in Oxford. *W* used to stay with him while at Oxford collecting information for the biography of William George Ward.

5

Wimbledon College, Wimbledon.
25 March 1899

My dear Ward,

I see Sidgwick wants you to reconcile your views with Strong's[1] doctrine of the Fall. I say 'Strong's doctrine' because I only want to remind you in case you have not noticed it already, that his view is the common one among orthodox Protestants and was fairly tenable for Catholics prior to the Jansenistic controversy, as seeming to have Augustine in its favour; but that controversy sifted it out, at least in its extreme form, and showed the other view to be more consonant with the 'Catholic Synthesis'—to use our phrase. According to the Calvinist view man fell from a normal state to a subnormal; and God 'could not have created the human race and intended it to be as we now see it;' and therefore we have in its present state a phenomenon which if it does not *prove* original sin at least makes it a needed hypothesis. According to the Catholic view (Suarez[2] gives it its extreme form) man fell from a supra-normal to a normal condition; God *could* have intended things to be as they are without prejudice to His justice or goodness, and there is nothing in the existence of sin and sorrow to demand the hypothesis of original sin. Things are now outwardly as they would have been had no supernatural intervention modified the course of the usual laws of evolution. This is of course a nut-shell statement. But at least it shows that the Fall is too unfixed a doctrine to be brought into more fundamental discussions. Notwithstanding Myers' rather ungenerous innuendo as to Williams'[3] orthodoxy, I think when our end is synthesis and agreement we ought all to minimise. See how Myers at once repudiated the 'Bridge of Light'[4] and most of the popularised presentment of *his* religion—and quite justly; since it is only the few who are capable of seizing the essentials of any system. Hence I don't feel inclined to fight for more of 'the Fall' than is absolutely needful; and though personally I incline to Saint Augustine, in controversy I would only stand up for Suarez lest I should lay needless burdens on men's shoulders. Forgive me if I have been sending coals to Newcastle
and believe me

Yours faithfully,
G. Tyrrell

Are there no 'rules' of the Synthetic? I am as yet quite ignorant of your modes of procedure, and fear I made a *faux pas* in taking the ball which Williams so unexpectedly threw in my hands.

Notes to Letter 5

1. Thomas B. Strong (1861–1944), was Dean of Christ Church, Oxford (1901–1920). He was a man with sympathies for the *Lux Mundi* school, i.e., the group associated with Charles Gore that wished to combine High Church traditions and some of the insights of emerging biblical criticism. This letter refers to a discussion on 24 March 1899 at the Synthetic; Myers gave the paper and Strong was a member. It is not clear what *T* means by "Strong's doctrine of the fall."

2. Francisco de Suarez (1548–1617), Spanish Jesuit philosopher and interpreter of Aquinas. He departed from Aquinas on some issues and some scholars discern Suarism as a system of its own, even in competition with that of Aquinas. In *T*'s day Suarez was considered the greatest Jesuit theologian and had many followers within the Society of Jesus. Allegiance to Suarez's interpretation of Aquinas became somewhat problematic in the light of Leo XIII's encyclical, *Aeterni Patris* (4 August 1879) which gave impetus to the Thomistic revival. *T* stood out among the English Jesuits for opposing Suarez's interpretation of Aquinas and preferring Aquinas, himself.

3. William J. Williams (1858–1930), friend and neighbor of *W*'s (*MW* I.360); he was a convert to Roman Catholicism and author of articles of interest to Catholics. He was also a friend of *T*'s and a Newman scholar. Williams gave the paper at the April 1899 meeting to continue the discussion with Myer's paper; it was not printed in *SSP* because it was deemed "too theological."

4. It is difficult to determine with utter certainty what "Bridge of Light" means, but I offer the following guess. It is not, so far as I can determine, a hymn. Henry Wadsworth Longfellow's poem, "Haunted Houses" ends with the stanza:

> So from the world of spirits there descends
> A bridge of light, connecting it with this,
> O'er whose unsteady floor, that sways and bends,
> Wander our thoughts above the dark abyss.

As Myers was a co-founder of the Society for Psychical Research and interested in "the world of spirits," Longfellow's words might represent a "popularised presentment of *his* religion."

6

31, Farm Street, London, W.
2 May 1899

My dear Ward,

[Through some blunder your Thursday's note reached me only this morning. I will let you have the paper[1] in time; though as yet I am in search of a thesis—partly owing to the vagueness I share with Professor Sidgwick as to the precise scope of the Synthetic Society. I suppose the idea is that given theism in common, we should—what shall I say?—labour together for the defence of as much religion as can be based on bare theism; or is it that we should strive to find out how much more we can hold in common? The latter would be apt to degenerate into controversy, unless the idea of 'synthesis' were taken in the sense of a desire to agree as much as possible and to minimise differences—somewhat in the spirit of Saint Ignatius'[2]][3] (I am afraid rather unjesuitical) '*praenotandum*'[4] to the *Exercises.*[5] ['Every good Christian should wish rather to save his neighbour's thesis than to condemn it.' But this requires more generosity and intellectual self-denial than can be expected in any mixed assembly; nor is it possible even for individuals to act on the principle if they cannot agree with their neighbour but the said neighbour begins to crow over what he considers an act of submission or 'adhesion' to his cause.][6] I think some expressions in Williams'[7] paper were unfortunate as having at least the appearance of theological colour, as is evident from the way Balfour[8] and Gore[9] understood them; and am therefore willing to believe that the sense of thunder in the atmosphere on Friday evening was due to that cause. But I cannot pretend that I was not somewhat disgusted at missing that sense of perfect immunity from rudeness which alone renders a Synthetic Society possible. I don't say the line was crossed, but one was expecting the catastrophe every minute. I am glad to see Mrs. Ward's book[10] so well received, especially by the usually implacable Athenaeum.[11]

Ever yours faithfully,
G. Tyrrell S.J.

Notes to Letter 6

1. *T* was preparing a paper for the 9 June 1899 meeting; it was not published in *SSP*. *W* was responsible for getting papers to the printer and distributed to the membership in advance.

2. Ignatius Loyola (1491–1556), founder of the Society of Jesus.

3. Bracketed material published in *MW* I.376.

4. "that which is to be known beforehand", i.e., a prefatory note to the *Exercises.*

5. The *Spiritual Exercises* were written by Ignatius as a series of meditations and rules designed to lead souls to conquer their passions and give themselves to God.

6. Bracketed material published in *MW* I.376.

7. Williams' paper, 28 April 1899—untitled and unprinted in *SSP*—led to charges of the Roman Catholic contingent proselytizing.

8. See letter 3 note 2. *W* reviewed Balfour's *The Foundations of Belief* (London, 1895) in the *Quarterly Review* 180 (April 1895):488–520. The review led to their meeting and eventually to the foundation of the Synthetic Society. Balfour and *W* maintained a lengthy correspondence—seventy-one letters from Balfour and one hundred twenty-one letters from *W*—which is preserved in the *WWP, SAUL.*

9. See letter 3 note 2 and letter 5 note 1. Gore edited *Lux Mundi*, "Studies in the Religion of the Incarnation" (1889) which was intended to put Catholic faith into right relation to modern intellectual and moral problems. It caught the religious imagination of the day and was the subject of lively articles and letters to editors. It interested *W* because it seemed to fuse two strains of Anglicanism which had heretofore been at enmity with one another, Tractarianism and Liberalism. *W* hoped that *Lux Mundi* augured well for the future of religion and that a new synthesis, a *via media*, might be found which could include the best of both worlds, i.e., the old traditions and some of the new, scientific thought. *W* wrote an article, "New Wine in Old Bottles" in the *Nineteenth Century* 27 (June 1890):942–56, in response to Gore's work.

10. *W*'s wife, Josephine Hope, daughter of James Hope-Scott, was a novelist who wrote mostly about Roman Catholic concerns. The book referred to here is *One Poor Scruple* (London 1899). It was reviewed by *T* in the *Month* 93 (May 1899):449–58, under the title, "Two Estimates of Catholic Life." In the review, *T* compared Mrs. Ward to Mrs. Humphry Ward, a comparison that was continually made.

11. The prestigious "The Club" founded in 1764 by Samuel Johnson, Joshua Reynolds and Edmund Burke. *W* was later invited to membership. *T* here refers to the journal published by the Athenaeum; in the 8 April 1899 issue Mrs. Ward is praised as the author of a "distinctly able book," p. 428.

7

Wimbledon College, Wimbledon
Saturday.[1]

My dear Ward,

If this is at all intelligible send it on to Spottiswoode.[2] I have watered it out easily into two articles for the *Month* and so it may well labour under the obscurity begotten of brevity. [Myers' note is amiable enough, but if his tone is 'turtle-dovey' I have hitherto misunderstood that bird.][3]

As to Gibson,[4] I expect he is the victim of the common fallacy of well-meaning zealous people,—that the end justifies the means. He believes there is no other way to bring the Roman authorities to what he considers their senses but to expose their present tactics to the scorn of the Anglo-Saxon whose good-will they are so desirous to propitiate; and thinks that the present harm will be abundantly out-balanced by the eventual good. As to the last point I hardly know what to think; but granting it, there remains the question as to the legitimacy of the means. I quite understand his irritation but, with you, I am sure such methods will only aggravate the disease. [The true 'liberalism' suffers always from such ill-judged advocacy. It is obviously the policy of the adverse school to drive the progressives to rash deeds and utterances, and if to apostasy so much the better. I believe it is by a sort of *e purchè si muove*[5] faith and steadfast obedience that such blind malice is best defeated. 'The kingdom of God cometh not with observation' is a Jesuitical principle—little account as Jesuits seem to make of it. Noise should be minimised.][6]

It would be a great good if one could systematise the doctrine of Newman as drawn from his entire works. Was there any truth in the vague rumour that you were going to do that long-desired biography?[7] If so, I hope you give as full a synthesis of his philosophy as the limits of a readable biography will allow. The danger will be of the work running to too huge a bulk.

I have just read—for the *first* time—Mivart's *Contemporary Evolution*,[8] more than twenty years in print. Its thoughts are admirable and should be continually reuttered. He has wandered off from that standpoint a good deal, but the written letter abides. I shall be here till Monday, when I go to Farm Street for a spell.

Ever yours faithfully,
G. Tyrrell.

Notes to Letter 7

1. Context of this letter—*T*'s paper for the Synthetic Society for 9 June 1899—places this letter in the last week of May or first week of June 1899.

2. The publisher which reproduced papers for the Synthetic Society meetings.

3. Bracketed material appears in *MW* I.368. There were periodic arguments and flare-ups of temper at the Synthetic Society and *W* usually tried to smooth

them over. Myers seems to have been involved in several of them (cf. *MW* I.376f). In dating this letter, *MW* suggests that it is in 1896, but references to Gibson place it in 1899.

4. William Gibson, Lord Ashbourne (1868–1942), published an antagonistic article in the May issue of the *Nineteenth Century* 45 (1899):785–94, entitled, "An Outburst of Activity in the Roman Congregations." Gibson argued that Roman Catholic apologetics were not directed at the outside world at all, but were meant to "suppress all that tends to produce uncertainty in the popular mind."

5. "Nevertheless it does move." Galileo was forced by the Inquisition to renounce his view that the sun is the central body in the solar system around which the earth moves. He is rumoured to have made this remark (about the earth moving) under his breath immediately after renouncing it for church officials. *T* quoted it often.

6. Bracketed material published in *A&L* II.104.

7. *W* finally wrote the biography of Newman and considered it his major work. *W* collected information about Newman for years and was known as a champion of Newman. *W*'s own work shows a conscious attempt to draw Newman's insights into a more modern arena where, *W* believed, they could illuminate and heal. The story of his troubles with the biography can be found in *MW* II.333–57, and in the massive correspondence about it in the *WWP*. See also Gilley.

8. St. George Jackson Mivart (1827–1900), a biologist and convert to Roman Catholicism (1844) hoped to reconcile contemporary scientific teaching with the doctrines of the church. *T* is here referring to his book, *Contemporary Evolution: An Essay on Some Recent Social Changes* (London 1876). Mivart was in trouble with church officials from 1892 until his death. In 1892 he wrote a series of articles and clarifications on "Happiness in Hell" which were put on the Index. His summary of that conflict can be found in "The Index and My Articles on Hell" in the *Nineteenth Century* 34 (December 1893):979–90. In October 1899 he criticized the Roman Catholic hierarchy for its failure to act against the obvious injustice in the Dreyfus case; see "The Roman Catholic Church and the Dreyfus Case" in the *Times*, 17 October 1899, 13–4. In January 1900 he published two articles—both of which *T* and *W* found extreme—which exacerbated his already tenuous position with church authorities: "Some Recent Catholic Apologetics" in the *Fortnightly Review* 67 (January 1900):24–44, attacked moderates like *W*; "The Continuity of Catholicism" in the *Nineteenth Century* 47 (January 1900):51–72, was his attempt to reconcile religion and modern science. The final outcome of his activity was a letter from Cardinal Vaughan requiring Mivart to sign a document about his faith in the Roman Catholic church. The document contained statements Mivart could not accept—e.g., that Scripture has God as its author and contains no error whatsoever—and his refusal led to his excommunication. See Jacob W. Gruber, *A Conscience in Conflict: The Life of St. George Jackson Mivart* (New York, 1960).

8 Wimbledon College, Wimbledon.
Monday.[1]

My dear Ward,

Our letters crossed. [I like every word of your article[2] which will do good precisely as from a known favourer of the 'large liberality.' There is some truth in your alternative that Gibson 'is not writing seriously;' but I think he has no business to be unserious when his pranks may set the house on fire.

A little wholesome and humble scepticism is the remedy for much of the difficulty you deal with; cocksureness of both scientist and theologian being at the root of it all. In the latter indeed it is more unpardonable since he deals *ex professo* in mysteries and not in phenomena accessible to the senses. Balfour's line will correct scientific rationalism and Newman's will correct theological rationalism which is every bit as far from that spirit of faith which stands related to scepticism as man is supposed to be related to his cousin anthropoids through a neutral ancestor. I have always accepted the charge that Newman's mind was profoundly sceptical, for this reason.

You suggest, though you don't develop, a more accurate sense of the expression: 'intrusion on the theological domain.' It is often misunderstood as though where a matter is common to theology and, say, history, history must stand aside as '*non audienda*'[3] e.g. the facts of the Gospel story. *You* mean by 'intrusion' the attempt of the historian to suggest or devise how theology is to be accommodated to the facts he supposes himself to have established: thus laying sacrilegious hands on the tottering ark. This sense is valuable; the other argues precisely that want of faith and humble scepticism which makes it possible for a man to rest tranquil with: *theologice constat—historice non constat*; or even, *constat quod non.*[4] This is the truth which I think underlies the Anglican defence of inconsistency and repudiation of logicality, which is only a slight perversion of Newman.][5]

I meant to make a few verbal comments on my paper in the reading and to illustrate diffuseness does not give objectors a fair chance of getting hold of one's precise point, and it is this that makes informal debating often so tedious and profitless; but of course the extremes meet.

Will you consider Farm Street my address for the future, as I am more there than here and letters are more faithfully forwarded thence here, than from here thence.

Ever yours faithfully,
G. TYRRELL.

Notes to Letter 8

1. Context of this letter—*T*'s paper for 9 June 1899—places this in early June, 1899.

2. *W*'s reply to Gibson appeared in the *Nineteenth Century* 45 (June 1899):955–61, under the title, "Catholic Apologetics: A Reply." *W* argued *ad hominem* against Gibson and, more persuasively, that Gibson's *modus operandi* made apologetics impossible. Gibson had argued that Roman Catholics ought to be able to engage in autonomous study without continually being supervised by Roman Congregations. *W* replied that Gibson's tactics were precisely the kind that made such freedom impossible.

3. "not by hearing"

4. it obtains (or holds) theologically—it does not obtain (or hold) historically; [or even] it just does not obtain (hold).

5. Bracketed material published in *MP* II.105.

9

31, Farm Street,
Berkeley Square, London W.
6 September 1899

My dear Ward,

I have not had leisure to meditate on the scheme as much as I should like; but one thing strikes me *prima facie*. The 'Concessions' seem more liberal than is necessary for the profitable discussion of the 'Questions.'[1] These are purely theistic; the former have a distinctly Christian bias—unless indeed Christianity be there taken in Mrs. Humphry Ward's[2] sense, which is not the dictionary sense. As better defining what we mean by theism and morality, I think the expression 'Christian theism' might stand in Concession 2; but not as implying that the theism of Jews and Turks has proved socially inefficacious. For the same reason, I am not satisfied with the parenthesis in Concession 1; if we take strictly that minimum which is common to Christians of *all denominations* we come down practically to Mrs. Humphry Ward's Christianity, which is simply the *theism* of Christianity—and is common to Unitarians, Jews and Turks together with dictionary Christians; i.e. to all who take the same views about God and righteousness as Christ did. If a bias towards Christianity in any more proper and restricted sense were assumed I suppose we should be deprived of Mr. Myers' illuminations; and indeed of the cooperation of many who though holding as much as Mrs. Humphry Ward, would not perhaps *call* themselves Christian; either in fact or in bias. I think there are two distinct lines which the Synthetic might take (1) Conceding theism, it might enquire about historical Christianity, or (2) Conceding less than theism, it might enquire about theism. The former line would lead through the quagmires of history; the latter through the fogs of philosophy. Yet the latter is I think the more pressing, the more profitable enquiry even in the interests of Christianity. Let us get now to the feet of Pope Conscience and God may look to the rest. I could wish the Synthetic were not so exclusively composed of Christians or 'post-Christians'; there are good heads among them of the circumcision.

I'll send you in a few days three articles[3] in which I developed my little Synthetic paper, with the usual result of finding that I had much less to say than I thought I had. I have just read a book by your namesake James Ward[4] on *Naturalism and Agnosticism* which shows me what I wanted to say said much better.

After the 25th I settle down for the winter, i.e. oscillating between this and Wimbledon.

Kind regards to Mrs. Ward

Yours faithfully,
G. Tyrrell.

Notes to Letter 9

1. Members of the Synthetic Society were sometimes asked to vote about policy matters and one of the most pressing questions at this time was the stand they should take on theism, i.e., must they hold to it as an underlying principle or suspend it for purposes of discussion. Henry Sidgwick prepared the "Concessions" and "Questions" and formally presented them to the membership prior to the January 1900 meeting (*MW* I.418–20; *SSP* 295–6). Sidgwick's action was taken as part of his duties as chairman for the coming year and was made partly in response to the unstructured debates of the previous spring.

2. Mary Augusta (Arnold) Ward (1851–1920), was an author of religious novels, the most famous of which is probably *Robert Elsmere* (London, 1888). She wrote about the lure of modern agnosticism and the seduction of the religious mind by the conclusions of the critical study of religious texts.

3. *T* is probably referring here to three articles he published in the *Month*: "A Problem in Apologetic" 93 (June 1899):617–26; "A Point of Apologetic" 94 (August 1899):113–27; the latter appeared in two parts, the final segment 94 (September 1899):249–60. The three of them were reprinted as "Adaptability as a Proof of Religion" in *FM* II.277–347.

4. James Ward (1843–1925), philosopher and psychologist. He was not a member, nor did he attend the Synthetic Society until 1900; his first paper for them was in 1902. *T* is here referring to *Naturalism and Agnosticism* (London, 1899), Ward's Gifford Lectures 1896–98.

10

Stonyhurst[1]
16 September 1899

My dear Ward,

As I am in the throes of a clergy-retreat, to be followed by another without interval, I return these[2] at once; and if any definite question occurs to me I will write later. As a year's programme the questions contain matter enough and to spare; but if it is a question of a perpetual programme, adjustments might be made when felt to be needed. The reform I was rather hoping for was relative to the actual conduct of the 'debates' (I am glad to see that word used definitely; for I thought they were rather intended to be very informal conversational discussions). Though too much formality may kill vitality, yet a right balance is desirable. I wish the *point* of each paper might be formulated at the beginning or end. In reading some of them over I had great difficulty in fixing the precise thesis, if any; and I can't help thinking that on some occasions (e.g. Williams' paper)[3] much of the discussion was wasted through this defect. Also, it might be well to secure one or two speakers *pro and con* beforehand in order to obviate the delay caused by each one's reluctance to speak until every one else has spoken. Beyond that, perhaps any greater formality might be tiresome and obstructive, but so much would I fancy be helpful.

Ever yours faithfully,
G. TYRRELL.

For the purposes of debate I'll concede anything. Else I should rather regret making evolution a stone in any building I wanted to last fifty years. I find it less satisfactory the more I try to get a clear and distinct idea of it, though I should be very glad to hold it, as it makes more for religion than the chaotic conception it has extended. At present I feel more disposed to admit it as a cause in the past which worked rapidly than as a cause now at work in any appreciable way. But I will show you soon the grounds of my doubt.[4]

Notes to Letter 10

1. Jesuit house of studies where *T* studied philosophy; he taught there 1894–96.
2. Policy questions for the Synthetic Society.
3. William J. Williams' paper for the Synthetic Society, 28 April 1899; see letter 5 note 3.
4. This whole paragraph is not marked with a P.S., but was attached to this letter.

11

114, Mount Street, Grosvenor Square[1]
London, W.
Sunday, 12 November 1899

My dear Ward,

Cremation is not a problem that has ever troubled me very much and so I can only give you my first thoughts on the matter. It was forbidden by the Inquisition in 1586 and I think once since some evasion of the law has been condemned. It seems a purely disciplinary matter; or if there is any quasi-dogmatic basis for the Christian custom of burial it is to be found in the reverence paid to the consecrated body of the baptised, a reverence that would seem to be hurt by the violent destruction of its remains by fire, instead of its merely permitted disintegration by natural causes. Perhaps the Christian position has some kinship with the Church's general attitude of protest against death and corruption which accounts for the otherwise very unreasonable desire to prolong life, even artificially, when unconsciousness renders such prolongation absolutely profitless. Here again rationalism and utilitarianism is adverse to the Christian sentiment. Also the mere force of custom is rightly respected by the Church, not as a supreme but as a very considerable criterion of right. The arbitrary customs of every society claim a degree of consideration. Christ and all the saints and all Christians have been buried and not burnt; nay, the custom is Semitic, as old as history, as wide as that race and wider. To try and connect the practice with the doctrine of the Resurrection as though the disintegration and dispersion of our dust presented any greater difficulty in one case than the other, is too ridiculous to think of. There would be more faith—more intelligent faith, in cremation, from that point of view. Custom and the sentiment founded on it, is doubtless the root-reason. Wherever Christianity came in, cremation went out. Cremation was no less associated by custom with paganism, than burial with Christianity; and it is just because its modern reintroduction has been inspired by a contempt for Christian custom and a sympathy with paganism that it has been forbidden by positive Ecclesiastical law.

On merely *rational* grounds I have no sympathy with those who *care* what is done with their own corpse or the corpses of their dear ones; for such *caring* introduces the element of *sentiment*; and for myself I like the idea of quietly mouldering away under the green sod in some quiet Catholic Churchyard with those *qui dormiunt in somno pacis.*[2] There is something violent and unrestful in the idea of being shot through a factory-furnace, as though men were glad to get rid of the last vestige of me. It is like 'The funeral will leave at 10.45 *sharp.*'

> 'Tis well, 'tis something, we may stand
> Where he in English earth is laid
> And from his ashes may be made
> The violet of his native land.
> This look of quiet flatters thus
> Our home-bred fancies: and to us
> The fools of habit, etc., etc.[3]

In fact I have as little sympathy with cremation as with a steam-tram-car, which is very useful for people in a violent hurry, but very ugly;—and why this violent hurry?

The sanitary argument is the only one I will listen to; or that the Church may ever listen to later. But I must first be convinced that burial is responsible for typhoid to a considerable extent; and then, that there is no other way out but cremation. Both are hard to prove.

I am afraid all this minutious sanitation is part of that 'cult of infirmity' which Arnold White attacks rather unpleasantly in the *National Review* (October or November).[4] My visit to Bruges this summer, where all the conditions of the most virulent typhoid exist, and no one seems to get it, point to the happy workings of the law of survival. All with any typhoid capacity have been killed off long ago and their breed has died out. Also I wondered how they got such robust health on wedges of tough veal, until the same law came to my rescue. The diet has secured a race of ostrich livers. The whole tendency of the interference of the medical art with nature's cruel-kind methods has been to increase the sum of sickness and pain and to degenerate the physical type. With savages when a man gets a cancer they burn it out with a red-hot poker; and if he survives he was worth preserving. I have just been reading Wilfrid Blunt's[5] 'Satan Absolved' and have perhaps caught his tone.

Kind regards to Mrs. Ward

Yours faithfully,
G. Tyrrell.

Notes to Letter 11

1. Another entrance to the Farm Street establishment.
2. who sleep the slumber of peace.
3. Quoted from Tennyson's *In Memoriam*, xviii, stanza 1.
4. "The Cult of Infirmity" in the *National Review* 34 (October 1899):236–45.
5. Wilfrid Scawen Blunt (1840–1922), poet and political writer. He and *T* were friends and Blunt was one of the few people to attend *T*'s funeral. For an excellent biography of Blunt see Elizabeth Longford, *A Pilgrimage of Passion: The Life of Wilfrid Scawen Blunt* (New York, 1980).

12 31, Farm Street, Berkeley Square,
London, W.
7 December 1899

My dear Ward,

I have these[1] over, so you need not apply to Manresa press.[2] So far there have been no anathemas, although the article was selected for refectory-reading at Saint Bernard's where the nose for heterodoxy is keenest. It is enough to tempt one out of one's prudence. I have a little venture on Hell[3] coming out in the *Weekly Register* for December 16 which may perhaps amuse you as out-Heroding Herod.

Kindest regards to Mrs. Ward.

Ever yours faithfully,
G. TYRRELL S.J.

Notes to Letter 12

1. Reprints of *T*'s article, "The Relation of Theology to Devotion" in the *Month* 94 (November 1899):461–73. This article signals a new phase in *T*'s thinking and the beginning of a radical departure from Newman and from *W*. He later recognized the article as a turning point in his life (see *S&C* Preface); it pointed to the interdependence of theology and devotion and argued that each is inadequate as a separate way of expressing religious truth. The article was reprinted in *FM* I.228–52, and reprinted as "Lex Orandi, Lex Credendi" in *S&C* 85–105. In 1902 *T* expanded his ideas in this article into a small book published under the pseudonym, Dr. Ernest Engels, *Religion as a Factor of Life*. He incorporated the Engels work into the "Lex Orandi" article and was able to secure an Imprimatur for it when he published *S&C*.

2. Manressa press, Roehampton, published the *Month*.

3. *T* here refers to his article, "A Perverted Devotion" which appeared in the *Weekly Register* 100 (16 December 1899): 797–800. It was reprinted in *EFI* 158–71. With this article, *T*'s troubles with censorship began. He was delated to Rome, his essay judged "offensive to pious ears" and he was dismissed from the staff of the *Month* and forbidden to publish outside its pages.

13 31, Farm Street, Berkeley Square,
London, W.
Thursday[1]

My dear Ward,

Thanks for both your letters. I quite agree that the article[2] was indiscreet and calculated to annoy; and would have willingly accepted the doom of perpetual silence however inproportionate to the offence. But the present terms are preposterous. My entire concern is the unripping of any good I may have done and the *scandalum pusillorum.*[3] The best hope is the insult given to the English Jesuit censors of my article; and to the whole province by the demand that my retractation must go to Rome for censorship as though none here could be trusted.[4] So far I have only written to say that I am going to contest the matter to the very last,[5] and am prepared to face any scandal of ill-consequences rather than say the thing which is not. They always modify their terms if they think one will fight; and when I get the price down to its lowest I will see if I can afford it. I should be glad of a talk about it if we can manage it.

Poor Newman! I sometimes wonder what his *inmost* thoughts were; and I read 'Who's to blame?'[6] yesterday. No one ever understood England and the English as he.

Yours faithfully,
G. TYRRELL.

I forgot to give notice of my intention to dine tomorrow;[7] if it is not too late you can tell me in the afternoon.

Notes to Letter 13

1. The context of this letter suggests that it was probably written on 25 January; the Synthetic Society meeting he refers to was scheduled for 26 January 1900.

2. "A Perverted Devotion" see letter 12 note 3.

3. scandal of the little ones.

4. The English Jesuit censors had read *T*'s article on hell and found no harm in it, but the Italian readers found it "damnable" (*A&L* II.455); the Italian verdict, therefore, could be construed as an insult to the integrity of the English Jesuit readers.

5. *T* wrote a reply to the Roman censors; see *A&L* II.121–5.

6. Newman's series of letters to the editor of the *Catholic Standard* in 1855 were collected and published as "Who's to Blame?" in his *Discussions and Arguments on Various Subjects* (London, 1872):306–62. There are eight letters on English constitutional principles and problems. The final paragraph answers his lead question: "Who's to blame for the untoward events in the Crimea? They are to blame, the ignorant, intemperate public who clamour for an unwise war, and then, when it turns out otherwise than they expected, instead of acknowledging their fault, proceed to beat their zealous servants in the midst of the fight for not doing the impossible."

7. With the Synthetic Society.

14

31, Farm Street, Berkeley Square,
London, W.
4 February 1908

My dear Ward,

I will be very pleased to meet Henry Sidgwick on the 23rd. Has Mrs. Ward seen Père Bremond's article in the *Études* on *One Poor Scruple*.[1] In case not, I send a *tirage*.[2] Bremond is 'a true Jesuit in whom there is no guile,' and wisely confines his pen to literary topics. My pitcher has gone once too often to the well, and our General is uneasy about my article on hell;* for hell is very near and dear to the Spanish heart. We all grab our religion differently; some, by the arm; some, by the leg; few, by the head; most, by the breech—a fundamental and serviceable part, but not the most honourable. Hell is the simplest of dogmas, if it be taken rudely, and therefore that on which the majority rest most firmly. To suggest that it is mysterious is to puncture their air-cushion. *Peccavi nimis*.[3]

Do you know what is to become of Williams' articles on Newman that were destined for the *New Era*? Why does he not send them to the *Register*[4]—the only blow-hole left for those who like a little fresh air. I fear now that Mivart[5] will throw everything back at least a decade unless reasonable people combine in some way to keep up a steady stream of healthy literature. I had a vague hope that the *Weekly Register* might become the organ of such a conspiracy; but on talking with Rooke Ley[6] I see no chance; so the ark must pass into the hands of the Philistines for the present. I have half a mind to send you some comments on Haldane's proposals[7] which you might circulate if you think they are worth it.

Kind regards to Mrs. Ward.

Ever yours faithfully,
G. TYRRELL.

* forgive rhyme

Notes to Letter 14

1. Henri Bremond, S.J. (1865–1933), a friend of Blondel's and of *T*'s. He left the Jesuits in February 1904, but not the priesthood. At this time he was editor of the literary review, *Études*. *T* is here referring to a favorable and lengthy review

of *One Poor Scruple* (see letter 6 note 10). About the *T*/Bremond friendship see Anne Louis-David (editor/annotater) *Georges Tyrrell Lettres a Henri Bremond* (Paris, 1971).

2. Off-print. For a long summary of the Bremond article see *MW* I.382–6.

3. I have sinned exceedingly.

4. The *Weekly Register*, a Catholic periodical of liberal leanings which published its last weekly edition 14 March 1902, became the *Monthly Register* April-December 1902 at which time it ceased to exist. Opinion is divided about its origins: Maisie Ward argued that it began with Cardinal Manning in 1881 (*MW* II.144–6); John R. Fletcher traces it back to the *Weekly and Monthly Orthodox* (1849); see "Early Catholic Periodicals in England" *Dublin Review* 198 (April 1936):284–310. For more precise details about its existence and problems at the turn of the century consult the Rooke Ley papers at *SAUL*.

5. See letter 7 note 8; Mivart was excommunicated by Cardinal Vaughan at the end of January 1900.

6. Frank Rooke Ley, editor of the *Weekly Register*.

7. *T* refers to Haldane's comment on the "Concessions" and "Questions" discussed at the 26 January 1900 meeting (see letter 9 note 1). *T*'s comments were presented at the meeting 23 February 1900 and can be found in *SSP*.

15

31, Farm Street, Berkeley Square,
London, W.
24 February 1900

My dear Ward,

On reflection it seems to me that as you are known to be my friend any 'stand' that I might possibly have to make would surely be put down to your influence were I to accept your kind invitation. As a fact [your influence is] quite the other way, namely [in the direction of that caution and moderation which one is so apt to throw to the winds in moments of irritableness and anger.][1] Perhaps you have a deeper responsibility for my mis-doings in that my decadence dates from your article on 'The Elasticity of Rome'[2] wherein you ended with a 'swipe' at the Society.[3] I felt that however the existing Society deserved the 'swipe,' yet 'elasticity' was the one dominant principle of Ignatius—the 16th century Hecker,[4] and that point I have since pressed and pressed in season and doubtless out of season. Perhaps my last and expiring effort will appear shortly in a booklet (too far advanced for suppression) called *The Testament of Ignatius Loyola*[5] which I have prefaced, epilogised and noted, all to the same tune. As I said once to His Paternity[6] if the bottle won't stretch it must burst—and the sooner the better. We know by faith, certainly not by sight, that the Church will stretch somehow or other, as she did when she swallowed Aristotle whole and entire with no worse result than a slight dyspepsia; but no other institution is so guaranteed as to be able to defy the ordinary laws of social growth, decay, and death. I wonder could you persuade J. Ward to give us the next paper.[7] I had a few words with him afterwards—I think he is much with us, and that he is completing the cycle of metaphysical development which will land us back at the starting point, namely the unformulated beliefs of *direct* thought. My idea is that God made our minds for very practical purposes and that it goes all right within those limits. Our first *reflexions* on its nature are the wrongest; and the last, if last be given, are the nearest to our direct and natural conviction. Between the extremes are infinite vagaries. Seth's Hegelianism[8] has forced this view upon me very much. In short it is Augustine's view about time; Don't ask me what it is and I know; ask me, and I don't know.

Kindest regards to Mrs. Ward.

Ever yours faithfully,
G. Tyrrell, S.J.

Notes to Letter 15

1. Bracketed material published in *MW* II.169.

2. *W*'s article was actually titled "The Rigidity of Rome" *Nineteenth Century* 38 (December 1895):786–804; reprinted in *PP* 66–98.

3. *W* argued that the Roman church is not rigid but adaptable and adapting. His argument hinges, in part, on his characterization of the counter-Reformation church as one in a state of seige, under martial law, a state he believed was no longer necessary. In the context of his argument he described the Jesuits as members of the papal army and discussed their military character. *W*'s remarks could be construed as implying Jesuit obsolesence as soldiers are unnecessary in times of peace.

4. Isaac Hecker (1819–1888), founder of the Paulists and associated, by a series of complex and misdirected moves, with the pseudo heresy of "Americanism." Hecker was a man ahead of his time, full of new ideas for adapting the

gospel to new situations. Presumably, *T* argues that Ignatius (and the Jesuits) are (or should be) on the creative edge of emerging traditions within the church and not the guardians of antiquated traditions.

5. *The Testament of Ignatius Loyola,* translated by E. M. Rix, with a preface by *T* (London, 1900). For an explanation of *T*'s use of this piece to "justify his own existence as a Jesuit," see Barmann, p. 162. *T* understood Ignatius' intentions to be mediating and therefore thought that contemporary Jesuits, in being conservative, betrayed the spirit of the founder. This theme recurs frequently in his letters to Bremond.

6. In-house reference for the General of the Society of Jesus.

7. James Ward (see letter 9 note 4); he first attended the Synthetic Society on 23 February 1900, the evening before this letter. He was asked many times to present a paper, but did not give his first Synthetic paper until April 1902.

8. Andrew Seth Pringle-Pattison (1856–1931), philosopher and member of the Synthetic Society. He sometimes co-authored articles with Haldane. He was a thoroughgoing Hegelian and gave two sets of "Balfour Lectures" in the 1880's. The second set of lectures was published as *Hegelianism and Personality* (London, 1887).

16

31, Farm Street, Berkeley Square
London, W.
Tuesday[1]

My dear Ward,

I am more sensible of your kindness in this affair; for one needs to have the word of another in support of one's own better judgment at such times; and one's best Jesuit friends can hardly advise with perfect freedom, having one eye on the order and only the other on me.

You may be quite sure that rather than give such a scandal I will yield everything on pressure, short of saying what I don't mean; but it must be 'on pressure', else the next thing would be to subject my other books to similar censorship, and so destroy any good they may have done. I was prepared (and am) to 'go under' and not write any more, and on first hearing of the matter I at once asked them not to trouble to judicate for that reason. I am afraid this more violent aggression was the fruit of my temperance. Silence was what they wanted; and when they saw I did not care, they wanted more. Odd as it may sound, I have no wish and should have much reluctance to split with the Society where my personal friends are so many and my affections consequently entangled—as I am a slave of habits and customs and would find a change as painful as being flayed alive. Also my view of vocation is that, those few who are free to choose have to make their choice of a walk in life, for better or for worse, at an early age when their experience is narrow and their judgment imperfect. Yet society requires and God wills that they should stand by their contracts when those contracts are of their nature irrevocable even though (as often happens in marriage) they may afterwards see that had they known differently they had chosen otherwise, i.e. supposing that there has been no substantial error, no after-inconvenience that was not risked in the very nature of the contract. A man's profession, or his order, or his wife seldom realises his first ideal. The Society is not less like Saint Ignatius, than Christians are like Christ. So I would not wish for release on that account; else I should in consistency have to go further. It is therefore only in the event of a sacrifice of truthfulness being involved that I will go to extremes; short of that I will yield inch by inch if hard pressed.

Ever yours faithfully,
G. Tyrrell.

Note to Letter 16

1. This letter and the following one are difficult to place with full accuracy. They are both written on the same kind of writing paper, a type and color different from all the rest of *T*'s letters and I surmise that they belong together. The context suggests two possible dates: 1) sometime in March 1900 (when Rome admonished *all* English Jesuits and when *T*, himself, was forbidden to publish anywhere except in the pages of the *Month*; see *T*'s letter to von Hügel 10 March 1900, or 2) sometime in May 1900 (as *T* was preparing a retraction of his ideas as set forth in "A Perverted Devotion," a retraction which appeared in the *Weekly Register* 1 June 1900). As it follows directly on the heels of the discussion in letters 12–15, I thought it best to place it here (in March) rather than in May. There is a certain internal coherence in this placement.

17

31, Farm Street, Berkeley Square,
London, W.
Friday[1]

My dear Ward,

It was immensely kind of you to take so much trouble[2] and I will really try to adopt a more severely scholastic style in my revision; for indeed there is no sense of the ridiculous at Rome. My temper is not angelic at any time; and if you only knew what I should *like* to write you would marvel at the modest dimensions to which I have reduced my contempt. But I am now less hopeful than when I saw you of a peaceful settlement; for between ourselves Father Gerard tells me that my 'admonition' was but a special section of a rebuke addressed to all the writers of the English Jesuit Province censuring them for 'being too anxious to conciliate the adversaries of the Church and not being sufficiently strong and courageous in their condemnation of heresy and error' and exhorting them to remember the traditions of the Society and to walk worthy of their vocation.[3] When one remembers that Fathers Smith,[4] Clarke,[5] Rickaby,[6] Thurston[7] are included in this *massa damnata*; and also that Father H. Lucas[8] was all but silenced a year since for having spoken depreciatingly in the *Tablet*[9] of Abbé Maignan's[10] style, it is plain that we are required to adopt the tone of the *Civiltà*[11] and of *La Croix*[12]; to return to the savagery from which we were slowly emerging. Father Gerard is, I can see, very sure about it; but he can do little in the face of such dark fanaticism. This verifies what I said to you—that the English Jesuit however redeemable independently, is hopeless owing to its connection with the main body; and cannot move forward till Spain, Italy, France, etc., have come up to line—and then it will be too late. Nobody can remedy it but the Pope, and he is as inaccessible and probably as impossible as the Mikado. And yet the Society of Jesus in England has great power to keep things back owing to its influence with women, and its repute for sanctity and safety; and to its real merits which are not few. Perhaps the best hope is that Rome may run its head against a stone wall, and so be waked up to sober realities. In a different spirit Monsignor Dunn[13] wished the other day that they would define the earth to be a flat plate and the moon made of green cheese and force it down the throats of these scientists. For once, I agreed with him we should then know where we stood.

Ever yours,
G. TYRRELL.

Is there any foundation for the report that there has been talk of submitting the *Essay on Development*[14] to censure? That would be a master-stroke; since it would show that Newman's conversion and subsequent position was based on a misapprehension.

Notes to Letter 17

1. See letter 16 note 1.

2. *W* apparently read a draft of *T*'s retraction and offered suggestions about it. For a text of the retraction see *A&L* II.128f.

3. Presumably their counter-Reformation identity as defenders of the Pope.

4. Sydney Smith, S.J. (1843–1922) author and an editor of the *Month*.

5. Richard F. Clarke, S.J.; see letter 1 note 2.

6. Joseph Rickaby, S.J. (1845–1932), philosopher and friend of *T*'s; see *A&L* II.59.

7. Herbert Thurston, S.J. (1856–1913) historian and *T*'s good friend at Farm Street.

8. Herbert Lucas, S.J. (1852–1933), he was also a friend of von Hügel's; see Anne Louis-David, pp. 140–3.

9. The *Tablet* was founded by Frederic Lucas in 1840. In 1900 it was owned by Cardinal Vaughan and was, in effect, the official newspaper for the archdiocese of Westminster. Herbert Lucas S.J. wrote an (unsigned) article attacking Maignan for uncharitable and unfair tactics; see "Father Hecker and His Critics" 93 (18 March 1899):403–5.

10. Abbé C. Maignan was involved in the Americanist controversy as an agitator. He was the author of an inflammatory article, "Le Pére Hecker—est-il un saint?" which appeared in the conservative periodical *La Vérité Française*.

11. *Civiltà Cattolica*, an Italian Catholic newspaper published twice each month by the Jesuits; it was highly conservative and against liberalism in any form.

12. *La Croix* was a French Catholic newspaper founded by the Assumptionists in the late nineteenth century to "become a powerful force against secularism in France." It was anti-liberal in tone and style and at the time of this letter was highly anti-Dreyfus in its editorial policy. See Robert J. Marion, *La Croix and Ralliement* (A Dissertation for Clark University, Worcester, 1958).

13. Thomas Dunn was the personal secretary of Cardinal Vaughan.

14. Newman's *Essay on the Development of Doctrine* (London, 1845) was written, for the most part, before his conversion to Catholicism. Accordingly, it belongs to his Anglican period, though it is sometimes said that it was issued immediately after his conversion "in defence of his change of allegiance;" see *Oxford Dictionary of the Christian Church* (1958 edition) p. 950. Apparently, he made no theological revisions in the text (on the advice of Cardinal Wiseman) because he hoped "it would be a more effective plea for the Catholic religion if it received no theological revision." See Ward, *The Life of John Henry Cardinal Newman*, II, p. 99.

18

31, Farm Street.
Monday, 13 March 1900

My dear Ward,

This[1] seems to me very opportune and calculated to reveal thoughts out of many hearts. Let me first notice a few trifles, and then put a problem which I have not yet cleared up, and which no-one seems to consider sufficiently.

1. There is an unnecessary appearance of repetition owing to your following the method: A, B, A2, B2, etc.; instead of A, A2, B, B2, and thus having to recur several times to A, viewed under a different aspect, which difference the ordinary reader will be obtuse to perceive.

2. pp. 9, 10, 15, etc. I wish we had an Academy to settle whether we should say *Metaphysic* or *Metaphysics*; and if the latter, whether to treat it as singular (like 'news') or plural.

3. p. 8. I suppose *Dionysius* and not *Clement* the *Areopagite*.

4. p. 30. 'Si quis dixerit . . . anathema sit.'[2] It sounds here as though they were *two* formulae.

5. p. 7. You might seem to the captious to approve of Gibbon's[3] contention, as much as of Newman's and Harnack's.[4] I suppose the formulation of the belief (not the belief itself, of course) is as unhebraic as possible and hails from the extreme East, eventually.

6. I think it is a good point to show that it is not the process of accommodation of dogmatic expression to science that is new; but the *rate* of that process. Yet this rapidity creates a difficulty that is distinct in kind and not only in degree; just as when single beats quicken into a musical note. The process was formerly quite insensible within the compass of one or several generations; but now elderly people who have followed the movement complain that all the old landmarks are gone; nor can any formulation of faith now remain long enough to take that firm root in the mind and imagination without which it is not very effective in the individual or in society. In fact it is held provisionally and conditionally and not categorically and finally; and though this is right as regards the Church corporately; I doubt if it does for the individual, or even the single generation.

7. p. 12. In fact, the Church first kills and then devours her foes, and digests as much of their constitutions as matter for her

purpose. No other philosophy of life is to live but herself; and she must rise and slay before she can eat.

8. p. 12, etc. Monsignor Moyes[5] is strong on the view that the strict *depositum fidei*[6] left by Church (as opposed to the whole body of Catholic teaching that has gathered round it) is subject, not to development, (as a seed develops) but to mere literal *evolution* or unfolding (as a moth's wing unfolds after the chrysalis breaks). This he gets from the preambles of the Council of Florence, which compares the process to the unfolding of a crumpled-up cloak. I suppose he explains Vincent of Lerins[7] as referring to the *tout ensemble* of Catholic teaching. It is on this view (at least, as misunderstood) that Father Clarke[8] asserts the Immaculate Conception (e.g.) to have been known to every pope since Saint Peter; at least *in confuso* or, as it were, in small type* needing only a closer glance. Hence, as far as the *deposit* goes, the only advance is from implicit to explicit; from confusion to distinction;—an advance wrought by the cavils and questions of heretics; by the curiosity of the faithful; but above all by the industry of scholastic theology which squeezes the last drop of juice out of the wine-press.

There is no growth in bulk; no putting out of new parts as in an organism. Thus Moyes.

We should all agree that when we speak of the growth of an idea we really mean the growing subjective accommodation of our mind to reality,—and not that eternal realities change. But whereas Moyes only admits a growth in the *mode* of our apprehension of revealed truth (a more distinct apprehension of the same area); you and Newman seem to admit a growth as to the extent and area of our apprehension. The difference is perhaps that between the ancient 'homunculus' embryology and the modern, applied to ideas. The latter would seem to Moyes to entail an increment in the substance and quantity of divine revelation, which has received no additional bulk since the Apostles' time. But I think he is the victim of a metaphor. For such an advance from confused to distinct knowledge, though it does not involve a growth or development of the thing known, does mean a real development of my idea and knowledge—a segmentation and taking on of parts and members, a process of organising which is not mere unfolding but veritable growth

* i.e., his subjective impressions being the 'small type' in question

from potential to actual knowledge. By re-reading and studying the same document I do not add to the bulk of its content, but I do add to the bulk and formation of my intelligence. Hence, keeping strictly to the *depositum fidei* I believe that the sub-apostolic Church (I leave out the apostles,[9] as being founts of revelation) did not and could not know all the potential contents of the deposit; that questions since asked and answered could not then have been asked or answered.

The fallacy that Moyes builds on is: Because what is seen indistinctly is really present in the object, it is really presented to the subject; because I can see a man a mile off, I can, by a careful examination of my impression, also see his waistcoat button. To see details, a nearer presentment is necessary, or else an intensified power of vision. It is through this latter condition that the Christian idea grows; and not, as Moyes & Co. think, through mere analysis and dissection of the cloudy impression of earlier times; that, will never give us the waistcoat button. Hence the Christian idea lives and grows because the light (*natural* and *supernatural*) lives and grows from strength to strength. Else, were logic alone needed, the Church could have done with Aristotle and without the Holy Ghost.

In all this, I speak simply of what is *De fide Divina*.[10] No one can deny development in so far as the Church takes new matter into her teaching *circa depositum*, or refers what is revealed to secular knowledge, and applies religion to the changing conditions of human life, etc.

9. pp. 28–29. "What remains unchanged in itself is the truth as it is the mind of God, and in the (imagined) consciousness of the Church . . . . in the ideal consciousness of the Church" cf. p. 34.

This is my principal difficulty. Taking Christ as the great and final revealer, he as man has direct but not comprehensive or adequate intuition of the reality and truth as it lies in God's mind; he clothed it in the swaddling bands of human forms and figures and words and gave those forms to his Church; and with them, the Holy Ghost to keep them in the Church's remembrance and to guide her into an ever deepening understanding of their significance—but not to *add* to them. The Church has no *direct* intuition of the reality in God's mind, but only *mediante Christo*,[11] or rather, through that expression of his human apprehension of the Eternal which Christ bequeaths, and which his spirit interprets to the Church.

Hence the truth is very differently in the mind of God or even in the human mind of Christ and in the mind of the Church. As by my own mind I mean not merely the present contents of my memory and the results of my past experience, but also the active power of dealing with those contents and of extending my experience; so by the mind of the Church, I understand not merely the present stage of dogmatic intelligence achieved in the minds of the faithful at large, but also the active principle of that and of future achievements—the Holy Ghost. And this gives concrete unity to the 'mind of the Church' as opposed to the abstract unity of the '*consensus humani generis*.'[12] But the truth is possessed by the Holy Ghost, as by God, yet as the active mind of the Church His function is but to safeguard and interpret the revelation [[given]] man by the Man Christ. '*Ille vos docebit omnia, suggeret vobis omnia quaecumque dixero vobis*.'[13]

Let me illustrate grossly the way I conceive it. A philanthropist desirous to bring the blessings of British civilisation to a stone-age tribe in the heart of Africa, betakes himself into their midst and learns their language—a few removes beyond the bow-wood type, no number beyond 3, etc., etc.

With great difficulty and using illustrations from their own social and material conditions he contrives to convey to a few of the more intelligent or less brutal some faint and grotesque notion of the material, social, political and religious conditions of Great Britain; he teaches them to put in practice such civility and morality as is within their present compass; and finally leaves them a record, in their own language, of all he has told them. After he has been killed and eaten, his few faithful disciples begin quietly working on his lines, and the practical benefits are such that opposition is conquered and the record becomes an oracle, to all future generations. Plainly, here, as soon as the immediate disciples die off, the earliest interpreters will be most hopelessly at sea; much of the record will seem sheer nonsense to them, yet because some is so valuable they will force interpretations of the rest. As their civilisation grows they will come to understand many things at first inexplicable; and thus be, in some way, in a better position than the first disciples to interpret and realise their benefactor's mind. But as living languages change rapidly it will be a great point to preserve the original meaning of the record—the sense it conveyed to the first hearers, for that is their *depositum fidei*, the third-hand presentment of the Reality namely British Civilisation.[14]

It is only in the lack of a Holy Ghost that this parable falls short of my purpose; also, the philanthropist's mind is fairly adequate to the reality he preaches; not so, the human mind of Christ which apprehended the Divinity human [[sic]]. Yet that lack is supplied by the natural upward growth of these savages in morality and civilisation and therefore in the power of sympathetic apprehension.

In the Christian Church there is, over and above the natural progress of the human spirit (whereby its power of vision is intensified and the objects thus virtually brought nearer) a supernatural progress in grace and faith (viewed subjectively as faculties) which brings the revelation of Christ home to us even more closely. And to me this is the most living proof of Christianity namely its anticipation of the results of our spiritual progress; the number of things that had no meaning for the past; and so much for us: 'Lo I have told you beforehand that when it shall come to pass ye may believe.'

In fine Christianity is in the hands of Christians like the *Imitatio Christi* in the hands of a child—it has no meaning for him now, but he may grow to its meaning when he has tried life and found it a failure.

10. p. 27. The ascription of universal infallibility to the opponents of a particular error is a theme worthy of independent development. Saint Augustine is a lamentable example.

11. p. 16. *In aenigmate* as opposed to *facie ad faciem*[15] hits off nicely the difference between the object of Divine and of ecclesiastical intuition. The Church 'intuits' the *aenigma* that Christ framed in Syriac language and symbolism and left with her as the rough cast of the impression created in his human mind by the vision of God.

12. Another complication in regard to development of the *deposit of faith* is that it includes all so-called *natural* theology; and this develops just like any other part of philosophy. Also it includes natural ethics which also grows in bulk of matter and not merely in distinctness.[16]

Notes to Letter 18

1. *T* read and made suggestions about an early draft of *W*'s "Unchanging Dogmas and Changeful Man" *Fortnightly Review* 67 (April 1900):628–48; reprinted in *PP* 99–132. *W*'s article was a conscious response to Mivart's articles (see letter 7 note 8) published in January 1900.

2. "If anyone says . . . let him be anathema" (condemned), a formula used in the proceedings of ecumenical councils to condemn those who teach the opposite of the council's canons.

3. Edward Gibbon (1737–1794), historian; this reference does not appear in the final version of the article.

4. Adolf von Harnack (1851–1930), German church historian; this reference does not appear in the final version of the article.

5. James Moyes (1851–1927), canon and theologian for the archdiocese of Westminster and current editor of the *Dublin Review*. Moyes was a conservative and likely to read or review *W*'s article. *T* was beginning to believe that the notion of an apostolic Catholicism which had developed through the centuries was unrealistic and that Catholics were going to have to deal with a *real* development of doctrine; yet, when he looked for like-minded theologians he found only people like Moyes whose notions of a literal unfolding of doctrine did not allow for a real development in the deposit of faith (as a seed develops into a tree).

6. deposit of faith

7. Vincent of Lerins (d. c. 450) laid down a famous three-fold test for Catholicity: *quod ubique, quod semper, quod ab omnibus creditum est* (what has been believed everywhere, always, and by all).

8. Not clear whether *T* refers to his confrere, Richard F. Clarke SJ (see letter 1 note 2) or to Robert F. Clarke (1844–1906), friend of *W*'s and later a member of the Pontifical Biblical Commission who was cited in the article by *W* as "a learned theologian and a man of science," i.e., the kind of man who could most effectively "answer" Mivart's questions.

9. *T* obviously thought that the Apostles *could* have known all future developments.

10. Of divine faith, i.e., the most solemnly defined dogmas of the Roman Catholic church.

11. by means of Christ's mediation

12. "consensus of the human race."

13. John 14.26: "[the Holy Spirit] will teach you and will remind you of all I said to you."

14. *T* later extended this parable into a booklet, *The Civilizing of the Maltafanus: An Essay of Religious Development* (London, 1902); see letter 20 note 3.

15. In a riddle as opposed to face to face

16. This letter has no closing and no signature.

19

31, Farm Street
16 March 1900

My dear Ward,

The article[1] is obviously and necessarily too compressed and contains matter for a considerable volume. As such it will miss the popular ear. But I think it will surely evoke discussion on one point or another; and then there will be a chance of developing some of the ideas; e.g. that 'practical' principles, like instincts and habits, are sound if the results are good *ut in pluribus*[2] and that a percentage of failure is naturally to be expected, as in the decisions of fallible authority. Or again, the idea that 'there is no error in what God *intended to convey* in scripture' and that one cannot begin to criticise till one has determined what that intention is. And I wish you had presented doctrinal development less as 'the means adopted by the Church, etc.,' and more, as the only *possible* means considering the psychological laws that govern the growth of mind.

Of trifles I only notice the following—

(1) p. 3. 1.22. 'The writer in question' i.e. Dr. Mivart

(2) p. 4. 1.26. 'Has not scientific—' I should have expected 'Is it possible to maintain that scientific—' Also, there should be a ? after science.

(3) p. 1. 1.2. from foot. Shouldn't it be 'that Copernicanism *was* heretical?'[3]

(4) p. 11. note. Pass la, not la lae.

(5) p. 13. middle. The Ascension was not merely a *verbal* but an *enacted* symbolisation, if we are to take *Acts* I as history. And a most significant thing is this *acted* concession to human categories of thought.

(6) p. 13. foot. The strange thing is that modern philosophy denies the very existence of that *substantia materialis*[4] which Scholasticism affirms will rise again, or is present in [the] Eucharist. If substance is merely a subjective category, an ideal peg to hang real appearances on, then transubstantiation coincides exactly with Zwinglianism, and yet every word of the *Lauda Sion*[5] is saved. There's a nice mess!

(7) p. 14. I think you will [[find]] all this *in substance* in most of the current treatises *De novissimis*; and I am pretty certain in Mazzella's[6] treatise. So look out for squalls.

(8) p. 16. middle. 'Encyclical,' not italics. The Pope's intention in the *Providentissimus*[7] was obscurantist to the last degree. If he left any breathing room it was merely by accident.

(9) p. 18. middle. I wish you wouldn't make the theologians an essential factor in the Church's life. I think it is rather in the subconsciousness of the faithful at large that God's spirit works; whereas theology is almost professed [[as]] a human and artificial instrument.[8]

(10) 19 7/8. Is Mivart an M.D. by profession?

(11) 20 foot. Isn't it rather by her parish priests and bishops than by the *Schola*?

(12) 21. 1.2. 'May' is a miosis. Surely the angels *must*

Forgive these crude lines, but I presume there is no time to lose.

Ever yours faithfully,
G. TYRRELL.

The articles in the *Pilot* (1 and 2)[9] on the 'New Age of the Roman Church' are good also. Lectures II and III of John Caird's 'Gifford' are suggestive on the Development theory.[10]

Notes to Letter 19

1. This appears to be *T*'s remarks on a *revised* version of *W*'s "Unchanging Dogmas and Changeful Man" (see letter 18).

2. in most cases

3. *W* used the Copernicanism argument and the Galileo case to prove his points throughout the article.

4. material substance.

5. Latin hymn by Thomas Aquinas used as sequence on feast of Corpus Christi.

6. Camillo Cardinal Mazella, S.J. (1833–1901), probably the principle author of the encyclical, *Aeterni Patris* (giving impetus to the scholastic revival) was the Prefect of the Congregation of Rites and the Pope's advisor on Biblical matters. He was a conservative and opposed to some of the new movements in theological thinking at the time, even moderate ones like *W*'s.

7. *Providentissimus Deus* (1893) was an encyclical by Leo XIII guiding the clergy on the Study of Scripture. When it was published there was a long debate on whether it was a forward-looking work or an obscurantist one. *W* believed it to be cautiously encouraging, with the emphasis on caution.

8. *T*, since his article, "The Relation of Theology to Devotion" (see letter 12 note 1) was thinking through a new understanding of religious authority. He agreed with *W* that an authority was necessary, but was more inclined to trust the saints than the theologians.

9. A series of eleven articles under the general title "The Next Age of the Catholic Church" began to appear in the *Pilot*, 3 March 1900. The author signed himself "Caractacus" and wrote on topics such as "The Temporal Power," "Censorship or Free Press?" and "The Pope Since 1870." They appeared regularly until the end of the year. *T* here refers to the first two of them: "Looking Backward" 1 (3 March): 16–17; and "Napoleonic Ideals" 1 (10 March):43.

10. John Caird (1820–1898), philosopher and professor of divinity at Glasgow. He had been influenced by the neo-Hegelian movement and was interested in Christian consciousness. His Gifford Lectures (1892–3, 1895–6) were published posthumously as *The Fundamental Ideas of Christianity*, 2 volumes (Glasgow, 1899).

20

31, Farm Street, Berkeley Square,
London, W.
Saturday, 7 April 1900

My dear Ward,

Destroy the enclosed when you have read it. It was in answer to one of mine declining to recover my reputation by an onslaught on Dell.[1] I said that I was too much in agreement with his main contentions to do so honestly; that I could hardly now deny that his representation to the Jesuit spirit was true of the greater and prevalent part of the Jesuits; and that with such I was absolutely out of harmony, just because I was in harmony with the elastic principles of Saint Ignatius; that the best refutation of Dell would have been the fact of my being allowed a free pen in advocating wider and more sympathetic lines. Gerard[2] is quite sincere in his agreement with my attitude, but the question of 'opportunism' comes in—the balance of good and evil, the proportion of uprooted wheat and tares; and I dare say I move too quickly for a Jesuit. Yet I feel that the 'inhibited' branch of writing is really the most important one and that for which I am best fitted, so that I am extinguished for the most part of me. I may however find a sort of issue in ethics and kindred subjects where my modernity will be less detected; besides which, anonymous work will always be possible if due secrecy be observed. Altogether things might be much worse. I believe I shall have to write some inane article with no reference to my previous one, to make it clear that I believe in eternal punishment and that I am not an agnostic.

As soon as I get it back you must read my type-written account of the Walla-washees,[3] where I have taken a leaf out of the *Tale of a Tub* to illustrate the meaning of ecclesiastical Christianity.

Forgive this soiled paper, as I began my letter in the dark and didn't notice it.

Kind regards to Mrs. Ward

Ever yours faithfully,
G. TYRRELL

I shall be invisible for a fortnight or so, and perhaps incapable of correspondence; having fallen into the hands of the surgeons.

Notes to Letter 20

1. Robert Edward Dell (1865–1940), a convert to Roman Catholicism (1897), journalist and editor of the *Weekly Register* from April to September 1899. In the April issue of the *Nineteenth Century* he published "A Liberal Catholic View of the Case of Dr. Mivart," the tone and substance of which did little to cool an increasingly difficult situation. *W* made a swift and scathing reply—"Liberalism and Intransigence" *Nineteenth Century* 47 (June 1900):960–73—upbraiding Dell for daring to speak for "liberal Catholics." Dell's article not only connected "liberal Catholics" with an extremist position, it connected *T* with Mivart at a time when von Hügel, *T* and *W* all wanted to distance themselves from him (*MW* I.323–26). In addition, trying to praise *T*, Dell put him in a very uncomfortable position by saying: "an English Jesuit Father whose views seem to be as much out of harmony with the spirit of his Society as his abilities are superior to those of his confreres." *T* had obviously been asked to "answer" Dell and refused; also, apparently, he sent the letter he received in response to his refusal to *W*.

2. John Gerard S.J. (1840–1912). *T*'s Provincial (religious superior) and later editor of the *Month*.

3. *T* here refers to an allergorical work which he wrote and gave to his friend, Alfred Raney Waller (1867–1922), to be published under Waller's name. It was published as a pamphlet, *The Civilizing of the Matafanus*. See letter 19, note 10. Maude Petre explains it as "the story of an attempt to civilize a tribe of gross and ferocious savages, the Walla Washees, by one of their number," and claims it to be *T*'s first writing on the Christological problem (see *A&L* II.309f). *T*, in deference to criticism changed the name of the tribe to Matafanus, but preferred Walla-washees. Also, see letter 18 note 14.

21

31, Farm Street, Berkeley Square
London, W.
31 May 1900

My dear Ward,

Thank you very much for your kind words in the XIXth[1] which may be as oil on the troubled waters. Your article is curiously parallel to that which I wrote on Dell ('Who are the reactionaries?')[2] in obedience to His Paternity, and which he could not find it in his conscience to publish. That the thing has been said so fully and clearly is therefore all the more gratifying to me. My revised version[3] of the declaration of orthodoxy has been passed; after six months of groaning and labour the seven hills have been delivered of a lean little mouse whose ineffectual squeak will be heard in the *Weekly Register* of Saturday. The Cardinal[4] sent for me the other day to hear the truth as to various rumours, etc., and though at first I had to listen patiently to the dangers of going too fast, it ended in his listening to the dangers of going too slow. In fact we ended in perfect agreement; but of course Moyes can blow the vane round in two minutes.

Ever yours faithfully,
G. TYRRELL

[Is there any news about Sidgwick? I am haunted by his terrified look.][5]

Notes to Letter 21

1. *Nineteenth Century*; *W*'s "Liberalism and Intransigence" (see letter 20 note 1) praised *T*'s work for which *T* was grateful; but the caustic tone of *W*'s article distressed both *T* and von Hügel. *W* never had an easy time thinking of himself as a "liberal" Catholic, but was able to accept the description so long as it put him in company with men like von Hügel and *T*; once it came to include people like Dell, however, *W* began to distance himself from it.

2. Written in response to Dell but never published and was apparently unknown and undiscovered until recently. *T* apparently sent it to *W* sometime—perhaps even before *W* published "Liberalism and Intransigence"—and *W* kept it with his papers. *W* clearly wanted Dell (and Mivart) to be "answered" and perhaps *T*'s refusal to publish *his* response to Dell disappointed *W* and inspired him to step in with his own article. See Appendix A for the text.

3. *T*'s retraction of "A Perverted Devotion" published on a direct order from the General of the Jesuits appeared in the *Weekly Register* 1 June 1900; the full text can be found in *A&L* II.128–9.

4. Herbert Cardinal Vaughan (1832–1903) archbishop of Westminster (1892–1903).

5. Bracketed material appears in *MW* I.377.

22 Catholic Church, Richmond, Yorks.[1]
2 June 1900

My dear Ward,

[That is really painful news; but quite explains my impression. I should less pity a man who had some theory of life in which suffering had a reasonable part to play. Still Henry Sidgwick is a good instance of the *anima naturalitur Christiana*[2] and would doubtless have been a Christian still had not that profession been made so disreputable, ethically and intellectually, by its loudest exponents. I said Mass for him the day after our meeting; and will do so again; for stoicism is a poor shield against suffering compared with the crucifix.][3]

Yours faithfully,
G. TYRRELL

I am here for as long as I can stay—possibly a month.

Notes to Letter 22

1. Jesuit house in Yorkshire where *T* stayed from the summer of 1900 until the end of 1905; after the publication of his retraction, he left Farm Street for good.

2. naturally Christian soul.

3. Bracketed material published in *MW* I.378. Henry Sidgwick was dying of cancer.

23 Catholic Church. Richmond.
18 June 1900

My dear Ward,

[I wonder who Zeta,[1] of the *Pilot*, may be. I think the quotation from *Loss and Gain*[2] might be retorted against him in the light of the later history of the Anglo-Catholic movement. Bateman's view[3] was not *then* held by any bishop, and had no historical existence; if referred to authority it would have surely been repudiated. But now it is largely accredited. Such changes never come from above but from below; and authority always yields with great reluctance at the last moment when it sees its very existence imperilled. We 'moderates' do not dream that authorities will ever cry *peccavimus.*[4] It is not desirable they should do so, lest the undiscerning many should take scandal, and withdraw all trust through a false inference. We rather foresee and feel that modern light and progress cannot by any possible device of obscurantism be kept out; that however the clergy may stick to their scholasticism and refuse to read prohibited books, and hope and pray that the sun may stand still, yet the lay mind will quickly be leavened with modernity; and (since our priesthood is not a caste but is recruited from the laity) a little later the younger clergy will be no less indocile to a system wholly out of harmony with their mental and moral needs. Hence a great danger of wholesale apostasy and revolt in the fairly near future. The Extreme Right hopes weakly in violent methods of repression; and strives to pitchfork back the incoming tide. The Extreme Left calls on them to surrender and cry *peccavimus* or demands what is not so much reform as a revolution—a breaking down, preparatory to building up; nor has it any very definite plan of reconstruction. If there is not a mediating party; these two will tug till the rope breaks and each is thrown backwards with disaster. I acknowledge in each of these extremes an inevitable factor of social or ecclesiastical progress; but another factor is needed; and that, is the *Juste Milieu* party.[5] Its policy is one of adaptation; it looks on both extremes as the terms to be harmonised; the new matter to be sorted and accepted so far as it will in any wise consist with the old forms; the old forms to be interpreted so far as they can be made honestly and consistently to cover and inform the new matter. While the Extreme Left call on the Extreme Right to jump down before all eyes from their untenable positions, the mediatorial party provides a gently inclined plane by which the descent may be accomplished unnoticeably, without hurting the pride of authorities (who are only too glad to escape honourably if they knew how to do so) and without destroying the confidence of the '*minores*' (i.e. of those who are led) in their appointed guides. Instead of first destroying and then rebuilding, it renews brick by brick as renewal is required. But its characteristic note is noiselessness. I think such a party is *toto coelo*[6] distinct in principle and aim from the *soi-disant* Liberal;[7] and not merely *in degree* (as Zeta thinks) as though we wanted only a little less than what they want, or were a little less violent than they—and were 'moderate' in the quantitative sense of the term. For this reason I should prefer 'mediatorial' to 'moderate' or to 'Juste Milieu' were I anxious to brand myself; for these latter imply a definite programme (e.g. with regard to the Index, Inquisition, Higher Criticism, Church Government) whereas all I want is a conciliatory spirit on both sides, each wishing to yield all that can rightly be yielded to the other in a spirit of true liberty. But since this can never be (seeing the one-sided character of the human mind which ever lurches to port or starboard), I think the function of the mediatorial party, which of course is always relatively a small one, is to try to interpret the extremes to one another; to act the part of heat in chemical combinations; and so it is through its instrumentality that the process of modification is gradually forwarded (i.e. forms are interpreted and new matter selected and assimilated). To ask of me a definite programme is, from the nature of the case, ridiculous, unless you can tell me where progress, mental, moral and social is going to end. I think, in general, that any accommodation that can be made without shaking popular confidence in the Church, ought to be made; and that this would allow of a great deal more liberty than is now accorded in many ways. It is the duty of so-called Moderates to think out the *how*, and to bring it home to the minds of those in power. It is surely unhistorical to speak, as Zeta does, as though the Church had not often gone through similar crises. From the nature of the case so large a body must lag behind the age but it moves *at the same rate*. The Church may *try* Chinese isolation; but it *cannot* succeed. Inevitably from below upwards the leaven of progress spreads; and the rapid current that swept the world along in the 19th century will most likely make itself felt in the Church in the 20th by a similarly sudden change of conditions. It is the sense of this impending crisis that makes those who see further than the end of their own noses anxious that the gale may not strike the vessel unawares; that the Extreme Right may not, by a lazy policy of inflexible rigidity, be responsible for the whole-sale defection of the Extreme Left. My difference then from both extremes is not one of degree; but of kind. My position is not a half-way house. My aim or programme is, whatever *unknown* issue may come forth from the working of the opposed but complementary tendencies, Right and Left; and to prevent the catastrophe of the exclusive predominance of either which would result from a schism. Is this more or less your view?][8]

Yours,
G. Tyrrell

P.S. There is no chance of the M.S.[9] seeing light after the General has rejected it.

Notes to Letter 23

1. In the 16 June 1900 issue of the *Pilot*, an Anglican newspaper with liberal leanings, there appeared an article, "A Plea for the Juste Milieu," signed by "Zeta." So far as I know, the identity of Zeta has not been conclusively established. The article was highly critical of *W*'s, "Liberalism and Intransigence."

2. *Loss and Gain: The Story of a Convert* (London, 1848) is Newman's novel about the Oxford movement.

3. Bateman is a character in *Loss and Gain* whom Zeta used to prove his point against *W*.

4. we have sinned. *T* may have been pushing *W* a little here to see just where he stood; the "Liberalism and Intransigence" article tended to put *W* more clearly in line with church authorities and with a kind of triumphalism that *T* disdained.

5. One striking a proper balance; it conveys some of what *W* intended with the notion of *via media*, but without some of the complicating problems that phrase brings with it.

6. by the whole heaven, i.e., infinitely.

7. self-styled liberal, a phrase *T* had used to describe some of the less cautious, more troublesome writers of the time (see his "Liberal Catholicism" the *Month* 91 (May 1898):449–57).

8. Bracketed material published in *A&L* II.109–11.

9. Very likely *T* is referring to "Who Are the Reactionaries?" which was refused for publication in the *Month*.

24

31 Farm Street, Berkeley Square,
London, W.
17 August 1900

My dear Ward,

I intended sending you a reprint of the article[1] as soon as I had one to send. I am sorry to say this does not mean any relaxation. This was an exception made for *Month* articles from the first, for the simple reason that there is as yet no one to take my place on the staff. On the contrary, in some sense, the restrictions have been made more difficult. I have now to obtain express leave from Rome *toties quoties*[2] to give a retreat etc.—which is a polite way of making the thing impossible. Under the circumstances one can only read and write and pray and wait. Of course the *Month* is still an outlet. Have you read Hatch's Hibbert lectures of '88 and his Bampton lectures of '81 [[sic]]?[3] They are full of suggestion, though he plainly is too anxious to explain *everything* by his hypotheses. I see *Zeta* is going on.[4] One does feel that the authorities hate us as much as they hate the extravagants and bully us more. I hear now that Père LaGrange OP[5] and his little school are delated. Would to God they would define the Ptolemaic astronomy to be *de fide* and have done with it. How instructive to find Dante saying "*fuori di tutti questi* (i.e., the inner heavenly spheres) *li Cattolici pongono lo cielo Empireo ...Questo e lo luogo dei Spiriti beati secundo che la Santa chiesa vuole che non puo die menzonga.*"[6] Of how many matters do we not speak in the same way which must eventually be quietly left behind! I am infinitely sad [[about]] Sidgwick[7] and wrote to him some time ago and got the enclosed? I don't mean sad about his future, but about his present. After all, life is very dear to such as he, and death and pain very perplexing. Kindest regards to Mrs. Ward. I am going back to Richmond[8] in a day or two to be quiet and think and write.

Ever yours,
G. Tyrrell

Notes to Letter 24

1. "The Mind of the Church" in the *Month* 96 (August 1900):125–42; reprinted in *FM* I.158–204.

2. each time.

3. Edwin Hatch (1835–1889), was an Anglican divine and specialist in the early Christian church. He was co-author with Henry A. Redpath of *A Concordance to the Septuagint and Other Greek Versions of the Old Testament, including the Apocryphal Books,* 3 volumes, (Oxford, 1892–1900). The Bampton Lectures (1880) were published as *The Organization of Early Christian Churches* (London/Oxford, 1881); one of his arguments is that bishops were originally financial administrators only. The Hibbert Lectures (1888) were later edited by A. M. Fairbairn and published as *The Influence of Greek Ideas and Usages on the Christian Church* (London, 1890).

4. See letter 23 note 1. Zeta continued to publish articles criticizing W. In the 7 July 1900 issue of the *Pilot* he wrote "The Juste Milieu Again."

5. Marie-Joseph LaGrange (1855–1938), a Dominican priest and Biblical scholar who founded the École Pratique d'Études Bibliques (1890) and the journal, *Revue Biblique* (1892). He was committed to the critical study of the Bible and was a ray of hope for those who thought the Roman church should adopt more progressive methods of Biblical scholarship.

6. From the *Convivio* (c. 1310). "beyond all these the Catholics assert the Empyrean heaven...This is the place of the blessed spirits, *according as holy Church which may not lie* will have it," (Book II.4.14, emphasis is *T*'s).

7. Sidgwick responded to *T*'s letter; the response is printed in full in *MW* I.378.

8. *T* was apparently visiting at Farm Street.

25

Catholic Church. Richmond. Yorks.
10 September 1900

My dear Ward,

I will not fail to send you the reprints as soon as I get them.[1] The articles were but part of a train of thought whose fuller development should lead to a clear sundering of two absolutely incompatible understandings of the Papal infallibility; of which neither has been stated purely without admixture of the other; one is that which unconsciously dominates in the mind of the ultra-Vaticanist; the other is that [[which]] was perverted by the anti-Vaticanists and led them [[to]] such a *species veri.*[2] The test question is: If the Scriptures and the Fathers and all written documents were destroyed (all allow that these are contingent) where lies the *depositum fidei*? In the pope's single brain, or in the collective brain of Christendom? If in the former, then the pope may say *L'église c'est moi*;[3] the spirit works directly on his mind; and only through it on the Church. If in the latter then the pope is infallible in declaring the general mind in cases of sufficient magnitude to threaten unity; in such matters as formerly justified an ecumenical council; when he publicly and notoriously does investigate the *depositum fidei* contained in the general mind; then, as the Catechism says, he speaks as Head and Teacher of the universal Church, in functional union with it; and not severed from it as a local bishop. It is, then, not a question of the 'form' of a document, but of a fact which justifies the form. The 'Immaculate Conception' was such a case obviously; the *Providentissimus*[4] was obviously not. The *L'église c'est moi* position is a perversion of the papal conception, due to an ambiguity; whereas the true conception is a legitimate and necessary development of the dogma of ecclesiastical infallibility, determining more exactly what was previously more vague. Is not all we are now suffering from Rome due the perversion aforesaid, to what is practically a belief in papal inspiration!

And this takes me to the projected memorandum. 'There is a method of freedom;' says Caractacus in this week's *Pilot*,[5] 'there is a method of repression.' The method of freedom has built up a strong Catholic Church in these Islands, in America, in Australia and wherever it has been given fair play. What has the other system built up? The mere shadow of it, falling across our English-speaking world in these latter years, has called out such a burst of 'No Popery' fanaticism, that we must go back to the Papal Aggression to find its parallel. But to the Italian ecclesiastic all this is simply incomprehensible; any concession he makes to liberty is not out of sympathy but out of diplomacy that he may later strangle it more effectually. An extract I copied from a letter of Ireland's[6] to a common friend is an amusing illustration; 'I have seen the Pope once; Cardinal Rampolla[7] three times; and I am at work seeing the other Cardinals at the rate of one a day. Well, *mon accueil*[8] could not possibly be better. It surprises me. The evident purpose is to make me understand beyond a possible doubt that I am in the highest favour, that they are all delighted with me; that they need my cooperation and are resolved to have it. The Pope told me to forget that letter on Americanism[9] which has no application except in a few dioceses in France. I am to see the Pope again, etc.' The Pope also told Archbishop Riordan[10] that the said letter was founded in misrepresentations. And yet if this was sincerity and not diplomacy why are not these things said aloud for everyone to hear? Why are not these slanderers rebuked and put to shame? Why were three of our fathers censured by the General for having been bodily present at Ireland's address in our own hall, as though he was under excommunication? Why was Father Lucas dropped on for daring to criticise Maignan's infamous book severely?[11] Why does Father Purbrick[12] write deploring the terrible uprising of American Catholics against the Church's authority; and implore me not to be led away by 'the higher (or high-minded) criticism' which he imagines to be intimately connected with Americanism? I take it that the Jesuits represent the mind of Rome far more truly, however for the moment it may be expedient to disown us. I cannot therefore think that the *memorandum* is likely to win its way by any arguments save those that appeal to diplomacy; and there, I am perfectly helpless. I do not see how the matter bears on the temporal power, though it may possibly do so. I can see how it bears on the progress of religion, on the salvation of souls, on the interests of truth, on the glory of God; but these are merely spiritual and unpractical considerations which go for nothing at Rome. My only hope is that things will get better by getting much worse; that the fever will come to a crisis and then burn itself out. With Rampolla for Pope, and Merry del Val[13] for Cardinal this may come about quicker than otherwise.

I am glad poor Sidgwick's agony was not prolonged R.I.P.[14] Our little society will be much enfeebled by the loss. The *Spectator* had a better appreciation of him; but you would treat another side of his strange personality. I'll stay here a little longer as I am writing a good deal more than would be possible in London.

Ever yours,
G. TYRRELL.

Notes to Letter 25

1. Probably part II of "The Mind of the Church" in the *Month* 96 (September 1900):233–40. *T* argued, in these articles, that the "mind of the Church" is the organ of tradition and growth and as such is the collective mind of the *whole* church—everyone in it—and that no single mind has that kind of authority. This letter elaborates on his position in the articles.

2. another order of truth.

3. I am the church, a take-off on Louis XIV's celebrated claim, "L'etat, c'est moi."

4. The doctrine of the Immaculate Conception, declared by Pope Pius IX on 8 December 1854, reflected the mind of the whole church, *T* argues. The encyclical, *Providentissimus Deus* (1893) reflected only the mind of the Pope and his advisors and is therefore not as binding. When it *is* interpreted as binding, *T* claims, one radically alters esslesiology to an "I am the church" papacy.

5. The eighth in the series "The Next Age of the Church" (see letter 19 note 9) was entitled "Statics and Dynamics" and appeared in the *Pilot* 2 (8 September 1900):430–1.

6. John Ireland (1838–1918), was the archbishop of St. Paul, Minnesota. He played an important part in the Americanist controversy.

7. Mariano Cardinal Rampolla (1843–1913), secretary of state to Pope Leo XIII.

8. my reception

9. Americanism was condemned via a papal letter, *Testem Benevolentiae*, from Leo XIII to Cardinal Gibbons on 22 January 1899.

10. Patrick William Riordan (1841–1914), was the archbishop of San Francisco and a close friend of John Ireland. Riordan was in Rome at this time.

11. See letter 17 note 10.

12. Edward I. Purbrick, S.J. (1830–1914), former Provincial of the Jesuits in England.

13. Rafael Merry del Val (1865–1930), became titular archbishop of Nicaea in 1900 and was made Cardinal and Secretary of State by Pope Pius X in 1903.

14. Sidgwick died in September, 1900. His "death almost brought about the [Synthetic] Society's dissolution" (*MW* I.379).

26

Richmond. Yorks.
17 September 1900

My dear Ward,

I will certainly look at the Appendix[1] you speak of when I get back. What alarms me about the tendency in question is that the 'L'église c'est moi' explanation of the papacy involves a distinct breach in that process of ecclesiastical evolution which Mallock dwells on:[2] or at least it involves an intervention like that by which the inorganic is raised to the organic; or mere life, to sentience—the equivalent of a new dispensation, an era, as some shamelessly say, of the Holy Ghost on earth, supervening on the era of Christ. I fully credit men like Father Purbrick or our own Father General with substantial good will and sincerity: and the better they are the more mischief they do. Indeed the disproportionate power that the Jesuits possess in the Church is due almost entirely to a reputation for moral sincerity which is not altogether undeserved. But a man may sincerely believe in the justice of his cause and for that very reason be unscrupulous as to the means by which he furthers it; and furthermore his belief however proximately sincere may depend on a certain blinding egoism or party spirit. Men who are humble in themselves find compensation in cracking up their party or nation. Corporate pride and vanity is a great problem. It seems a condition *sine qua non* for the success of a cause yet ethically it is as indefensible as personal pride. The body lives in each of its members; and for its honour and well-being they think whatever is expedient is lawful. I suppose in the process of evolution the moralising of bodies and societies must necessarily lag behind that of units and individuals. Don't you think that in the repression of Christ the Pharisees and Priests may for the most part have been founded by genuine high motives; that their blindness was not due proximately to personal wilfulness but to the accumulated little insincerities of generations crystallised in the tradition which they inherited? This is what I feel with regard to many of [[the]] narrow-minded zealots. It is their traditional mode of acting and judging that I dislike; and though they have not formed it, but inherited it yet I feel they *ought not* to take an attitude of lazy acquiescence which says: 'Of course *we* are all right.' It is the difference between a man who lies; and one who swallows a lie when he can and ought to criticise.

Yours ever faithfully,
G. TYRRELL.

Notes to Letter 26

1. Unfortunately, since *W*'s letters have been destroyed, it is not possible to say what appendix he was referring to.

2. William Hurrell Mallock (1849–1923), published *Doctrine and Doctrinal Disruption, Being an Examination of the Intellectual Position of the Church in England* (London, 1900). Charles Gore reviewed it for the *Pilot* 12 May 1900 and *W* responded to Gore with a long letter to the editor on 26 May 1900. Mallock argued that science alone can supply no basis for religion, a position *W* believed to have been worked out by Newman in 1838. In a letter to his wife, 15 August 1900, *W* said, "Tyrrell's article on the 'Mind of the Church' appears to me, from a *résumé* I have seen, to be taken from my short letter to the *Pilot* on Gore and Mallock. What a wonderful assimilator he is—but of course he has worked out what I only sketched very slightly. I suppose I have no more right to speak of his borrowing from me than of my borrowing from Newman" (letter *not* in *WWP*, but in private hands).

27 Richmond.
23 September 1900

My dear Ward,

Here are couple of reprints.[1] The final paragraph is 'wrote sarcastic' for them that have eyes to see.

Your estimate of Henry Sidgwick in the *Spectator*[2] is a needful supplement to what has already been said.

I think it would be a good thing if the paper-readers, like the Presidents, of the Synthetic were chosen alternately from the opposite camps. If it were needed I would make a stand for Blondel's[3] thesis or for the experimental character of religious philosophy in the individual i.e. Religion is the only solution to the problem of action which every man has to solve positively or negatively; truly or falsely.

But I don't feel clear enough yet to be very anxious for a hearing.

Ever yours,
G. Tyrrell.

Notes to Letter 27

1. "The Mind of the Church," (see letter 24 note 1 and letter 25 note 1). *T* argued sarcastically against theologians who were misusing the evolutionary metaphor. In the final paragraph he (tongue in cheek) repudiates evolution and modern scientific conclusions while extolling arguments from the First Cause; he ends the article with these words: ". . . endeavours are being made to bring the age back once more to the simpler thought forms of Aquinas and Aristotle." *T* hoped to caution those who would rush to adjust the doctrines of the Catholic faith to modern science; he believed they were making the same mistake as the medieval theologians who linked Roman Catholic doctrine to Aristotelianism. Medieval science changed and, says *T*, so will modern science, thus an artificial union should be avoided.

2. The *Spectator* published an article on Sidgwick when he died, and a week later there was a letter about him from "M." On 22 September, *W* published a long letter about Sidgwick, mostly in response to the letter from "M" 85 (1900) 371–2.

3. Maurice Blondel (1861–1949), French philosopher famous for his work, *L'Action* (Paris, 1893) which attempted to shift the focus of philosophy away from abstract thought and idealism to "action," i.e., to the whole person and the concrete experiences of thinking, feeling, and willing. *T* read Blondel's *Lettre sur les exigences de la pensée contemporaine en matière d'apologetique et sur la méthode de la philosophie dans l'etude du problème religieus* (Saint-Dizier, 1896) in the fall of 1897

(*A&L* II.45); in November 1899 von Hügel gave *T* a copy of *L'Action* and *T* finished reading it by the first week in September (*T* to von Hügel, 7 September 1900). *W* was attracted to Blondel, but not to the same extent; *W* thought Blondel was indebted to Newman and that there were some similarities between them (see "Liberalism and Intransigence").

28

Richmond.
2 October 1900

My dear Ward,

You are quite right as to my altered position about the *depositum*; I wondered faintly if any one read me carefully enough to spot it. Still I see that the wording on p. 5 of the September reprint is misleading.[1] I should have said: 'nor yet that expression which the faith received in the mind of its first hearers, *nor yet* the present day expression of the faith in which that former expression is at once lost and preserved as the child is in the man, *but rather those identical truths and realities which were expressed and seen less perfectly* (relatively to me) *through the earlier forms, more perfectly through the later and more transparent forms.*' My former notion (in 'Theology and Devotion')[2] was that the Church guarded infallibly the primitive mental, if not verbal, *expression* of the faith, re-translating it into the thought forms of later ages, that her concern was not directly with the *fact* implied in (e.g.) *Hoc est corpus meum*,[3] but rather with the sense those words conveyed to the sub-apostolic Church (I say *sub*-apostolic to escape the complicating condition of apostolic inspiration). But this view did not allow for the *third* kind of development (l.c.; p. 1) due to the growth of the power mental vision which should be allowed for in the Church as in the individual; in consequence of which the primitive expression becomes, as it were, a more transparent medium for us. To revert to my illustration: Dr. Gardinar's History primer[4] means much more to him than to the schoolboy for whose use it is written, or than it will mean to that boy in later life, when by the growth of his mind it will have become a more transparent vehicle of the facts signified. According to my former notion the *deposit* consisted not perhaps in the text of the primer, but in the sense it conveys to the mind of a boy—which sense might be translated into many languages and subjected to many comments—the Church having no concern directly with the facts but with Tommy's view of the facts; and judging other expositions only by this criterion. This view relieves us from the dogmatism that credits the Pope with a direct intuition of eternal realities. According to the view on p. 5 (*as amended*) the deposit is just that section of historical *fact* to which the primer gives expression, not the expression itself nor the imperfect understanding which Tommy derives from it. And now we must make the violent hypothesis that Tommy though otherwise advancing in all branches of education has no other access to that period of history for the rest of his life. He has probably lost the work long ago, but remembers the substance of it quite faithfully though not the words. Let him every ten years sit down and write an essay on that period and I think you will have a very strict parallel to the development of ecclesiastical dogma. The facts dealt with are the same throughout *in substance*, but more clearly and fully seen; not only more clearly (as Moyes would admit or any other theologician) but more *fully*, as real development requires. None of these essays *is* the deposit, but all contain it. This view relieves us of the miracle of a *direct* reading of the mind of [[the]] sub-apostolic Church, which in default of all documentary evidence would be as marvellous as an intuition of eternal realities. It shakes us more free of the criterion of primitiveness, and not only equalises the living Church of today with that of the earliest times, but exalts her. It excludes 'finalism' of dogmatic expression as effectually as the other view, and involves less of a separation from the natural laws of mental progress.

Ever yours faithfully,
G. Tyrrell.

Notes to Letter 28

1. "The Mind of the Church" (see letters 24–26). *T* had been revising his understandings of the "deposit of faith" since he wrote "The Relation of Theology to Devotion" (see letters 12, 23). Maude Petre suggests that the "Mind of the Church" articles were used by *T* specifically to work out some changes in his views, especially with regard to his interpretation of Newman (*A&L* II.210).

2. "The Relation of Theology to Devotion" in the *Month* 94 (November 1899):461–73; reprinted in *FM* I.228–52 and reprinted as "Lex Orandi, Lex Credendi" in *TSC* 85–105.

3. The words of consecration of the Eucharist in the Mass, "This is my body."

4. Samuel R. Gardiner (1829–1902), was a historian who wrote several histories of England, some of which were used for textbooks.

29 Richmond. Yorks.
6 November 1900

PRIVATE

My dear Ward,

Boland[1] having got into Parliament is retiring from the *Weekly Register*. Ley writes to me:[2] 'In a week's time I shall be the sole owner of the *Weekly Register*; and I have made arrangements by which I shall be able to carry it on for two years on my own account; though *able* I am by no means *willing* to do so; unless I can rely upon the support of those Catholics whose interests Boland and I thought we were securing by taking over the paper, it is useless sacrificing further time and money. If I could secure the co-operation of one or two others—(I have no belief in a multiplicity of owners of a paper)—willing to invest in the undertaking, I should be prepared to give them proportional shares. I absolutely refuse to make an appeal *ad misericordiam*;[3] the appeal must be solely on the *merits* of the paper, on its past and present work in the cause of educated Catholic opinion. If the leaders of the Catholic thought in this country regard the paper as having done harm rather than good, or wish to do the work on their own account then I only ask to be told so in order that I may retire without further outlay of time and money,' etc., etc. Personally I am inclined to turn my thumb down as far as advice can do it; but I should like to know how the thing strikes you. One feels naturally that the *Weekly Register* was the sole organ for the *legitimate* expression of intelligent Catholic thought, and which made recourse to non-Catholic organs less excusable;—for to stop such utterance by more repression is futile and dangerous; if it loses one outlet it will find another. Anonymity is inexcusable under a free government, but lawful under a despotism; but it is a thing authorities should dread. The death of the *Weekly Register* will be viewed in both camps (liberal and illiberal) as a triumph of the Cardinal's principles[4] as to ecclesiastical journalism—principles which issue in clericalism of the strictest and narrowest type. It will be taken as the failure; if not as the repression; of the moderate or mediatorial party. This of course is hard, because the *Weekly Register*'s failure is really due to the 'extremism' into which it has lapsed at sundry times; and to the displays of undignified temper and bad taste that have more than once blotted its pages, and have caused it to be boycotted by the timorous. But the truth is there is no Catholic public to demand or supply such a journal as you or I should wish to see. On the one side there are the devout Clericalists who have got the *Tablet*, if they are Tories; the *Catholic Times*,[5] if they are Fenians; on the other, the anticlericals who love the flash and report of gun-powder. No one wants, even if anyone could supply, a Catholic *Pilot*;—at least, only individuals here and there; nothing that could be called a public. At all events with Ley himself as editor—competent as he is in many ways—I don't see how the paper could be kept *consistently* moderate and self-restrained; for he is not only very hot, but also too proud to take advice, except of the most indirect and tactful kind.

[My article in this *Month*[6] is to lead up to another suggested by what the Cardinal said to me regretting your anxiety to make Catholicism intelligible to men like Balfour, Sidgwick, etc.; on the score, that Christ preached to the poor and ignorant and scorned the learned. I objected that the learned he scorned were the theologians of his own church, the pedants, scribes, canon-lawyers, etc., not the educated as such; also, that these, bad as they were, were the natural guides of the masses in default of someone with evidently miraculous claims to a special revelation; that for any one less than a Christ (and so for us) the right order would have been to work at the roots of social belief and practice instead of nipping off buds. I feel I have put a bigger problem than I can deal with comfortably and have half a mind to leave my own question unanswered.][7] I am loth to leave Richmond where leisure is so abundant.

Kindest regards to Mrs. Ward

Ever yours faithfully,
G. TYRRELL.

Notes to Letter 29

1. John Pius Boland (1870–1958), member of Parliament from Kerry (1900–1918) and later general secretary of the Catholic Truth Society (1926–1947).

2. On 11 June 1901 Frank Rooke Ley, editor of the *Weekly Register* sent a memorandum to various people about the history and future of the paper. He reminded them that he and Boland had purchased the paper in April 1899 from Wilfrid Meynell and informed them that Boland's position as an MP constrained

him to sell his share of the paper to Ley. Ley, who assumed editorship in September 1899 (after Robert Dell's brief editorship [see letter 20 note 1]), hoped to foster Roman Catholic interests and open a forum of opinion on all matter legitimately open for discussion. He hoped the paper would serve the Catholic cause in England and raise the level of Catholic thought somewhat, but all his hopes depended on the infusion of some new capital into the venture; at the present time, Ley said, the paper lost more than 550 pounds each year. His plea was twofold: he wanted complete editorial control, and financial support. For more information about the paper consult the Rooke Ley papers, *SAUL*.

3. to mercy

4. Cardinal Vaughan published a pastoral letter 22 February 1900 which set forth, briefly, his principles of Catholic journalism: "The office and the honour of a Catholic journalist is religiously to follow the lead of the Church in matters that concern the Church; to strengthen her action upon the world; to defend the faith and Catholic interests with skill and with courage; *sentire cum ecclesia* in all things; so to inform and convince his readers that they may intelligently and joyfully co-operate with the Episcopate, and thus present to outsiders the spectacle of a Church knit together not only in one faith, but in the discipline of a common spirit."

5. The *Catholic Times* was a later extension of the old *Northern Press and Weekly Times* (1860–1870). The *Catholic Times and Catholic Opinion* (1876–1925) was published in Liverpool with a London edition.

6. "Tracts for the Millions" in the *Month* 96 (November 1900):449–60; reprinted in *FM* II.136–57. *T* noted the intention of some to write for the many, but said, ironically, that the few (the sophisticated audience) needed help as well.

7. Bracketed material published in *MW* I.361.

30

Richmond.
13 November 1900

My dear Ward,

I felt pretty sure what you would say about the *Weekly Register* and hardly see what else can be said. [As to the Synthetic, in a few words I once had with Haldane we agreed that our debates could never issue in any true *rapprochement*, but at best in a clearer definition of our several standpoints and fundamental assumptions. Of course by a *rapprochement* each one secretly means a conversion of others to his own view. Haldane felt that there was no hope of getting the Synthetic to worship the subject-object; I, that Leo XIII stood as poor a chance. But, seriously, I think Haldane in the discussions over Sidgwick's programme, showed a failure to catch what I imagined to be the idea of Synthetic, and was all for a metaphysical Society. For myself, I think the educative value of mutual understanding with a view to better self-understanding is simply enormous, and having little of the apostolic proselytising spirit I find satisfaction where Haldane finds disappointment.][1] Hence I should regret not only the permanent, but even the temporary suspension you speak of.[2] The latter, because, what with deaths and other departures, the continuity of so feebly rivetted a society is seriously impaired by an interval even of a year; and its life in the thoughts and interests of its members is so diluted that it will hardly ever have energy to reassemble itself. Again I cannot see how a year's intermission will heal the wound which Sidgwick's death has inflicted on us. We cannot grow another Sidgwick in a year or in fifty. That is the danger of [[a]] strong leader in every society; when he goes everyone collapses and looks in dismay at his neighbour. Still unless there is strong general feeling in favour of going on, I see no use in dragging on simply to keep up appearances, and I fancy that many are, like Haldane, disappointed because they realise, what it were worth going on to realise still more, that many men have many minds. How fearfully dull and silent we should be, if they had but one.

Ever yours,
G. Tyrrell.

Notes to Letter 30

1. Bracketed material published in *MW* I.372.
2. The Synthetic Society was suspended for one year after Sidgwick's death.

31

Catholic Church. Richmond. Yorks.
22 January 1901

My dear Ward,

I think the bishops' pastoral[1] much worse than irritating because it implies throughout a conception of Church-authority which can in no sense be explained away as a development of older ideas—the Church is cut clean in two; on one side a living, active *Ecclesia docens*[2] (reducible to the Pope; for the bishops have no assignable *raison d'être* save as papal delegates); on the other, a purely passive dead *Ecclesia Discens*[3] with no participation in the thought, will and action of the organism; its duty being to contribute money, obey blindly, and ask no questions. The Pope (or the *Ecclesia docens*) is not the inherent head of the organism, a part (albeit principal) of that whole body of moral *persona* whereof Christ is the Spouse; but he is vicariously the Spouse himself, an *alter Christus*,[4] a personality distinct from that of the Church, outside and above her, as a husband set over a wife. This is a different kind of Headship altogether from that which results from a gradual differentiation of the organism, unless we take Aristophanes' view of the origin of the sexes. Again there is no attempt to limit the delegated power of the Church. The pope is Peter; Peter is Christ; Christ is God; therefore the pope is God; and the practical corollary is absolutism unqualified. If all this is not innovation and heresy I don't know what is. We must by all means get a straight answer to the questions suggested by this pastoral. If this really be Romanism then I have never been a Romanist for five minutes; and I am sure numbers have been under a like illusion. Fawkes' letter in the *Pilot*[5] simply irritates me by missing the point—as though it were simply a question of more or less; not of a complete *transitus in aliud genus.*[6]

I am still here; reading and writing. Father Colley[7] our new provincial and his new consultors are of the most orthodox Stonyhurst type, and have doubtless been selected to do what the recalcitrant Gerard could not be got to do. The former has already written to ask if, seeing that Divine Providence (i.e. Father General) does not approve of my methods of doing good, I do not think it would be for God's greater glory (i.e. Father General's greater convenience) that I should resume parochial work at Saint Helens[8] for a time (i.e. *sine die*).[9] I replied, in effect, that nothing could be more for God's glory than to let sleeping dogs lie; which I put so delicately and firmly that he has decided to do so.

[The decision about the Synthetic was ingenious and happy; Professor [[James]] Ward's paper in 1902 is a solid rock on which to anchoi our hopes of reassemblage].[10] I trust that by that time I shall be in London again, but I can foresee nothing clearly, especially through the fog that hangs about this Pastoral.

Father Gerard gave me leave to republish a volume or two of *Month* articles as these would not need censuring, as already published; so I have made a selection. But I fear Father Colley may object.

Kindest regards to Mrs. Ward. Have you left Eastbourne?[11]

Ever yours faithfully,
G. TYRRELL

Notes to Letter 31

1. The Cardinal Archbishop and the Bishops of the Province of Westminster, "The Church and Liberal Catholicism: A Joint Pastoral Letter" published in the *Tablet* 62 (5, 12 January 1901):8–12, 50–2; dated 31 December 1900. See Appendix B for text of the pastoral.

2. The church teaching.

3. The church learning.

4. another Christ

5. Alfred Fawkes (1850–1930), a convert to Roman Catholicism from the Anglican priesthood, was known mostly as an author and preacher. He was a friend of *T*'s and associated with hopes to move the church more in touch with the spirit of the age. He returned to the Anglican church in 1909 in the aftermath of the condemnation of "modernism." Fawkes was the author of the "Correspondence" entitled "The Roman Bishops on Liberal Catholicism" which was signed "A Roman Catholic Correspondent" 5 January 1901, 13–4. Fawkes' language was strong and his points clear and sharp: the bishops do not understand the modern mind, they do not know their opponents, they have sunk to harsh and exasperating language, given us no clear dogmatic teaching and couched it all in unrealistic rhetoric. He predicts that the liberal position will maintain its place in "Latin Christianity."

6. passage to another class.

7. Reginald Colley S.J. (1848–1904) succeeded John Gerard as Provincial in December 1900.

8. A Jesuit mission in Lancashire. *T* spent a year there in 1893 in pastoral ministry and some argued later that he "ought never to have left St. Helen's." For an analysis of this remark see *A&L* II.34–9.

9. indefinitely

10. Bracketed material published in *MW* II.412.

11. *W* moved to Dorking, near London, in 1900.

32

Richmond. Yorks.
28 January 1901

My dear Ward,

When I reviewed your book on the *Catholic Revival* some years ago in the *Month* I said (I forget the exact words) that the Pope was infallible in *reading* the mind of the Church. One or two of 'ours' objected, but on the whole it seemed to be the accepted view. I thought that Dr. Ward's view had been practically discarded by every clear-minded theologian, and that it had done good work in formulating a position in such a definite way as to secure its rejection for ever. But since then I have learnt that this is just the view which is being pressed everywhere steadily by Jesuits and other ultra-montanes; and now the Joint-Pastoral inspired from Rome gives it official utterance—not, I trust, final. This view can no more blend with Newman's, than oil with water. If one is all right, the other is all wrong. Here indeed is a definite line of cleavage between the Israelites and the Philistines; the making of as real a schism as one could wish to see. As directed against turbulent malcontents and *soi-disant* liberals the document is as insignificant as it will be ineffectual; its true significance is in its assumptions and presuppositions.

I like your letter on the Temporal Power[1] better than anything I have yet seen on that disagreeable subject. You imply that such independence is a condition for the de-nationalising of the Papacy. That of course is just what we want—deliverance from Italianism or any other 'ism;' a truly cosmopolitan Church and a representative Curia. Extensive territories would give birth to a nation, but such as you advocate could never become a temporal power to be weighed against others in the political balance—a condition of things conducive to the slavery and not to the liberty of the Church as the Middle Ages often exemplify.

Ever yours faithfully,
G. TYRRELL.

P.S. Forgotten in the post bag till today.

1 February 1901.

Note to Letter 32

1. "The Duke of Norfolk and Papal Independence" in *The Times* 18 January 1901, 10e. There had been an outcry over the Duke's address to the Pope and *W* here claims that the press coverage was unfair and biased (see article about this in the *Table* 97 (1901):122). In his letter to *The Times, W* summarized an Italian pamphlet on the restoration of the temporal power and quoted a speech by Lord Boughman to the House of Lords (1849); both items argue that the Pope should not be under the domination of an individual foreign power, i.e., Italy, and that the Pope should be free to exercise his spiritual ministry.

33

Richmond, Yorks.
5 February 1901

My dear Ward,

Honestly I know absolutely nothing of the authorship of the letter by K.[1] in the *Pilot*; and I should be glad if you would contradict any reports on the subject. Not only the sentiments but the very phrasing are so much my own, that I began to think I wrote it in a state of somnambulism. I quite allow that the bishops analysis of what actually happens is false; but I do not quite find comfort in that diagnosis of their mistake because when a false analysis is widely imposed and widely taught in the Jesuit schools, and widely accepted by the unintelligent and indifferent majority of the faithful it hardens into a false doctrine and theological error. It is as in art; the first products of genius are independent of art rules; but false analysis gives false rules; and these rules govern and vitiate subsequent production. The bishops are imposing their false analysis upon the Church and its future life and government will be, and is now being, fashioned upon that analysis. This pastoral is in justification of recent episcopal absolutism, and elaborates a theory of which that kind of government is the legitimate consequence. The difference between 'false analysis' and 'theological error' is therefore, I think, the difference between a tadpole and a frog. If I don't want the frog I must go for the tadpole. Is it possible that F. W. Myers is dead,[2] as some one writes to me, or is it his brother? I am going to bring out two of past volumes *Month* articles.[3] It will make the undiscerning public think I am quite free to write. I see the fraud, but for reasons of my own I am willing to acquiesce in it.

Ever yours faithfully,
G. TYRRELL.

Notes to Letter 33

1. "Liberal Catholicism: A Rejoinder" signed "K" appeared in the *Pilot* 3 (2 February 1901):142–3. Alfred Fawkes (see letter 31 note 5) was probably the author of the letter.
2. Myers (see letter 4 note 3) died early in 1901.
3. Refers to *Faith of the Millions* (London, 1901); see letter 35.

34

C. Church. Richmond. Yorks
16 February 1901

My dear Ward,

Just a line to say how satisfying I found your article on Newman[1] in the *Weekly Register*. But of course I have to ask with *Zeta* of the *Pilot*,[2] is it what our bishops say: is it what they say at Rome? These are rhetorical questions needing no answer for the answer is obvious. The Pope has blessed and approved the Joint-Pastoral.[3] Still I believe: *Magnus est Newman et praevalebit*,[4] though it will not be in our time. The *Apologia*[5] which I am re-reading for the nth time is more significant, more irresistible than ever. What is going to be done for the Newman centenary? I should suggest [the assassination of Father Neville[6] and the appropriation of his goods by Wilfrid Ward.][7] There is no one who could do the work as you could and it would be for you *monumentum aere perennius*.[8] [I was surprised that you chose the *Weekly Register* as I thought you had banned that luckless periodical. But I was also glad, for I have always felt it a pity that there should be splits in so small a party].[9] Of course the Dellites[10] are impossible and Ley suffers from his past association with them and from his own heat and bitterness to boot; nor will he brook interference of any kind. [I can hardly wonder at his exasperation, but it is plain that exasperation in print does harm always, and good, I think never. Rather than that [[the]] *Tablet* should flap its triumphant wings over us all and be the only voice of Catholicism in this land, I think we should do all we can to keep this last blow-hole open. I was also glad to see Dr. Brownlow's[11] signature in the same number, for the same reason. I am going to write to Ley—for he will take more from me than from anyone—to urge him to suppress the [[bitter note]] once and for all and to try to make the *Weekly Register professedly* Newmanian in its tone and tactics and views. At all events the effort is worth making.][12]

Ever yours faithfully,
G. TYRRELL.

Notes to Letter 34

1. "Cardinal Newman" in the *Weekly Register* 103 (15 February 1901):196–8. 1901 was the centenary of Newman's birth and W's article was a general portrait of the man with some focus on Newman's views on authority.

2. Zeta continued to publish in the *Pilot* (see letter 23 note 1); here *T* probably refers to two letters, one 19 January 1901 and the other 9 February 1901. In the first one Zeta argues and concludes that "Liberal Catholicism and official Catholicism are enemies by nature and cannot be reconciled;" in the second Zeta says that the Catholic church has always appealed to antiquity and asks how a liberal Catholic can justify a departure from this rule. In a letter to von Hügel (20 February 1901) *T* mentions Sydney Smith (see letter 17 note 4) in conjunction with the arguments set forth by Zeta.

3. Cardinal Vaughan had been encouraged to write the Joint Pastoral Letter by Merry del Val who, apparently, assured him that the Pope would approve it officially (see Gary Lease, "Merry del Val and Tyrrell's Condemnation," unpublished paper, presented at the American Academy of Religion Annual Meeting, 1979). Pope Leo XIII did write a letter of congratulations to the English bishops which was published in the *Tablet* (23 March 1901):441.

4. Newman is great and will prevail

5. The *Apologia pro vita sua* (London, 1864), Newman's account of the Oxford movement, was published after a public controversy with Charles Kingsley.

6. William P. Neville (1824–1905), was Newman's sole literary executor and the person with whom *W* had to contend for every inch of the Newman biography; see Gilley.

7. Bracketed material published in *MW* II.336.

8. a monument more lasting [than bronze].

9. *T* may have meant the *true* liberals as distinct from the self-styled ones. He and *W* had both argued in print that real liberalism was for the very few.

10. See letter 20 note 1.

11. W. R. Brownlow (1830–1901), Roman Catholic bishop of Clifton.

12. Bracketed material appears in *MW* II.145, though most of the names are not given; Bishop Brownlow's name does appear in her book.

35 Richmond. Yorks.
1 August 1901

My dear Ward,

I hasten to tell you that you will receive a copy of my last-born,[1] lest misled by the title you might purchase it under the impression that it contained something new. *Faith of Millions*: is almost a *lucus a non lucendo*[2] title for a book addressed to the few; but my own title was found to be in the market after the books had been bound and one had to choose another in a hurry. I sent Gerard a list and he chose the worst, at Longman's[3] advice. [I have read your *Edinburgh*[4] article with great interest but would have to write something twice as long to do justice to it. Like your "Doctores Ecclesiae"[5] I feel that it implies principles that may carry, not us, but those who follow us hereafter, much further than we can now distinctly see. Obviously it points to a radical change of view as to the sphere of Ecclesiastical infallibility. This will come about not through any analysis of theories or refinement of definitions such as was attempted in the recent *Weekly Register* controversy anent Halifax's article,[6] but simply through the opening-up of the past by historical research. It will be impossible to pretend that the Church or the Pope are infallible in departments where they have erred over and over again. It was not individuals, but all that we mean by authority that for centuries has ignored, if not overtly denied, evolution in the Church and has projected the present backwards to apostolic times, taking a bird's-eye view of the tree and seeing its crown of foliage thrown, as it were, flat on the earth. We justly point out to Anglicans that no error in doctrinal detail can be so deadly as an error touching the rule of faith and the nature of the Church herself; yet we forget that the mechanical 'creationist' view of the Church still held by men like Gallwey[7] and Humphry[8] and Lescher[9], who believe that Christ said the First 'Mass' and that Saint Paul paid triennial visits *ad limina*,[10] is only a survival of what was once universally held. When history has done its work it will be hard to imagine men ever trusting the church as she now demands to be trusted—with that naive faith in the Pope which is just what attracts so many converts to us desirous of certainty in matters of quite secondary import, or less. I think we shall be drawn back to the view I put forward in the 'Walla-washee' romance namely that the Church will infallibly right herself and that it is safer in a storm to cling to an inverted life-boat than to sit comfortably in one that is not capsized; or, paradoxically, it is better to be wrong with the Pope, now, or in detail, than right with his adversaries; that taken in conjunction with the whole organism of truth, what were separately a lie, is truer than what were separately the truth. This is a hard saying; but Newman says much like it. Of such details I can say reasonably: 'I believe them in a sense, though I don't know what sense: I believe the whole system of which they are the undeveloped parts—rudimentary, grotesque, inexplicable at present; what they mean I know not now but later times shall know.'

Your 'Doctores' raises the obvious question: 'Who are the experts, if a distinct class from officials and not designated by the officials?' If it is presumption in me to call myself an expert, it were equally presumptuous for me to decide who are experts. But in no view can one exclude the need of private judgment somewhere or other. I look for a clearer solution in recognising that in every realm of thought the active minds are the few and exceptional, and the passive and receptive are the many: that the Church is for the many and not for the few, or rather an instrument for distributing the wealth of the few in a form suited to the needs of the many. While for all, the sense of the Church of today is the loving rule of faith: those who are interested and activeminded will read that rule for themselves with individual variations; but the masses who only ask to be taught will take the official formulation literally and without discussion. The more forward minds will be in sympathy with the Church of the future rather than of the present. Were there none such, I don't see how there could be any evolution since this demands a principle of variation for selection to work upon. A heresy is only a rejected variation; but the principle of heresy is a principle of progress and life.][11]

You see I cling to Richmond—for many reasons. I suppose it can't be for ever; yet I see no reason why not. I am allowed to publish now without foreign censorship; but they have appointed thirty-two home-censors of whom twenty-five are Stonyhurst schoolboys in sacred orders; so that the chances against the four chosen being of the seven adults are very small. However I sent up a book[12] the other day to see how much they will have of it. I have also another on the stocks[13] *de omni re scibili et aliis*;[14] but I shall hardly see the end of it this side of seventy. So there is plenty to do. I feel the ecclesiastical atmosphere of Farm Street would be stuffy beyond endurance. Also I have a scruple in dealing with those many clients whom I could help on my own lines, since in so doing I only make them discontented with the kind of advice and direction they get from 999 priests out of a thousand. It is not fair to educate people above their station. Those who cannot come into the Church or stay in it on the ordinary lines will save their souls better outside; nor again have I any authority to speak save as representing the mind of Cardinal Vaughan or of the Society of Jesus. These would not tolerate my line for a moment; and I cannot be regarded otherwise than as a representative. That is where you as a layman have the advantage of me.

Altogether, while the present fashion prevails—and it will not change soon—I am better out of it. My superiors are only too thankful that I stay quiet and will, for self-interested reasons, leave me in peace. I had a delightful time with Bremond[15] up here. It was the first sympathetic converse I had enjoyed for a year; except a brief visit from Maude Petre.[16]

Give my kindest regards to Mrs. Ward. I hope you will do all you can to keep the *Register* alive and healthy.[17]

Ever yours faithfully,
G. TYRRELL.

Notes to Letter 35

1. *Faith of the Millions* (London, 1901), two volumes. By this time *T* was writing with one eye to the censors and yet still following his plan as formulated five years earlier in "A Change of Tactics," *Month* 86 (February 1896):125–27. He retitled that work—"A More Excellent Way"—and reprinted it as the lead essay in this collection. He hoped to call the collection *Essays Toward a More Excellent Way* but told Maude Petre, "Gerard is afraid of the smack of Liberalism in that title" (*A&L* II.163). *T* wrote "A Change of Tactics" with much the same argument in mind that W had delineated in "The Rigidity of Rome." Both of them argued for an end to the siege mentality of the church and hoped that the Catholic church would learn to invite and not compel attention and devotion.

2. a grove from no light (i.e., a ludicrous derivation or, in this case, an inappropriate title.)

3. *T*'s publisher.

4. *W*'s article, "Time Spirit of the Nineteenth Century" appeared in the *Edinburgh Review* 194 (July 1901):92–131.

5. *W*'s response to the Joint Pastoral Letter (and surrounding arguments); it appeared in the *Pilot* 3 (22 June 1901):774–6. In the article *W* tried to explain

the pastoral away by making distinctions that did not lie in the pastoral itself: he hoped to lay the groundwork for a more workable conception of the doctors of the church, for theologians and (the few) experts who are really entitled to speak out and to work with the bishops. He could see that the pastoral letter left men like himself no room whatsoever to speak and write on religious issues and hoped here to deny those implications and secure a place for the continued work of people like himself and *T*.

6. "The Recent Anglo-Roman Pastoral," *Nineteenth Century* 49 (May 1901):726–54. The article was ostensibly written by Lord Halifax (1839–1943), president of the English Church Union and strong promoter of Anglo-Roman reunion. In fact, the article was written by *T*, himself (see Thomas Michael Loome, "A Bibliography of the Published Writings of George Tyrrell (1861–1909," *Heythrop Journal* 10 (July 1969):305). For a more detailed analysis of *T*'s arrangement with Halifax see my "George Tyrrell and the Joint Pastoral Letter."

7. Peter Gallwey S.J. (1820–1906), a conservative colleague of *T*'s.

8. William Humphry S.J. (1839–1910), a conservative author whose articles were often about the need for papal power.

9. Wilfrid Lescher (1847–1917), a Dominican pamphleteer and lecturer described in an obituary in the *Tablet* as one who "followed the papal line."

10. to the threshold [of the apostles]. The phrase is often used for bishops visiting Rome. Since the council of Trent, diocesan bishops have been required to report to Rome every five years, *ad limina Petri et Pauli.*

11. Bracketed material appears in *George Tyrrell's Letters* (London, 1920), edited by Maude Petre, p. 72.

12. *Oil and Wine*, which *T* completed in 1900 and kept back. He gave the manuscript to his friend, Robert Dolling (1851–1902) to "do with as he pleased." In June 1901 *T* apparently told his Provincial, Father Colley, that he had given the book to Dolling, and Colley managed to get *T* to submit it for approval. The Jesuit censors passed it, but Cardinal Vaughan's censors found it "full of mischief" and insisted that it be sent to Rome for approval; it was turned down by the Roman censors. *T* then had it privately printed (1902) for private circulation only; it was published in 1907.

13. It is not clear which work *T* refers to here.

14. concerning everything knowable and other things besides

15. *T*'s friend was visiting him in Richmond a week in July (*A&L* II.163).

16. Maude Dominica Petre (1863–1942) was from an old Roman Catholic family in England. She was noted for her philanthropic works and is remembered as *T*'s friend and patroness; she provided a place for him when he left the Jesuits and supported him until he died. In the letters in *A&L* she is "V." Her autobiography, *My Way of Faith* (London, 1937) presents the reader with information about her background. She was the sixth of eleven children in a family which had money on both sides; she had, one surmises, considerable financial resources at her command. She entered a religious community in her early twenties and was made superior, but later left it. She never married and was, she says, never "in love" until she met *T*.

17. The *Weekly Register* became the *Monthly Register*, April-December 1902, at which time it ceased to exist. *W* was a member of the board of directors for the *Monthly Register*, and both W and von Hügel tried to get people to write articles for it. For details about it and its demise, consult the Rooke Ley Papers, *SAUL*.

36 Catholic Church, Richmond, Yorks.
7 September 1901

My dear Ward,

Von Hügel sent me *La Vitalité*[1] some time ago with some marked passages which I read; but I will now read it all. As to Laprune's[2] optimism the school he represented was too weak in those days to have drawn out into light the strength of Rome's opposition as we now experience it. But the tide will come in, in spite of Pope Canute[3] who will prudently push back his chair when he finds his feet getting wet; men will not venerate bones in these days without knowing whose they are and whence they come. I like Father Schobel's[4] criterium of the mind of the Church very much. It is plain that the 'one man one vote' fallacy must be avoided; that opinions are to be weighed as well as counted; that in regard to questions still in dispute the numerical majority is sure to be wrong; and the few pioneers, right; that even in the worlds of science or history or art there is an *Ecclesia docens* and *discens*. But in those worlds I suppose it is to the press we should go—to the current periodicals and monographs—in order to get at the general mind rather than to individual doctors or learners. And similarly, in the ecclesiastical world. Maude Petre tells me you have a vague idea of taking up Newman's biography independently of Neville. I do hope this is true; I feel sure that ought to be the great work of your life; and it will give you scope for all that you are best at. Perhaps too it might stir the old gentleman up to unlock his treasures which I believe he hoards through mere miserliness and love of possession.

As to the Joint Pastoral I think the issue of all the correspondence is that it will be quietly shelved and forgotten in some cupboard together with the bones of King Edmund.

Kindest regards to Mrs. Ward

Ever yours faithfully,
G. Tyrrell.

Notes to Letter 36

1. *La Vitalité chrétienne* (Paris, 1901) a work by Olle-Laprune.

2. Leon Ollé-LaPrune (1839–1898) was a French philosopher with some affinities with Newman, especially in his stress on the limits of a purely intellectual approach to faith.

3. An ironic reference to Pope Leo XIII as King Canute (d. 1035) who, legend claims, once rebuked his courtiers' flattery by commanding the tide to cease its advance.

4. Victor Schobel (1848–1915), had been a professor of dogmatic theology at Oscott Seminary and at the Oratory in Birmingham (see *MW* II.141).

37

Richmond, Yorks.
23 December 1901

My dear Ward,

You will guess whence Mr. Waller[1] has derived the document from which he compiles; and I need not ask you to be silent. Things are better with me as to the Jesuits—all restrictions are withdrawn; though I do not mean to use such parlous liberty more than I can help. Having fought a volume[2] through our censors His Eminence[3] blocks the way by demanding a fresh censorship by his own men. The onus is bad enough without having it doubled. Besides as it now stands corrected it is the work of our censors as much as mine, and it is hard that they should be subjected to Moyes or Gildea.[4]

Is the Synthetic dead, now that Gore is translated?[5] If not I think I should make its seances a pretext for visiting London now and then—in order to check the gossip that my prolonged, but quite voluntary absence gives rise to.

Kindest regards to Mrs. Ward and with best Xmas wishes

Yours faithfully,
G. Tyrrell. S.J.

Notes to Letter 37

1. Alfred Raney Waller, *T*'s friend and publisher (see letter 20 note 3) who had published *The Civilizing of the Matafanus*; *T* had obviously just given him the *Oil and Wine* volume for publication and private circulation.

2. Cardinal Vaughan had given his Imprimatur to *Faith of the Millions* which was reviewed in *Church Review* 41 (7 November 1901):711 under the title, "Liberalism Again." The Cardinal, no doubt, resolved to be more careful with *T*'s works in the future.

3. Cardinal Vaughan. He eventually sent the page proofs to Rome (*A&L* II.172) where it was judged unpublishable.

4. William Gildea (d. 1915), canon and theologian for the archdiocese of Westminster.

5. Charles Gore (see letter 3 note 2 and letter 6 note 9), was made Bishop of Worcester in December 1901.

38 Richmond, Yorks.
28 January 1902

My dear Ward,

On the 21st I shall be giving the ordination retreat at Oscott[1]; and cannot bilocate. My reasons for prorogation of the Synthetic [[are]], first, the selfish one that it would be difficult; if not impossible for me to attend, living so far away. Secondly, Gore's resignation of the presidency combined with yours of the secretaryship all on top of the [loss ot our '*principium formale quo*'][2] i.e. Sidgwick. [Who is there left to lead and push?][3] Balfour is, I suppose, tired of it. Yet [I should *greatly* regret its collapse.][4] I wish it could be carried on by an intermittent organ; it would not cost much more than the papers do; and we could meet and eat once in a blue moon. If Rochester[5] presided why could not Worcester?[6] Lyall[7] is getting too sleepy I suppose; and Lodge[8] is too busy—else he has plenty of 'go,' which is more wanted in an official than subtlety. I hear Neville has yielded you some of his spoils; is it true? Why not all? I should think a revision of the *Catholic Revival* brought up to date very opportune just now, when the egg is showing signs of chipping. Williams sent me a badly constructed but most interesting study of John Henry Newman's philosophy a short time ago; I hope you have seen it. I wish you would show how and why it is possible for *both* the Williamses to claim him as their prophet. I should say it is because his noetic training underlay his very attack on the noetic; that he used the liberal method in defence of the conservative position; that he was a liberal in intellect and conservative in sentiment. But his development though applied to more recent data would have 'carried him whither he would not.' Hence our Eastbourne Williams has the spirit of John Henry Newman on his side; while Herbert Williams has the letter[9]—John Henry Newman as he was and not John Henry Newman as he would be now. Isn't Mignot's *Discours sur la méthode*[10] a bold utterance—'le dernier mot pour la théologie orthodoxié'[11] says a French correspondent pathetically. Also, the selection of the commissioners is significant. What could do more to restore waning confidence in Rome than an extension of this commission[12] system to all departments touching the confines of theology? What the educated feel now is that the theologians decide without any knowledge of the factors of the problem; that the individual expert can be bullied and 'hooshed' away. But if the consentient voice of a body of experts can be ensured a hearing as chief witness in the suit, the process will be less of a farce than hitherto. The theologians may not be converted but at least they will be kept at bay. In fact the system provides a legitimate channel for the influence of the *Ecclesia Discens* on the *Ecclesia Docens.* If the Church will listen to the experts (not as to judges of doctrine, but as to witnesses to facts of which they and not the Church are judges) the people will listen to the Church. Else they will listen to the experts and effect the conciliation for themselves as best they can between faith and science. When my book[13] is in type I will send it to His Eminence and offer to put his corrections by way of notes in an appendix so as to have my text intact. If he objects then I will withdraw it for private circulation with a preface explanatory of all the circumstances. He is an impossible man but when he goes we may easily get an impossibler. However, I will not give him another chance of obstruction.

Kindest regards to Mrs. Ward

Ever yours faithfully,
G. TYRRELL S.J.

Notes to Letter 38

1. St. Mary's seminary at Oscott, Birmingham.
2. formal principle; bracketed material published in *MW* I.362.
3. Bracketed material published in *MW* I.362.
4. Bracketed material published in *MW* II.413.
5. The Anglican bishop of Rochester was Edward Stuart Talbot (see letter 3 note 2), a member of the Synthetic Society.
6. The Anglican bishop of Worcester was Charles Gore (see letter 37 note 5), a member of the Synthetic Society.
7. Sir Alfred Lyall (1835–1911), member of the Synthetic Society.
8. Sir Oliver Lodge (1851–1940), physicist and member of the Synthetic Society.
9. The Eastbourne Williams is William J. (Willie) Williams (see letter 5 note 3), whose interpretation of Newman proceeded along lines which *W* and *T* both thought good and helpful in terms of accommodating the church to the modern world. J. Herbert Williams (d. 1931) was a lawyer and an author whose interpretations of Newman tended to be more conservative. In the *Weekly Register* (22 February, 1 March, 8 March and 29 March 1901) there was a public argument between them precipitated by Herbert Williams' letter attacking *W*'s interpreta-

tion of Newman in his article of 15 February (see letter 34 note 1). Willie Williams defended W and Herbert Williams counterattacked; Willie Williams had the last (published) word in the 29 March edition. Two letters from *W* to Williams and twenty-four letters from Williams to *W* are in the *WWP* at *SAUL*.

10. Eudoxe Irénée Mignot (1842–1918), Roman Catholic archbishop of Albi in France. The "Discours sur la methode" was an address delivered at the solemn opening of the Institut Catholique de Toulouse in 1901. It was published (Paris, 1908) along with his *Lettres sur les études ecclésiastiques*, five letters to his clergy.

11. the last word for (on behalf of) orthodox theology

12. The Pontifical Biblical Commission was announced in the *Tablet* 99 (4 January 1902): 10. It was established by Pope Leo XIII to consider questions pertinent to Biblical studies. The original twelve scholars appointed to the commission gave rise to some early hope and enthusiasm, but they were soon joined by twenty-eight other men most of whom had little scholarly or biblical training. See Barmann, pp. 87–93.

13. *Oil and Wine.*

39

Richmond
7 February 1902

My dear Ward,

I will not intrude words upon you except to say that I have heard of your sorrow and will say Mass tomorrow for your boy and for you and Mrs. Ward the next day.[1]

Ever yours faithfully,
G. TYRRELL

Note to Letter 39

1. *W*'s eldest son died of complications of pneumonia in February, 1902. He was ten years old.

40

Richmond. Yorks.
21 February 1902

My dear Ward,

Though I am not at Oscott, yet, and for the same reason, I shall not be able to put in an appearance at the Synthetic meeting. The cold has got into my marrow and paralysed my vital functions throughout. As my every word at Oscott would have been put under a theological microscope and in doubtful cases, sent for analysis to head-quarters, I am not at all sorry to escape that ordeal. I liked Rashdall's paper[1] immensely, having just come to a similar issue myself in a private study of my own,[2] in which I conclude that religion—unlike every sort of science, deals with the real world and that Reality means a will-system of which the divine will is source, centre, and end. It is merely an essay of my own, and for myself, with a view to seeing how far religion can be preserved and yet severed from its present troublesome entanglement with positive knowledge. One gets weary of compromises with criticism over divisions of territory. To have yielded so much as we have had to yield to physics, biology, history, etc., makes it daily more difficult to draw a firm line, and put a limit to possible concessions in the future. Is there then some new orientation which will make it possible to be almost indifferent not merely to what criticism has done, but to anything it could conceivably do? I suppose, at present, we should have to say: 'No; Christianity would fall with the denial of certain facts of the positive order.' Yet, for hypothesis' sake, I have endeavoured to find a way. But I am quite aware that in doing so I have come close to two heresies against which I have written (1) A. Sabatier's[3] view of dogma and (2) 'Rationalism in religion.'[4] Against the latter I feel I have raised a firm wall of partition; but as to the former I am not so sure; though I think if Sabatier explained himself better, he might be held in a Catholic sense. Of course it is all premature and at best a hundred years before the time; still here and there are to be found Catholics who could be saved by such a *modus vivendi* were it at all tolerable. I venture to send you the brochure[5] in a post or two, in case you might have leisure to look over it at any time. It was suggested by a very practical little scheme of life that I was asked to criticise by a certain Countess Zamoyska[6] of whom you may have heard. I began it in defence of her ideas but ended in a sense of their inadequacy. I hope most sincerely that the kindly narcotics of time and preoccupation will soon take the worst edge off the sword of your recent sorrow. One knows that interests are the remedy; but the difficulty is that, for the time being, they are all killed. Still, with whatever repugnance it is best to resume them as quickly as possible.

Ever, dear Ward,
Yours faithfully,
G. TYRRELL S.J.

Notes to Letter 40

1. Hastings Rashdall (1858–1924), moral philosopher of the liberal school of Anglicanism and member of the Synthetic Society. Rashdall made a distinction in his paper between God and the Absolute, a distinction which *T* used in some of his later work (see Schultenover, chapter 6).

2. The private essay was *T*'s pseudonymous *Religion as a Factor of Life*, published privately by A. R. Waller (1902); *T* used the pen name Dr. Ernest Engels. The essay was *T*'s first attempt at a philosophy of religion and was later printed almost verbatim in *Lex Orandi; or Prayer and Creed* (London, 1903).

3. Auguste Sabatier (1839–1901), French Protestant theologian who applied historical criticism to the New Testament. *T* reviewed his *The Vitality of Christian Dogmas and their Power of Evolution: A Study in Religious Philosophy* (London, 1898) in the *Month* 91 (June 1898):592–602; reprinted in *FM* I.115–35. *W* reviewed the same book along with Henry Sidgwick's *Practical Ethics* (London, 1898) and John Henry Newman's *Oxford University Sermons* in one of his most daring articles: "The Ethics of Religious Conformity," *Quarterly Review* 189 (January 1899):25–36. *W*'s review was published anonymously and never reprinted anywhere; *W* found Sabatier's views very close to those of Newman.

4. *T*'s essay appeared in the *Month* 93 (January 1899):1–16; reprinted in *FM* I.85–114.

5. *Religion as a Factor of Life.*

6. Hedwig Zamoyska (1831–1923). *T* reviewed her work, *Ideals in Practice, With Some Account of Women's Work in Poland* (London, 1903) for the *Monthly Register* 1 (May 1902):55–7. At first, it seems an unlikely book to catch *T*'s interests, but he was excited about it, and wrote to both von Hügel and *W* about her. He found her work practical, and called her experiment "a novitiate for life in the world." He reviewed it again, in tandem with a book by Rudolf Eucken, in "Religion and Work" in the *Month* 102 (December 1903):561–71. Both Eucken and Zamoyska apparently influenced *T*'s emerging philosophy of religion (see Schultenover, chapter 6).

41

Richmond. Yorks.
4 March 1902

My dear Ward,

Miss Petre asked me to return you the enclosed, which is pleasant reading from a man like Eucken.[1] What think you of the *Monthly Register*?[2] and on what lines do you think it should run? I should hope it will be as far as possible the organ of Newman-Catholic thought. I wanted Ley to direct the *Weekly Register* in that channel long ago, but he had not the men, who could or would help him. As for myself if I write anonymously it is a certain risk of a scrape; if under my own name it means the delay and worry of our domestic censorship; so I am practically a dead man. In case you did not see Fonsegrive's[3] reply to Monsignor Turinaz[4] I enclose it. I hear that Monsignor Mignot has also replied, but I have not seen it. What was the upshot of the Synthetic meeting?

Ever yours faithfully,
G. TYRRELL

Kindest regards to Mrs. Ward. I do hope she is not too utterly broken by her sorrow.

Notes to Letter 41

1. Rudolf Eucken (1846–1926), professor of philosophy at Jena, Switzerland. He had written *W* a letter praising his "Time Spirit of the Nineteenth Century." *T*, who began reading German at von Hügel's insistence, was beginning to read Eucken's philosophy. Eucken's letter to *W* is in the *WWP* at *SAUL*.

2. Successor to the *Weekly Register*; his hope that it be an organ of Newman-Catholic thought may be carrying coals to Newcastle since *W* was on the board of directors of the new paper and a clear promoter of "Newman-Catholic thought."

3. Georges Fonsegrive (1852–1917), author and director of the Catholic periodical, *La Quinzaine* which was established to demonstrate that Roman Catholicism was not incompatible with science and/or democracy.

4. Charles François Turinaz (1838–1919), Archbishop of Nancy and Tours in France. He was a reactionary polemecist who published *Les périls de la foi et de la discipline dans l'Église* (Nancy, 1902).

42

Richmond. Yorks.
8 April 1902

My dear Ward,

Countess Zamoyska has just sent me a little work of hers and begs me to write something about her Institution. Of course the document I sent you, which grew out of such an attempt, is absolutely useless for her end; but it contains some things directly bearing on Zakopani[1] that I want to reproduce; and so, I want you to let me have it back, at least for a bit. I was much interested in your Newman-Renan article[2] in the *Monthly Register* and think I agree i.e. I think the mystical or religious interest, the ethical interest, the aesthetic interest, and the intellectual interest are very separable and separate things even where they coexist in the same man; and that men are to be classified according to that which predominates and uses the others. Chateaubriand,[3] Newman, Renan,[4] Turgot,[5] etc., are easily discerned as of one type or the other, I should say the mystic in Newman was stronger even than the ethical. A strong ethical interest seems often to exist in men of no religious sympathy whatever. Take e.g. Sidgwick; and perhaps J. S. Mill[6]—though his *Essays on Religion* make me doubt whether he was not a mystic in desire. His Eminence called my latest book[7] up for re-censorship and sent it to three Roman theologians who were of course unanimously against it. The points they marked recur over and over again in my other books which have His Eminence's *Imprimatur*[8]—of which he himself has written to me eulogistically. I think of recalling them all and giving my reasons. Did you see *La Question Biblique* by Albert Houtin[9]—a record of a century of bible-squabbles in France? I think so, from one or two remarks in your article. If authority were *occasionally* on the wrong side in that matter, it would be no difficulty; but that it should be so always and systematically makes one pause.

Ever yours faithfully,
G. TYRRELL.

Notes to Letter 42

1. Zakopani was a small community (population 18) south of Krakow, purchased by the patriot Wladyslaw Zamoyski, husband of the countess. She operated a training school there and thought young women could live a lay Christian vocation in a socially stratified world. She was not a philosopher, but apparently was a friend of Ollé-Laprune's, and undoubtedly had a profound effect on *T*. Her school was practical, and she put an emphasis on Scripture in her teaching and advice for living.

2. "Newman and Renan" in the *Monthly Register* 1 (April 1902): 10–4; reprinted in *PP* 283–300. In the article *W* compares their temperaments and finds in Renan "no sign of any disposition for patience and humility in his theological inquiries."

3. François René Vicomte de Chateaubriand (1768–1848), a French Romantic writer famous for his brilliant rhetorical defense of Roman Catholicism in *Génie du Christianisme* (Paris, 1802).

4. Joseph Ernest Renan (1823–1892), philosopher and apostate theologian involved in biblical criticism and famous for his *Vie de Jésus* (Paris, 1863).

5. Anne Robert Jacques Turgot (1727–1781), economist and *philosophe* who contributed to the Enlightenment concept of progress.

6. John Stuart Mill (1806–1873), utilitarian philosopher.
7. *Oil and Wine.*
8. A declaration that a book has been passed for publication by some censoring authority.
9. Albert Houtin (1867–1926), French priest, disciple and friend of Loisy's; he eventually left the priesthood and wrote books and articles about the period and about the modernist movement: *Histoire du modernisme catholique* (Paris, 1913) and *La question biblique chez les catholiques de France au XIX*[e] *siècle* (Paris, 1902). *T* reviewed the latter book in "The Bible Question in France" in the *Monthly Register* 1 (October 1902): 227–8.

43

21 December 1902[1]

My dear Ward,

Forgive this inconvenient cheque; I can no other. ['La Synthétique c'est Toi;'[2] all the rest seem to have been rapt from the fickle and the frail, caught up to the heavens or to the episcopate or to the ministry. We have become practically unworkable. I still think if each of us circulated an annual paper either commenting on some previous one or starting a new hare, it might partly serve the purpose. Then we could, once a year, put together the collected scraps of deity and worship it in common.][3] Indeed I am thinking that theology will end in being an experimental science—a sort of psychophysics; an affair to be settled not by discussion but by thermometer. 'Let us pray' will be the experiment e.g. Haldane will wrestle with the subject-object and then we'll take his temperature; and so with the rest.

What think you of Loisy's little book?[4] I fear it is a forlorn hope to try to show that the synoptics meant by the Kingdom of Heaven what we mean by the Church. The Parousia *as instant* is the key that explains them. But the problem is too grave and intricate for a letter. To treat that belief as accidental or incidental is very like trifling; to accept it honestly is to land ourselves into a perfect network of theological barbed wires.[5]

Kindest regards to Mrs. Ward

Yours faithfully,
G. TYRRELL

Notes to Letter 43

1. No place of origin given for this letter.
2. The Synthetic, it is you. *W* was the most able to keep the Synthetic Society alive at this point, *T* suggests.

3. Bracketed material published in *MW* II.413.

4. Alfred Firmin Loisy (1857–1940), French modernist and biblical scholar. The "little book" was *L'Évangile et l'Église* (Paris, 1900), which was written as a reply to Harnack's *Das Wesen des Christentums* (Leipzig, 1900). Harnack argued on the analogy of a kernel/husk, that the essence of Christianity lay in the fatherhood of God and the brotherhood of man and that all the rest was husk, i.e., added later and non-essential. Loisy countered with an astonishingly novel defense of Roman Catholicism which argued that the essence of Christianity lay in the faith of the developed church as it expanded under the guidance of the Holy Spirit. In the process of his defense, Loisy denied some of the dogmatic foundations of the church and began an argument that eventually led to his excommunication, years later. On 17 December 1903 five of Loisy's works were placed on the Index, including *L'Évangile et l'Église*.

5. *T* may have been beginning to feel himself trapped, and in any case was in the throes of a severe depression during Christmas of 1902 (see his letter to Bremond 29 December 1902 in David, p. 142).

44

Richmond
27 April 1903

My dear Ward,

Non possumus;[1] our prelate has gone off for his retreat and my Mass is indispensible in consequence. I wish you could persuade the 'officials' to accept your doctrine of the relativity of Catholicism and not to impose their own aspect of it on others—an aspect that strikes me rather as a speculative *maximum* than a practical minimum. However, it is no use kicking a dead dog—even the offense to one's nostrils will soon be a thing of the past. Who is the *Edinburgh* article on Acton by?[2] It sounds like Mr. E. Grant-Duff.[3]

Are you getting on with John Henry Newman or has Acton ousted him for the present?[4]

Ever yours,
G. Tyrrell

Notes to Letter 44

1. We cannot. *T* could not attend the 30 April 1903 meeting of the Synthetic Society.

2. "The Late Lord Acton" in the *Edinburgh Review* 197 (April 1903):501–34.

3. Mountstuart E. Grant-Duff (1829–1906), statesman and author.

4. There was a request by Lord Acton's children that *W* undertake to write a biography of their father. *W* ultimately refused to do it because he did not feel

sufficient sympathy with the man. In the *WWP* there is one letter from Annie Acton and nine from Richard in addition to five letters from Mary Drew (Gladstone's daughter) about the use of letters and documents. *T* here alludes to the request from the Acton children in light of *W*'s own work on the Newman biography.

45 Richmond. Yorks.
1 August 1903

[My dear Ward,

I have read your *Hibbert* article[1] twice, and find myself in agreement with most of it. My chief objection is to the use (Balfour is responsible) of the term 'authority,' for two things so generically diverse as intellectual originality and official jurisdiction in regard to truth. The natural laws of collective mental growth divide the Church, like every other society, into the teachers and the taught, the leaders and the led. No one I suppose denies that the young and inexperienced should listen to the old; and laymen, to experts and doctors. The real problem of Romanism lies in the assumption that by mere official appointment, independent of all personal gifts and attainments, certain 'laymen' should be considered fit to sit in judgment upon experts or at least to determine whether or not the conclusions of experts are legitimate developments of the common belief. To do this they must themselves be experts unless by official appointment they receive some divine *charisma* of infallibility. This of course is just what our Church teaches; and so is quite logical in summoning the expert to the tribunal of the ignoramus and in deciding juridically what *naturally* only admits of intellectual decision. It is no use I think shirking this 'miraculous' factor in Church Authority, or in trying to bring the whole system within the compass of reason. Deny miraculous infallibility and still I see the *ex officio*, as distinct from expert, teacher would serve a useful purpose, like that of school-masters; but their teaching would not be the supreme rule of doctrine; the teachings both of Pope and Council would be always revisable by the judgment of theologians and saints. All that we must complain of now in the cramping of originality by officialism is traceable to the Vatican conception of Church authority; to the belief that Rome possesses a short-cut to truth independent of experience and reflection; that her infallibility is *not* explicable by the natural law of the human mind. Now this is either true or not true. If it is not true, we must go behind the Vatican Council and cry '*Peccavimus.*'[2]

Again, I agree with you very much when you make the saints the teachers of the Church (unofficial, of course); it certainly *ought* to be that those who live the life should know the truth experimentally and instinctively. But is it really so? Are there not saints in every religion; nay in every sect of the Christian religion? Have not canonised saints swallowed down, even more than others, every current superstition of their place and day? Is not their very reverence, humility and obedience the reason of the mental passivity and incapacity of criticism? It seems to me, the truths which feed sanctity are few and simple and common to all who possess the light of conscience. And then, who is to decide who are the saints and who are the experts? Men who are neither one nor the other *ex officio*, and whose only claim to inerrancy rests on the supposition of miraculous intervention. But given such intervention, why not dispense with the experts altogether? Thus I think the mingling of these two disparate conceptions of authority make it impossible to state our position clearly; and still more to bring it within the limits of philosophy. The importance of Newman's line is that it prepares an ark in view of the coming deluge; it prepares a philosophic and rationalistic theory of Church-authority which will (or may possibly) stand when the 'miraculous' theory shall have gone the way of all fond illusions. Then and only then will it be possible to give to 'official' teaching (*versus* expert) the respect and value which is its due, and to recognise its necessity and utility—and indeed, its divine authority.][3]

Ever yours faithfully,
G. TYRRELL.

Notes to Letter 45

1. "The Philosophy of Authority of Religion" in the *Hibbert Journal* 1 (July 1903):677–92.

2. "We have sinned."

3. Bracketed material appears in *George Tyrrell's Letters* (London, 1920), pp. 74–6.

46 26 October 1903[1]

My dear Ward,

The book is to hand;[2] I will have a review ready for the December *Month* but whether the editor will have place for it then God only knows. My present idea is to criticise it from a Renan's standpoint[3] rather than a Rampolla's[4] though it matters little from which extreme one criticises a *via media* since Pilate and Herod shook hands across Christ.

Yes there is a curious analogy between Halifax and Hügel, both lay churchmen, terrible to their respective ordinaries; both moving for reunion by yielding to the enemy all that the authorities hold most sacred; both slightly lacking in humour and deadly earnest about it all, full of confidence to the ultimate realisation of paradox.

Fawkes comes from Friday next till Tuesday. We shall talk ourselves hoarse. I send another Post Mortem.[5] Don't bother to write about it; it is only *Month* padding.

Kindest regards to Mrs. Ward.

Ever yours,
G. Tyrrell

Notes to Letter 46

1. No place of origin given for this letter.

2. *W*'s collected essays, *PP*, was sent to *T* for review in the *Month. T* used the occasion to force some of the issues provoked by the Joint Pastoral Letter and to distance himself from *W* somewhat. His style was ironic because, he said, he wanted to tease some issues out into the open; his target was *W*'s dream project, finding a *via media*, some kind of moderate strategy for issues of religious discourse. *T* had, by this time, given up on any kind of *via media* and was surprised (if not distressed) that *W* continued to hold out for one. In a letter to Maude Petre 11 April 1903 he said, "The moderate men being exasperated cease to exercise restraint on their immoderate disciples, and what might have been an orderly and dignified retreat from untenable positions has become a pell-mell flight. And yet I doubt more and more if there be an honest *via media* with clearly defined limits such as W. Ward is trying to tinker up out of John Henry Newman" (in *Selected Letters* 107–8). *T*'s review, "Semper Eadem" appeared in the *Month* 103 (January 1904):1–17. For some discussion of the rift caused between *T* and *W* by this review see *MW* II.165–7.

3. That is to say, a critical or unorthodox one.

4. That is to say, one which holds to a conservative or papal line (see letter 25 note 7).

5. "Post Mortem," *Month* 102 (October 1903):367–78 was *T*'s review of Frederick W. H. Meyers, *Human Personality and its Survival of Bodily Death* (London, 1903).

47

Richmond, York
9 December 1903

My dear Ward,

Yes you have just spotted the camel.[1] Not that I have really committed myself but that I have suggested the bare possibility of such a view. As my preface says towards the end, I am working out Catholic results as far as they can be worked by a new and less definite method—really I am seeing how far the results of Catholic and liberal theology can be made to tally. To this the rabidest Roman STL[2] *ought* not to object since the essence of apologetic effort is to take the outsider on his own ground, his own hypotheses and exclusions and still corner him.

Privately and personally I quite see that *Catholic* theology is tied absolutely to certain historical beliefs and equally to certain philosophical categories. I also feel that to make so vital a thing as religion is for every man depend on conditions so contingent and disputable would be quite intolerable except so far as the truth of the said faith and categories had some sort of supernatural guarantee like that offered by the theological presuppositions of a miraculous revelation miraculously guarded. Within the limits of that presupposition Catholic theology works according to the ordinary laws of mental development. But that presupposition is, rightly or wrongly, being choked by the *Zeitgeist*; and so it is of some interest and perhaps even of practical importance to see how much of Catholicism will be left standing on the presuppositions and exclusion of liberal theology, i.e., of theology working on purely scientific or philosophical methods and ignoring the limits of a deposit of faith, and ecclesiastical charismatic authority. 'Newmanian' insofar as it implies 'mania' I never was, I hope. Newmanist I am and hope to remain in the deepest sense, i.e., by fidelity to his liberal and progressive spirit, not by a cultus of the *littera mortua*[3] of his positions. What worse fate could we wish him than to be imposed like another Aquinas on future theologians as lessons by heart? He represents a great stride forward in Catholic thought—a veritable renaissance, but he would be the last to claim finality for his results. Similarly, many of us go through a Newman phase or fever which is a purgative and constructive state in our mental history, but it is not the end.

It is when the fever passes and the power of criticism revives that we begin to reap the benefits of the innoculation. It was when my scholasticism began to collapse that the *Grammar of Assent* drew me out of this mire of empty verbiage and set my feet on the solid rock of reality. The anti-Anglican Newman[4] interests me slightly if at all. As *ad hominem* I admire the *Essay on Development* but I think some of its admissions disastrous absolutely, e.g., that violence and disingenuousness have gone with orthodoxy while charity and intelligence have usually been heterodox. And then though he makes out Catholicism to be a true development of the earliest patristic Christianity, yet he leaves the first and more important phases of growth wrapped in darkness (necessarily) and we are left wondering whether what he describes be not a side by side development of wheat and tares later oversown in that dark period which is now the subject of so much anxious study. Newman will be an everlasting source of light if he is studied critically in relation to his own past, present and future, if his necessary limitations are carefully defined and recognised; if the original and the traditional elements of his mind are separated—I am afraid that means if he escapes the fate that follows great men exactly in proportion to their greatness.[5] When is W. J. Williams going to give us his mind on Newman.[6]

Ever your faithfully,
G. Tyrrell

P.S. Loisy writes quite hopefully.

Notes to Letter 47

1. *T* almost certainly refers to *Lex Orandi* which was available by late November 1903. *T* squeezed his Engels work (letter 40 note 2) for all he could get from it. He wanted to revise it as a series of articles for the *Month*, a project von Hügel warned him against (von Hügel to *T*, 4 December 1902); but *T* finally decided, as he told von Hügel, "I am writing a sort of expurgated and amplified Engels for the orthodox multitude which I am going to offer to the censors" (*A&L* II.181). This project was published as *Lex Orandi*. It passed the Jesuit censors in August, and the diocesean ones—Cardinal Vaughan had died (19 June 1903) and his successor, Archbishop Francis Bourne, not wanting to begin his reign by overriding the Jesuit censors, approved it. *T* hoped to be protected by this double approval lest/when his authorship of *Religion as a Factor of Life* (Exeter, 1902) was discovered. That work had been reviewed already in a French journal as a "compendium of agnostic theology" (see Eugène Franon, "Un nouveau mani-

feste catholique d'agnosticisme" in *Bulletin de littérature ecclésiastique* (Toulouse) 3rd series 5 (June 1903): 157.

2. Ecclesiastical degree, a Licentiate of Sacred Theology; probably meant here as a term of contempt.

3. dead letter

4. Probably *Certain Difficulties Felt by Anglicans in Catholic Teaching* (London, 1876) and/or *The Present Position of Catholics in England* (London, 1852).

5. *T* had been having some problems with Newman's theories for some time; he articulated some of them in "The Limitations of Newman" in the *Monthly Register* 1 (October 1902): 264–5. *T* believed that the theory of development devised by Newman loyalists like *W* failed to provide the hoped-for *via media*; Newman could *not* be used, *T* thought, to effect a plausible synthesis between faith and reason because Newman (and *W*) understood faith and reason to be on the same plane and thus capable of conflict and in need of synthesis. *T*'s inclination was quite different: for him faith and reason were different, had different roles and led to different kinds of religious expression. *T* argued, in his article, that *W* gave the lead to the *head* in religion, whereas *T* focused on action and the *heart*. All this leads back to a point *T* had been pressing for some time, *viz.*, that the real teachers are the saints. There is a *real* development in the lived relation between God and people, not just an unfolding (as Newman's theory would have it). "As the church prays, so she believes" he said in *Lex Orandi* (p. 214).

6. Willie Williams published *Newman, Pascal, Loisy and the Catholic Church* (London, 1906).

48 — 11 December 1903[1]

My dear Ward,

Your two letters give me so much to say that I will follow Devas'[2] example and inflict a voluminous epistle on you in a few days. My article on your book will appear in January and I want to present the key thereto, for writing on such topics in the *Month* is like whistling with one's mouth full of flour. I am *so* glad Mrs. Ward is satisfied with L.O.[3]

Ever yours,
G.T.

Notes to Letter 48

1. No place of origin given for this card and postmark not legible.

2. Charles S. Devas (1848–1906), economist and distinguished convert to Roman Catholicism.

3. *Lex Orandi*

49 11 December 1903[1]

[My dear Ward,

A last word as to Newmanism. You say his 'principles' will never die; I say his 'spirit.' I fancy these are but two aspects of the same thing; that 'spirit' lays a little more emphasis on the moral tone and temper; whereas 'principle' emphasises the corresponding mortality. If we differ substantially, it is that, while I agree with you that Newman's prophetic insight foresaw *in the vague* the intellectual revolution which is now upon us and with which e.g. Loisy is, I think vainly, trying to cope, he did not and could not have anticipated and prepared for the precise problem which is now presented to us, and which I try to state as definitely as possible in my coming article.[2]

Apart from the purely *ad hominem* and *anti-Anglican* values of the *Essay on Development*, it was a great service to show clearly, as he did, that the Church had practically and implicitly (and to some extent explicitly) acknowledged that same principle of Development which is the dominating category of modern science and philosophy; that she had in the same measure repudiated the rigid *semper-eadem* conservatism of the Eastern Churches and of the high Anglicans; and was, so far, more liberal, more progressive than they. But then (and this takes me to my article) the Church, as John Henry Newman would be the first to acknowledge, has no intention of being dominated by this development category; she adopts it only as an *ancilla theologiae*;[3] it is like a wild horse caught in the prairies and put to work on tramlines, in blinkers, up and down, down and up. In the present instance the tramlines, the blinkers are the presupposed facts of a miraculous revelation and of a no less miraculous magisterium by which the workings of development are limited and infallibly corrected.

The Church has 'adopted' development, just as she adopted Aristotelianism i.e. she has enslaved it. The alternative would be for her to be enslaved by it; to submit her presuppositions to be criticised by i.e. to be accounted for and explained away, as by Harnack and Co.

Development is common to the Church and to modern thought, as wood is common to a table and a tree; or rather as growth is common to wall-fruit and wild fruit-trees. Neither (the Church nor Modern thought) can absorb without destroying the other; neither can yield to the other without suicide—I do not speak of given conclusions and details but of the vital principles of the two systems.

Hence in my article I have laid them side by side like two snakes eyeing one another. Amalgamation in some larger synthesis that is neither, is difficult to believe in. All that I dare suggest in the *Month* is the pacific *modus vivendi* at which you hint once or twice namely diversity need not mean hostility. Let them move each in its own plane, by its own laws; let us all acknowledge the confessedly *ex hypothesi* and abstract character of a philosophy which but works out the necessary consequences of certain questionable presuppositions and exclusions; and let us not fear to see how far Christianity fits into such an artificial synthesis and how much of it stands after the miraculous has been excluded (as in *Lex Orandi*). This is all I have committed you to, though I know you mean more and at least *hope* for, if you do not see your way to a synthesis.

What is my own hope?

Throughout the article I speak advisedly *not* of Catholicism, but of Catholic Theology which is related to the former as man's theory about his own nature and character is related to what he really *is* before God. It is ultimately and in the last resort to this theology that we owe what is intractable and harsh in the conceptions of the Christian revelation and the ecclesiastical magisterium. Proximately we quote decrees and decisions; but it is theology that determines the value of these decrees, and gives us our theory of the *Ecclesia Docens* and to which the *Ecclesia Docens* must appeal for defence of its claims. What to us seems preposterous in Father Coupé's recent letters to the *Tablet*[4] about the *sub gravi* obligation of interior assent to the expediency of the Temporal Power (a theologoumenon which the Bishop of Liverpool[5] has just made the text of a Pastoral), or in the notorious Joint-Pastoral of 1901 is I am convinced the necessary and legitimate development of the two presuppositions of Catholic theology, which is always and essentially 'logical' if nothing else. But, with you, I believe that in one or two of its admissions it contains (because of its very logicality) the seeds of its ultimate dissolution; even were there not thousands of Coupés and Moyeses working out its *reductio ad absurdum* as fast as they can. First of all the 'Deposit' is professedly a presentment of strictly supernatural facts and experiences (seen once for all and then withdrawn from view) in the terms of things natural. All we hold is this *deposited expression* of doctrine; not the facts and experiences; in other words; all we hold is an analogue or metaphor of those experiences. Now there is no valid inference from analogues; the conclusion is vitiated with all the inexactness of the premise. Hence all those explications and applications of the *deposit* which constitute the edifice of theology are affected with the quality of their principle i.e. the truth-value of the whole system is that of analogy.

Secondly; there is the distinction between *definita propter se* and *propter alia*.[6] The whole end of the latter is the protection of the former i.e. the preservation of the original sense of the deposit of faith as it was understood by those to whom the apostles committed it and who had no direct touch with the supernatural experiences expressed by it. Definitions fall, *not on the realities revealed*, but on the form in and under which they were deposited; they are directed to the guarding of the deposit. Hence the Ptolemaic Astronomy might really be inseparably part and parcel of the mental language of the *depositum fidei*; might be necessary for securing the preservation of the impression produced by Christ's revelation on the sub-apostolic mind; might be *ecclesiastically* true, as part of a symbolism through which alone certain truths are known to us.

Thirdly; It is certain that nothing is *de fide divina* but what was actually (however confusedly) contained in the sub-apostolic mind; nothing that a theological microscope could not have detected there in all its form and fashion. It is also admitted that (e.g. the form and matter of the sacrament of Orders; in the decree of Eugenius IV[7] *ad Armenos* [[sic]] mistakes may and have been made as to what is accretion, and what primitive nucleus. Now, pin theologians to these admissions and then apply the history of the development of dogma to point after point and I predict a considerable and liberating contraction of the area of *de fide divina* doctrines, and a transfer of much that now passes as such, into the category of *definita propter alia*. Theologians will say as Bellarmine said; If the earth moves, that must be what the scripture meant; if facts won't fit theology theology must be made to fit facts.

For all their inadequacy we owe a good deal to the intransigent presuppositions of theology. For if there had been no canonised immutable doctrine, no canonised interpretation, what would have happened to Christianity? It was the fiction of an unchanged and unchangeable nucleus of sacred tradition that saved the Christianity of the apostles from being quickly transformed out of all recognition. As it is, it is possible for us with our improved historial methods to reach back across the centuries to the historical Christ, to understand him better and not worse in the impress he has made on generation after generation; to sever the wheat from the tares; to distinguish the life-giving imperishable principles from their contingent and defective applications. All this we owe to theological intransigence,—to the desperate efforts to keep up the *semper eadem* fiction, to the struggle of conservatism against the irresistable laws of change and growth. Amid all the protective theological accretions the nucleus of Christianity has been preserved like a fly in amber or like a mammoth in ice; while outside theology the spirit of Christ has lived and developed in the life of the faithful collectively.

[[I cannot but think that if the church is to live it will be through the very converse of what occurred as to Aristotelianism i.e. through its absorption of our theology into the contemporary philosophical synthesis.]][8] For then the church stood for civilisation and culture; but to-day she stands to culture as she did in the first centuries—an outsider and apologist, asking to be heard by them, so now she must stoop to conquer, or die to live. That she would live and survive such a transformation may seem questionable to most; but to me it is a matter of more than hope and nearly of faith.

If you don't want to keep this letter will you let me have it back as I have no time to copy it, but might wish to refer to it later.

Ever yours faithfully,
G. Tyrrell

P.S. On re-reading, I only wish to reiterate that I am not speaking as in *Lex Orandi* of the lived Christianity of the faithful or of the beliefs implied in that life, but only of the intellectual life of the theological schools of the rationalized presentiment of Christianity elaborated by the purely speculative thirst of theologians. Also when I say Loisy labours 'in vain,' I mean if he does not distinguish between Catholicism and Catholic theology or imagines that the latter could even think of 'coming to terms' with modern thought or could by any process of development find room for the results of his criticism. 'New bottles for new wine.' I hope the context of the article itself will clear up what is obscure in these notes.][9]

Notes to Letter 49

1. No place of origin given for this letter.
2. Probably, "The Abbé Loisy: Criticism and Catholicism," *Church Quarterly Review* 58 (April 1904):180–95, a comprehensive review of Loisy's *L'Évangile et l'Église* (Paris, 1902), and *Autour d'un petit livre* (Paris, 1903) along with T. A. Lacey, *Harnack and Loisy* (London, 1904), and Auguste Sabatier, *Les Religions d'autorité et la religion de l'esprit* (Paris, 1904).
3. handmaid of theology
4. Charles Coupé, S.J. wrote pamphlets for the Catholic Truth Society. In the *Tablet* 102 (1903) he wrote three very long letters on the temporal power; see pp. 696, 766 and 856.
5. Thomas Whiteside (1857–1921), wrote a pastoral letter on the temporal power arguing that Catholics may not have an open mind on the issue. The letter was printed in the *Tablet* 102 (1903):939f.
6. defined for its own sake and defined for the sake of something else.
7. Eugenius IV (1383–1447; Pope from 1431) presided over the council at Florence (1439) which temporarily re-united the Greek and Roman churches. This council issued the instruction *Pro Armenis*, instructing the Greeks on the sacraments.
8. Double bracketed material published in *MW* II.166, i.e., this one sentence.
9. Bracketed material, i.e., the whole letter plus the post script, published in *A&L* II.215–9.

50

Richmond, York
22 December 1903

If you have not read it you should read *La Psychologie des Foules* par G. Lebon[1] (Alcan. Paris—pp. 190 2 Fr. 50). It bears deeply on Balfour's theory of 'authority' raising issues that Balfour hardly notices. In some respects a *hasty* book; but still 'considerable.' I have been sent a charming edition (Dent's 'cloister library') of John Henry Newman's *University Education*[2] and am re-reading with quickened admiration.

Yours,
G.T.

Notes to Letter 50

1. Gustave LeBon (1841–1931), wrote books on the psychology of various things, this one on the psychology of crowds.
2. *On the Scope and Nature of University Education* (Dublin, 1852).

51

4 January 1904[1]

[My dear Ward,

By this, Longmans will have sent you the January *Month.*[2] I had feared that I had exaggerated the theologians' case; but half a dozen letters of approval from some of our hitherto most hostile theologians proves that I have not done so. 'I am sure it will do a lot of good by helping thinking minds to focus,' says one. Another. 'You express what I often wanted to say and could not.' 'Felicitations on admirable article in *Month*,' says a red hot ultra Thomist. 'Your article has given great satisfaction here?' (at. Saint Bueno's). 'A splendid article,' says my principle delator, Father Slater,[3] 'it is most orthodox. If he would only write often like that!' 'The Provincial, and Father Gerard and the rest are perfectly delighted with your article.' Etc., etc. all this in one day. Surely they are children in wisdom if not in malice; innocent as serpents and wise as doves. I will wait to gather in all the adhesions I can before suggesting that they have been somewhat premature. I have carefully (very) studied John Henry Newman's sermon on *Theological Development*[4] and have no doubt whatever that he held the pre-scholastic and patristic idea of the *permanence* of revelation in the mind of the faithful, and never quite twigged[5] the school theory of a mere formula of a long-past revelation as the subject matter of theology. He puts theology on all fours with natural sciences and its relation to its subject matter. It formulates certain subjective immanent *impressions* or *ideas* exactly analogous to sense impressions which are realities of experience by which notions and inferences can be criticised. *In principle* (with one or two unimportant modifications) this is *Liberal* theology.[6] It cannot (and this is what I do not think you see clearly enough) combine with this impossible school-theology which ties us to the categories and thought forms of the last twenty centuries. If Catholicism is to live, the school-theology must go. See 'L 'affaire Loisy' in the current *Pilot* by Lord knows who.[7] Will you answer my article or will you let it slide?[8] If you answer it I hope you will wait a little to let it soak in and to let Moyes and Co. commit themselves by exposition of their position. Also, I should very much like to submit a rough draft of the sort of answer I think would do most good.

With best New Year wishes

Yours faithfully,

G. TYRRELL][9]

Notes to Letter 51

1. No place of origin given for this letter.

2. *T*'s review, "Semper Eadem," *Month* 103 (January 1904): 1–17; reprinted in *S&C* 106–32. In the review *T* criticizes *W* because he "had not found a *via media* between scholastic theology and science—between the old theology and the new." The criticism begs the question, however, as it was not *W*'s intention to find such a *via media*, i.e., a final synthesis but to use the *via media* idea to argue for moderation from all sides. At the same time, because *W* could not always see the consequences of some of his tentatively "liberal" positions, he was vulnerable to *T*'s criticisms. *T* claimed to be ironical in this review (see *MW* II.164–70; *T*, himself, stated his aims to John Gerard, editor of the *Month* and to Charles Devas (see Appendix C for copies for those letters).

3. Thomas Slater, S.J. (1854–1928), had been a professor of moral theology and canon law at St. Bueno's from 1892–1901.

4. Sermon XV in the *Oxford University Sermons.*

5. Victorian slang for understood.

6. Given the climate of religious authority at the time, and the heated discussions following the Joint Pastoral Letter condemning "liberal Catholicism," the very word *liberal* was a dangerous one. *T* meant to distinguish between liberal *theology* and liberal *Catholicism*, but was not able to make the distinction clear. At the root of the problem, however, were two different interpretations of Newman which had finally broken into open conflict. For an interesting related case see *MW* II.176.

7. "Lord knows who" and so did *T*, who wrote the letter himself and signed it "From a Correspondent" in the *Pilot* 9 (2 January 1904): 10–1 (see Loome, p. 306).

8. *W* contemplated a response to *T*, but never published one (see *MW* II.168); Charles Devas, in a lengthy letter (*WWP* at *SAUL*) advised *W* against publishing a response to *T*.

9. Bracketed material published in *MW* II.167–8.

52 12 January 1904[1]

Dear Ward,

I am doing a Part II to 'Semper Eadem'[2] so suspend your judgments if you have any. I could not have believed that with *Lex Orandi* and all my writings and past history before them the Philistines could have been so blind as to mistake the statement of a dilemma for a contrast of false and true. I had to explain to Gerard today that 'liberal theologians' such as Caird, Sabatier and Gardner[3] are *not* 'liberal Catholics,' that if I had 'liberal Catholics' in mind at all it was such as Newman and my grievance was that they were too conservative and left us tied to obsolete categories as much as ever. I hope in Part II to put such misapprehensions out of reach—though of course in the *Month* one can not speak freely.

Yours ever,
G.T.

Notes to Letter 52

1. No place of origin given for this postcard, and postmark not legible.

2. *T* worked on and wrote a second part, "Semper Eadem II" but it was not accepted for publication in the *Month.* It was finally published in America as "The Limits of the Theory of Development" in the *Catholic World* 81 (September 1905):730–44; reprinted as "Semper Eadem II" in *S&C* 133–54.

3. Percy Gardner (1846–1937), professor of classical archaeology at Oxford and a friend of von Hügel's. He reviewed *L'Évangile et l'Église* in the *Hibbert Journal* 1 (April 1903):602–6. In the process of his review, he remarked, "It is strange to say of a church which degrades or rejects all who dare to think differently from the Roman Curia that it can adapt itself to modern conditions" (p. 604).

53 14 January 1904[1]

Dear Ward,

It is plain that my article was overdone and has been misunderstood as an attack on 'Liberal Catholicism' which even Gerard seems to identify with 'liberal theology' such as Sabatier's. Also he seems to think that I question your *via media*[2] as tending to slip over to liberal theology and not rather as tending to slip back to 'school' theology. My mistake was in calling the latter *Catholic* seeing there is a liberal and a conservative Catholic theology. Of course they at once identified Catholic theology with official Catholicism and liberal theology with liberal Catholicism. I will correct all this in my part II. I quite believe that the dilemma exists only for those who hold a childish mechanical view of the fact of revelation as an oracular utterance in the past; but this *is* what is not taught in the schools and is presupposed by the Vatican theory of apologetic. What I want to bring out is the *need* of a via media and of a modification of that mechanical view.

I will write more fully after my February article.

In haste,
yours ever,
G. TYRRELL

Notes to Letter 53

1. No place of origin given for this letter.

2. Associated with Newman and originally put forth in Tracts 38 and 40 of the *Tracts for the Times* (1834), Newman dismissed it as "a paper theory" in Tract 41. His early views on the matter were meant to ascertain and articulate the glory of the Anglican church which, Newman said, "has taken the VIA MEDIA, as it has been called. It lies *between* the (so-called) Reformers and the Romanists." The term, therefore, can be taken to suggest a fruitful tension between those on the critical/creative edge of the theological enterprise and those whose position requires them to defend the old order. *W*, however, applied it to what he thought was a fruitful tension between late nineteenth century liberal Catholics and a conservative church authority. He, himself, was clearly more at home in and eventually identified with the old order, with those who preserve and transmit traditions. For a brief period, however, he associated himself with the new, with those searching for a critical new theological method: his friendship with von Hügel and *T* and his understanding of their similarity of aims helped him to think of himself as a "liberal Catholic," even though the word liberal was never comfortable for him. The crux of the argument between *T* and *W* on the *via media* issue was a profound difference of interpretatoin of Newman and of the role of a *via media*. *W* usually refers to Newman's *via media* as a position of moderation (a position he, himself, hoped to occupy); *T*, on the other hand, believed the *via media* to require a more daring pushing of premises to logical conclusions. *T* eventually rejected a *via media* because he thought it was being used to establish a final synthesis, a task he had given up as impossible.

54 19 January 1904[1]

My dear Ward,

This is most annoying, most disingenuous, most characteristic of [[the]] Jesuit *ménage*.[2] I have written again to Gerard as explicitly as possible without actually calling him a fool and have put the case clearly in two or three different ways. The fact is they don't know what Liberal Catholicism means and won't take the trouble to think. It stands for any view of anything that is broader than their own. The word 'liberal' is to them a red rag and sets their passions aglow and they can see nothing but freemasonry. I told him it will cause just indignation if you have to defend yourself elsewhere than in the *Month* and that he should suggest to you to suspend your reply till my second article is out, of which I will send you the proof in a day or two. It is just possible that he may refuse to insert this when he sees how it divests the previous one of its supposed character of an onslaught on Liberal Catholics in general and most notoriously on Wilfrid Ward. I reminded him how in offering the article to him I had said that it was 'neither an attack nor a defense of *any* school, neither of "liberal theology" nor of those whom you (John Gerard) call "theologians of the wooden old school;" but an attempt to clear the *status quaestionis*.[3] If it was *against* anyone, it was against those who hoped they had found a *via media*— "Liberal" Catholics who failed to distinguish themselves *in principle* from the extreme left; or against Ward who—*meo judicio*[4] had failed to distinguish himself *in principle* from the extreme right.'

The truth is you underrate the self-complacent ignorance and stupidity of the clerical mind. Infallibility has no reason either to read or to reflect.

Yours,
G.T.

Richmond
20 January 1904

I did not mean *Liberal-Catholic* theology but liberal *Catholic-theology*. I should never use the term 'liberal' of myself *in print* because it is perverted by Catholic usage into a synonym for

'Masonic.' But *in my own mind* I use it for lack of any better. Why don't you invent one to distinguish John Henry Newman from Mazzella?[5] 'Broad' won't do; it suggests 'latitudinarian.' Corrance in the *Hibbert*[6] calls his position 'Progressive' Catholicism; but then he *is* a liberal in the fuller sense. We want a label for your position. It is the only protection against misunderstanding.

G.T.[7]

Notes to Letter 54

1. No place of origin given for this letter, but P.S. postmarked Richmond.
2. The *Month* refused to publish *T*'s second part—"Semper Eadem II"—and, though *W* had asked to reply in the pages of the *Month*, and had just cause, he "consented to forego his right to reply in deference to Fr. Gerard's difficulties" (*MW* II.169).
3. state of the question.
4. in my estimation
5. See letter 19 note 6.
6. H. C. Corrance, "Progressive Catholicism and High Church Absolutism," *Hibbert Journal* 2 (January 1904):217–34; the article was concerned with the Loisy controversy (for further information see Barmann, p. 129).
7. This postscript was written the next day, but included with the 19 January letter so as to constitute one letter.

55 25 January 1904[1]

My dear Ward,

Things are rather mixed up. Gerard wrote on Friday to say he could not find room for me in February; that he did not agree with my exegesis of the University Sermon, etc., etc., and wanting to know what my own *via media* was. I replied that my attitude was expressed in the last four or five paragraphs of the January article, i.e., there is no urgent necessity to press in at all between Scylla and Charbydis,[2] we can drop anchor and wait for a pilot. I said a false impression had been created by his (and others') quite inexcusable identification of 'Liberal theology' (which I carefully defined and exemplified) with Liberal Catholicism; that the article was not an attack or defence but an exposition—objective, impartial, irrespective of and counter to my actual sympathies; that still less was it an attack on you as incarnating liberal Catholicism (or liberal theology) but a criticism of your hoped-for (not affirmed) *via media* as vitiated by the same instability as that of Liberal Catholicism but *in a contrary direction.* I showed him that I had identified your actual (versus your hoped-for) position with my own *modus vivendi.* I said I would write to the *Tablet*[3] at once and protest against these three false inferences. Which I did; and as I was rushing off to Ambleside[4] I had no time for censorship so I let Colley know what I had done and why. On returning just an hour ago I find he writes begging me to wait another week and have the letter censored; and that you write suggesting that you may be replying yourself. I have written and complained to Colley that Gerard will neither let you justify yourself nor let me justify you; and that such justification is imperative and beyond his powers to prohibit; that I will attend to any reasonable censorship of the letter compatible with such justification but no more. If you write, deal with my article in its *true* (versus its superficial) sense, i.e., as I have here and elsewhere explained it. I will search my memory and send you as close a reproduction as I can of my *Tablet* letter.

Ever yours,
G.T.

Notes to Letter 55

1. No place of origin given for this letter.
2. In Greek mythology, Scylla and Charybdis were two dangers to searfarers traditionally located in the straits of Messina, between Italy and Sicily. Scylla was a six-headed monster and Charybdis a dangerous whirlpool. *Through Scylla and Charybdis* was the title of a book published by *T* in 1907: the Scylla (or rock) of tradition and authority and the Charybdis (whirlpool) of progress and liberty. This was precisely the dilemma *T* addressed himself to in "Semper Eadem."
3. *T* wrote a lengthy letter to the *Tablet*, but it was never published. It can be found in *MP* II.221–3, dated 22 January 1904. What *was* finally published in the *Tablet* (30 January 1904) was a brief explanation of two points: 1) that by liberal theology he did not mean liberal Catholic theology but the work of men like Sabatier and Caird and 2) "that so far as the position taken up by Mr. Ward in his book is concerned, I do not see that *in principle* he has dissociated himself from what I have called 'theological intransigence.' " p. 177.
4. Village in Westmorland.

56 10 November 1904[1]

Dear Ward,

Just a line; for we are both swamped with work. Of course by 'Catholic theology' I *meant* Jesuit theology as now dominant; the theology that anathamatizes you and all your work no less than me;[2] not the theology of the Church taken historically in all its varying moods. If you can kill this Jesuit theological parasite with a pill or by weakening purgatives, do so as soon as possible. But I think that unless it is more rudely dispatched it will kill all intelligence out of the Church. Japan may be crushed, but her best chance was to break off endless and futile negotiations.[3] [As to Loisy's position, I don't think you quite seize it. His question is, e.g., *not* was Christ conscious of his Godhead? did he foresee and foreplan the Catholic church? did he teach the atoning value of his death? but rather, can all this be *demonstrated* from the Gospels according to the received principles and methods of scientific criticism.][4] Undoubtedly it cannot, and much that points to contrary conclusions presents a problem to the critic not *as* critic, but *as* Catholic. To suggest a solution to that problem is Loisy's work *as apologist*; *as critic* he simply disengages the data from which the problem arises. I have this from himself. Surely it is [[a]] clear unassailable and commendable position.

'*Catholicus*' of the *Times*[5] is that rascal of a David Fleming.[6] He knows well that Loisy lost his chair at *l'Institut*[7] for the assertions which he says we are free to hold. So too, he wants to defame Loisy in Protestant eyes by ignoring his distinction of *qua* critic and *qua* Catholic as I have just put it.

Yours ever,
G.T.

Notes to Letter 56

1. No place of origin given for this letter.

2. *W* always considered himself more cautious and was, in fact, more sanguine than *T* about the probable consequences of a cautious progressiveness. *W* believed that his explicit loyalty to Roman Catholicism meant that he could never be condemned; *T* points out that *any* progressive theology, cautious or not, can be condemned.

3. Reference to precipitating factor in Russo-Japanese War (1904–5). Russia had penetrated into North Korea and Manchuria and Japanese countered with negotiations. The Russian government would not move and assumed that the Japanese would be quickly crushed in any armed conflict. On 6 February 1904 Japan broke off negotiations with Russia; a series of quick and astonishing Japanese victories followed, culminating in the destruction of the Russian fleet by May 1905.

4. Bracketed material published in *MW* II.171.

5. Responding to an earlier letter in *The Times* (21 January 1904) about Loisy, signed "*Vidi*"; the letter signed "*Catholicus*" appeared 25 January 1904. For more details see Barmann, pp. 115–8.

6. David Fleming was the secretary to the Pontifical Biblical Commission. An Irish Franciscan, he had served on the committee which declared Anglican Orders to be invalid and, in the matter of Loisy, represented a quasi-official position.

7. L'Institut Catholique of Paris. Loisy finished his studies there and remained as a Professor of Hebrew and Exegesis from 1884–93. He was, at that time, among the forerunners of Catholic biblical scholarship, but, because he began to apply critical methods to Scripture, was an object of suspicion to some of the conservative religious authorities in Paris. On 25 January 1893 his rector, Monsignor d'Hulst, published an article in *Le Correspondant* in which he hoped to "defend" Loisy. The article, however, caricatured Loisy's position so badly that he was ultimately dismissed from his position.

57

Richmond, Yorks.
1 December 1904

My dear Ward,

[I don't pay much heed to gossip; but I think there is now a sort of consensus or accumulative proof to the effect that in spite of my letter to the *Tablet* last February you consider you have a grievance against me in regard to the 'Semper Eadem' article. I quite see that Gerard might, as he does, consider himself aggrieved. For though in my letter, proposing the article, I fully warned him of its ambiguous sense, and said that those who were foolish enough to see heresy in *Lex Orandi* would be *foolish enough* to see reaction in 'Semper Eadem;' yet in expressing my dissent from your 'medial' position about development I left undetermined the side to which I inclined. Had I done otherwise I could not have got the article in at all. His controversial greed made him swallow the bait and the hook. He jumped at the idea that it was an onslaught on Liberalism all round and on you in particular. To suppose that in one moment the author of *Lex Orandi*, etc., should execute such an astonishing *volte face*[1] argued a very childish judgment both in him and in all those who, knowing me, took the article as a plea for the blackest obscurantism: *Nemo fit repente nequissimus.*[2]

If your grievance lies in the fact that I gave a false impression of you as ultra-Liberal in the eyes of the undiscerning, you know at least how completely that impression would have been erased by my second article had it been published; and how I wrote then to the *Tablet* and made it beyond doubt what I meant.

If however it is because I have expressed my conviction that a compromise between static and dynamic conceptions, between the philosophy of mental development and the patristic conception of the deposit is impossible and even dangerous, I do not see why you should be aggrieved any more than I should were you to express your conviction of dangers of liberal theology. Subsequent reading and reflection has confirmed me in the conclusions I then reached. [[Gerard tells me I misread Newman's *Oxford Sermon* and *Essay*; you tell me the same, but in a diametrically opposite sense; neither of you have adduced any sort of reason so far. Besides it is not a question of Newman but of truth.]][3]

Of course I feel that our paths have long since bifurcated and are bound to diverge more and more; that my faith in the *bona fides* of our officialdom is as weak as yours is strong; still, while recognising your unwillingness to be identified with me as quite reasonable under all the difficult circumstances, I should be most sorry to leave you with the idea that I had in any intentional way been unfair or unfriendly towards you. At the most I have been awkward owing to the difficulties of my absurd position which deprives me of the power of free utterance and explanation which you enjoy as a layman.

Yours sincerely,

G. Tyrrell.][4]

Notes to Letter 57

1. turn around
2. No one turns bad all at once.
3. This sentence is omitted from Maisie Ward's transcription with no indication that she has made an omission.
4. Bracketed material published in *MW* II.169–70.

58 Richmond. Yorks.
4 August 1905

Dear Ward,

I had only a hasty glance at *De Profundis* and have read nothing else of Wilde's whatever, and only know him through gossip.[1] So I doubt if I am fit for the task of a psychological analysis though it would be fairly congenial.[2]

If you can give us an objective Newman you will do a great service to truth. On that basis we could fight profitably about our various Newmanisms afterwards. To add one more interpretation to the many would be a small good in comparison. I hope your work will be a classical source for all impartial enquirers.

[I am afraid the *Dublin*[3] will give you more trouble than it is worth. One has seen death in the eyes this many a day.][4]

Yours faithfully,
G. TYRRELL.

Notes to Letter 58

1. *De Profundis* (London, 1905) is a drastically cut version of a long letter from Oscar Wilde (1854–1901) to Lord Alfred Douglas. It was published in 1905 and *W* asked *T* to review it for the *Dublin Review*.

2. It is perhaps a gesture of reconciliation on *W*'s part to write to *T* after nearly a year, and to ask him to write reviews for the *Dublin Review*.

3. *W* assumed editorship of the *Dublin Review* in 1906 and held that post until 1915. (see *MW* II.200–38)

4. Bracketed material, in a slightly different form, appeared in *MW* II.202.

59 Richmond. Yorks.
11 August 1905

Dear Ward,

If you want the review *without fail* for January I had better decline it, as I *may* be very crowded with work these next four months. I hope you will give me the offer of doing something for April. I shall be able to tell in two or three weeks what my engagements are; and if I am freer than I expect, I will write and arrange about something for January.

Yours faithfully,
G. TYRRELL.

The Baron[1] is here, in great form.

Note to Letter 59

1. Von Hügel.

60

Pension Bellevue, Gunterstalstrasse,
Freiburg i. Br.
21 March 1906

My dear Ward,

I was very glad to get your letter with its expressions of sympathy and goodwill. I think this issue was inevitable; and that my position as a Jesuit was almost unfairer to them than to me.[1] It was only the amount of kindness and even agreement I found in the English Province that made me insensible to the general character of the bulk of the order. I began treating for a quiet 'secularisation' last August, but as the conditions promised to be fatal to my literary liberty and still more as so very many of my friends (even the Baron[2] and Semeria[3]) thought it a weaker line to move than to be moved, I put my *whole* mind before the General,[4] withdrew my plea for secularisation, and threw on him the onus of dismissing or retaining me. Had he retained me I was willing to write no more but stay on quietly at Richmond till the end—for I felt that to be so *active* in favour of the opposite camp as I had insensibly become was equivalent to treachery. Should he dismiss me (as a Jesuit and 'unsecularised,' with all my vows upon me and therefore suspended) I should at least have the advantages as well as the disadvantages of my vagrant condition. I had put that to him December 31. Then January 1 either God or the Devil published some extracts from one of my most nefarious private brochures in the *Corrière della sera*[5] (*absolutely defensible* statements, but the sort of things one says to a man who admits next to nothing; medicine for a desperate case, not bread for daily use). Ignoring my dilemma of December 31 the General demanded a wholesale repudiation of the quoted extracts. I wrote an explanation of the first, which was mistranslated preposterously and maintained all the rest as my sincere opinion and as defensible from authority. The prompt reply was my dismissal. I do not believe this was the General's own wish at all; but I have since learnt beyond doubt that a *mot d'ordre*[6] had been given to the General of the Dominicans (and therefore of course to that of the Jesuits) to help the Pope to uproot Liberalism root and branch. There have moreover been several plain indications of this same effort since. From what I know of the sudden spread of the Liberal movement among the young clergy in Italy (as well as France) I am not surprised at their alarm. Unfortunately their own lack of education prevents their being able to deal with the trouble by other than quasi-physical, self-defeating methods of expression, while owing to the rottenness of seminary training the *giovane clero*[7] develop a Liberalism of the shallowest and most aggressive type, a fanaticism *à rebours*[8] quite as bad as that of the *Civiltà.* But while we have a *buon paroco*[9] for Pope and a Stonyhurst schoolboy for his Secretary and advisor,[10] we can expect no remedy. Both *Civiltà* and *Études*[11] have begun dissecting me before my corpse is cold, but so offensively as to do me good rather than harm. Still I intend to try to answer the latter in its own pages just to show that one can leave the Jesuits and yet not suffer moral and spiritual shipwreck to the extent implied in the '*Hélas*!'—'*le triste évènement*'—*la fatale* issue,[12] etc., etc., with which the walrus-editor deplores while he devours me—not to speak of his implying that I got an *Imprimatur* for *Lex Orandi* by a trick. Also I want to tell him that I am, at Easter, bringing out '*Lex Credendi*, a sequel to *Lex Orandi*,' in case he might like to attack them both together. Please thank Mrs. Ward for her kind message.

Ever yours faithfully,
G. TYRRELL.

I shall be here for a couple of months, most likely; till the storm is over it is no use building a nest. Probably I may settle in Italy and spend three months a year in London—if I can afford it; and my market is not too badly damanged by my ecclesiastical bankruptcy.

Notes to Letter 60

1. *T* was dismissed from the Society of Jesus, 19 February 1906.
2. Von Hügel.
3. Giovanni Semeria (1867–1931), Barnabite priest and Scripture scholar who was a friend of both von Hügel's and *T*'s.
4. Luis Martin, S.J., General of the Society of Jesus; for a copy of the letter see *A&L* II.458–99.
5. Late in 1903 *T* published the anonymous *A Letter to a University Professor* (n.p., n.d.); later published as *A Much Abused Letter* (1906). Late in 1905 sections of it were leaked to the Italian press and were published in *Corrière della sera* (Milan) 1 January 1906. The passages published were a questionable translation and out of context, but the author was identified as "an English Jesuit." Once Jesuit officials learned that *T* was the author, it was not long before his dismissal from the Society (see Loome, pp. 288–90; *A&L* II.193–6).
6. word of command or password
7. young clergy
8. in reverse
9. a good parish priest, perhaps used here as a term of derision, i.e., just when what is needed is a Pope who understands some of the issues involved in higher criticism and the needs for some accommodation to the modern world, the church gets a good pastor.
10. Merry del Val (see letter 4 note 7 and letter 25 note 13). He was educated by the Jesuits, but not at Stonyhurst; but *T* is probably using this description as an in-house insult.
11. *T* wrote to Maude Petre 9 March 1906 to tell her he had learned that the Pope, personally, wished to rid the church of the "liberal neo-Catholic movement" and had instructed superiors of religious orders and bishops to help him. One of the results of this new vigilance was a series of articles attacking *T* personally, two of which appeared in *Études* (to which *T* responded in the issue of 5 April 1906) and *Civiltà Cattolica*.
12. "the sad event"—the fatal issue.

61

Freiburg i. Br.
8 April 1906

My dear Ward,

[Many thanks for the *Dublin*[1] and for the kind mention therein. With your own criticism, as with so much of the attitude of George Sutcliffe,[2] I agree in the abstract. What I always feel is that Rome has duties as well as rights; and that in the concrete she takes all you say about loyalty, and the value of authority as a matter of course but will not hear a word on the subject of those duties which are correlative to her rights. I do not believe that men of the average soil would ever deny her her rights of loyalty and submission if she showed any decent consciousness of her duties; and that it is because she has for centuries traded on their faith and loyalty, grabbed everything and given nothing, that she has now lost her authority beyond recovery. Of course I am smarting under the assassination of Laberthonnière.[3] Correlative virtues should always be preached and apprehended and practised simultaneously measure for measure. When has the Roman Church ever, by word or action, emphasized what she cannot deny, that there are limits to obedience and authority? When has she ever censured excessive claims on her behalf; or checked the violence of men like Turinaz; or condemned a book as uncharitable and ignorant if it made for her power? *One* sign of that kind would do more to restore her lawful authority than a hundred self-interested condemnations however just—*non enim qui seipsum commendat probatus est sed quem Deus commendat.*[4] The truth is she has *no faith*; in her heart, she does not believe in her cause; her sole hope is in advertisement. *Real* faith begets faith. Because they detect the tremor in her voice men cease to believe in her. And then they cannot but feel the 'business-value' of her claims. It may be lawful but is it expedient to tie such disparate interests together? Not only evil but the appearance of evil may be wrong. Saint Paul thought so, and declined his temporal rights while claiming them. Mrs. Ward will say I want to make the Pope a Baptist minister. That is to prejudice the case by importing a vulgarisation that is no consequence of my belief. Christ was not vulgar in his poverty and simplicity; in the robes of Caesar he would have been vulgar. It is perfectly fair to ask: If Christ or even Peter came on earth to govern the Church today, *in propria persona*,[5] do you believe for one moment that they would assume the Byzantine pomp of the Vatican or claim temporal power? I am afraid if you said yes I should not believe you—so perhaps it is *not* a fair question. To me the mixture of revelation and theology; and of spiritual and temporal power are two manifestations of the same fallacy. I believe in revelation as a man of faith; I believe in theology as a man of reason; I believe each helps and depends on the other; but the bastard progeny of their mixture is not *a priori* only, but historically the enemy of both, the parent of unbelief and ignorance. So too the authority of Church government is lawful and necessary: it is ministerial to spiritual authority—but it is not "divine" in the same direct sense any more than theological thought is divine in the same sense as revelation. What is due only to the spiritual is claimed for the natural. The Church's chief officer is called His *Holiness* and *as such* claims what belongs only to the natural; and thus we get a parallel mixture with parallel ill-results. If I do not recognise myself in George Sutcliffe so of course neither in Paul;[6] though undoubtedly I am nearer to him of the two. But in no case is he a religious man; his interest is primarily intellectual and theoretic; whereas I care about a synthesis only because I care about religion. I feel a far deeper fraternity and sympathy with any religious nonconformist (even a Baptist minister) than I do with Abbé Loisy or Houtin or Gibson or Williams (obviously this is not for quotation); and if I swear by the Baron or Miss Petre or Laberthonnière it is just because with them too the life is more than the theory; and because with them I still hope that Catholicism offers a fuller and richer life than any form of Protestantism and perhaps than Anglicanism can offer to those who want it. If in any other point I were like Paul, it might be in retiring to save my soul in peace 'Where the Churches cease from troubling and the weary are at rest"[7]—not to the Dominicans (God forbid) nor perhaps the Carthusians; but quite away. The book is certainly interesting and actual. I am told that Paul is the Baron, is Gibson, etc., etc. Plainly he is a mosaic; and probably even that unconsciously. Sutcliffe is more obvious—at least I think so. I am very pleased indeed to receive it and still more the sympathetic and friendly letter that accompanies it which I must answer as soon as I can. As to my vows I could easily get 'secularised' by a little trouble and perhaps intrigue; but it seems to me rather undignified to petition for favours from those [[from]] whom one has suffered unceremonious handling. *They* ought to see that it does *them* harm to leave me suspended. For my own devotion I always preferred hearing to saying Mass[8] and to occupy the layman's part of the Church; being too democratic even to enjoy the 'superiority' of sacerdotal dignity. A Roman collar always chokes me though I wear it still for propriety's sake.][9] With best wishes to Mrs. Ward

Ever yours faithfully,
G. TYRRELL

After Thursday address
16, Rue Cassini Paris

Notes to Letter 61

1. The April issue of the *Dublin Review.* On p. 409, *W* reviewed a book by Charles Devas, *The Key to the World's Progress* (London, 1906) in the course of which he mentioned "Father George Tyrrell's invaluable contributions to Catholic thought."

2. George Sutcliffe was a character in the novel, *Out of Due Time* (London, 1906), by Mrs. Wilfrid Ward (see Appendix D). Sutcliffe was pretty much modeled on *W* himself; see *MW* II.238–53.

3. Lucien Laberthonnière (1860–1932), Roman Catholic priest and modernist theologian. He edited the *Annales de philosophie chrétienne* (Paris, 1905–13), when it was placed on the Index and he was forbidden to publish anything more. In the *Annales* he developed a pragmatic view of religious truth; this view can also be found in his *Essai de philosophie religieuse* (Paris, 1903) which was placed on the Index in April 1906 (and, presumably is what *T* refers to here). For more about Laberthonnière see Alec Vidler, *A Variety of Catholic Modernists* (Cambridge, 1972), pp. 82–90.

4. not he who commends himself is approved, but he whom God commends (2 *Corinthians* 10.18).

5. in one's own person

6. The central character of *Out of Due Time* is Paul, the Comte d'Etranges. Mrs. Ward later claimed strenuously that the character was based on Félecité de Lamennais (see *LL*, xxxix) and that she had never known anyone like him, but it is not difficult to see why many readers at the time suspected that he was based on Baron von Hügel, with touches of *T.*

7. A paraphrase: in *Job* 3.17 it says, "There the wicked cease from troubling and the weary be at rest," a line that Tennyson chose to modify slightly at the last lines of his *The May Queen* (1832): "And the wicked cease from troubling, and the weary are at rest."

8. On 7 February 1906, Richard Sykes, S.J., the Provincial, informed *T* that he could no longer celebrate Mass.

9. Bracketed material published in *George Tyrrell's Letters*, 99–102.

62

[[Postcard]]
Damgan Morbihan Vannes
9 July 1906

Many thanks for the kind and judicious review of LC:[1] I will take due account of its useful criticism. I hope it won't hurt the *Dublin Review*—though perhaps the day of prudence is past for it as for me. Here for a day or two more. I am flying from correspondence, so don't discover me needlessly.

Ever yours,
G.T.

P.S. Bremond's *Newman* series[2] has been simultaneously crowned by the Academy and denounced to (not by) the Index. It is said that they will condemn not Newman but the Newmanism of every sort that matters. *Sinite eos; caeci sunt* etc.[3]

Notes to Letter 62

1. *Lex Credendi* was reviewed by *W* in the July issue of the *Dublin Review*. He praised the book and *T*, but disagreed with *T*'s interpretation of Newman and his assessment of Newman's theory for the development of doctrine. The disagreement about Newman, which began in 1904, grew increasingly sharp and bitter.

2. Henri Bremond published several works about Newman for the series, "La Pensée Chrétienne" (Paris). The books *T* refers to were: Newman: *Le développement du dogme chrétien* (1904), revised with a Preface by Monsignor Mignot (1906); *Newman: La psychologie de la foi* (1905); *Newman: La vie chrétienne* (1906); and *Newman: Essai de biographie psychologique* (1906).

3. Let them alone, they are the blind [leading the blind (*Matthew* 15.14).]

63

[[Postcard]]
Damgan Morbihan
16 July 1906

Would not it be good to get a French translation of your criticism of Bremond into the *Annales*?[1] Laberthonnière would be very glad. It is most desirable that these two readings of Development (according to John Henry Newman) should be at last clearly stated, and opposed in the interest of criticism and truth.[2] You ought to base your observations on the fourth edition of the *Développement du dogme chrétien* (with Mignot's Preface)[3] and which I think is more explicitly opposed to you. I dare say the difference may resolve itself into a logomachy. But whether real or merely verbal, it ought to be cleared. Although Henri Bremond's *Newman* is delated, I cannot help thinking that his reading of Newman would be more acceptable to Rome than yours—in so far as he makes a present of him to the Philistines in the matter of development. My own position is that Faith (Dogma) and Theology have different laws of development answering to their quite different natures:[4] that the hybrid monster called dogmatic theology looks in vain for a single law of growth.

Yours ever,
G.T.

Notes to Letter 63

1. *Annales de philosophie chrétienne*, edited by Laberthonnière (see letter 61 note 3).

2. *T*, true to his style of trying to get all positions out into the open, was here trying to start what he hoped would be a constructive argument between *W* and Bremond. He may also have been trying to get *W*'s views more clearly into the public forum where they could be refined and criticized.

3. See letter 64. *W* did write a critical review of Bremond's work, but chose the first (badly translated) edition of the *Essay*.

4. See letter 47 note 5; *T* separated dogma and theology in order to explain what he understood as a *real* (not apparent) development in the relationship between God and humanity. He had been working along these lines since "The Relation of Theology to Devotion" (see Letter 12 note 1).

64

Boutre, Vinon, Var.[1]
17 August 1906

My dear Ward,

As you will perceive, Bremond is riled up considerably,[2] needlessly so I must say, for after all we who take the pen must be prepared to perish by the pen. I of course am Francophil; [3] it was better a cool man should answer. If you had attacked his biography of John Henry Newman you would have had a good case, but you choose a volume written immediately under the influence of Semper Eadem Part II. i.e. in the conviction that the *Essay* was simply the common doctrine without the remotest approach to Hegelian Development; all put forward nervously and obscurely by one who is feeling his way and dreading to give a handle to Liberalism. Then [you certainly mistook a paraphrase for a translation. I admit the French custom is abominable, especially when they use inverted commas.][4] Still the very palpableness of the alterations, the equipollent for the major, the particular instance for the general, ought I think to have given you pause. Altogether you were unfortunate both in the choice of the volume and of the particular sentence if you wanted to discredit Bremond as a too liberal interpreter of Newman. Indeed he stands entirely on the other side. Michaud[5] is an ass and you should not have quoted him. He would eat you up just as easily and eagerly as he did Bremond. *Personally* (not controversially) I agree with you that Newman's is too concrete a mode of thinking for the French mind, and that cumulative arguments and balances of probabilities will be of more use for us mist-dwellers and mist-lovers. Nor do I think that any single categorical statement *is* either quite true or quite false, for which reason I dislike theologians. *You* did not *make* the epigram about John Henry Newman but you quoted it with approval as the foundation of your attack, and must take the consequences. No, his comrades did not really mistake Thomas for an ox, but they meant he was just as dumb and silent, and so the joke about Newman 'described the man.'[6] [Your worst sin of course is that you seem to claim a monopoly of the understanding of Newman and to warn others off the field][7] by representing it as a task of superhuman difficulty to which you alone are equal. I am sure there is nothing of this in your mind; but it is palpable in your style when you write about him. I think it better to tell you so frankly, as it alienates a good deal of sympathetic attention from what you have to say on the subject. As the biographer of Newman your place will, I trust and believe, be quite unique; [as an interpreter of his thought you are one of many. I do not agree with you on many points, and what is more to the purpose neither do Williams, nor Loisy,[8] nor Dimnet[9] nor heaps of others who are professed Newmanists, which I am not.][10]

I wish you had chosen any French organ but the *Verité*.[11] It is as though I were to accuse you of liberalising in the pages of the *Civiltà*, and to enlist the sympathies of my own enemies against you.[12] Bremond has written some reply but I have not seen it yet. However let the matter drop. We are equally damned now-a-days, moderates or immoderates, and it is not a time to split so small a party into smaller fragments still. So the Pope has declared for war.[13] He is nothing if not consistent. It is quite analogous with his war against the incoming irresistible tide of criticism—admirable faith and courage worthy of the opposite cause. Twelve years ago and ever since I have prophesied that the Church would not wake up till she butted her head against a stone wall. I think the wall is at hand. My own affairs are *subjectively* settled. I have accepted the *impasse* as chronic, and refused the proffered terms. Perhaps in a future pontificate I may re-enlist in the clerical army, but at present it is best to retire.

Ever yours faithfully,

G. TYRRELL.

Notes to Letter 64

1. Bremond's home where *T* was staying.

2. *W* published "Newman Through French Spectacles" in the *Tablet* 108 (21 July 1906):86–9. The editorial note advertized it thus: "Mr. Wilfrid Ward vindicates the memory of Cardinal Newman against grave misinterpretations of his teaching on the part of a certain French critic" (81). *W* concentrated on Bremond's *Newman: Le développement du dogme chrétien* in the unrevised, first edition rather than the later translation/edition recommended to him by *T*. *W* argued that Newman's careful and nuanced use of the English language made him hard to interpret, especially, he suggested, for Frenchmen. He used the review to focus on part of the Preface of the book, a paraphrase of part of Newman's ideas about development. Bremond paraphrased—did not quote—Newman, but the words paraphrased are put in quotation marks and introduced with Bremond's judgment that these are indeed "paroles extraordinaires." *W*'s point, accordingly, was that Bremond mistranslated Newman, misunderstood his thought and misled readers. In evidence of this last point *W* cited a hostile review by an Old Catholic, M. Michaud, whose review proceeds from exactly this passage. *W* also gave his readers the impression that Newman was extremely hard to understand, especially in his philosophical thought and that Bremond surely didn't understand Newman's philosophy; in fact, he hinted, Bremond might not understand English all that well (see *MW* II.172–7).

3. *T* responded with "Newman Through French Spectacles: A Reply" in the *Tablet* 108 (4 August 1906):163–5, signed "Francophil." His reply mixes wit and anger and claims that *W* misinterprets both Newman and Bremond, and that Bremond was clearly *paraphrasing*, i.e., *W* made a mountain out of a molehill.

4. Bracketed material published in *MW* II.173.

5. Michaud's review appeared in *Revue internationale de theologie* (1905). Michaud was an Old Catholic and, *T* argued in his reply, hostile to any notion of development whatsoever. *W* argued, however, that Michaud was hostile only to the counterfeit Newman presented to him by Bremond.

6. *W* responded to "Francophil" with a letter to the Editor on 11 August, pp. 215–6. In his review *W* quoted some college friends of Newman who said Newman "could never be got to pronounce any single categorical proposition to be simply true." He clearly noted it as an old story by college friends, yet in *T*'s reply these words were quoted as if they were *W*'s own, a charge *W* defended in *his* letter; here *T* gets the last word.

7. Bracketed material published in *MW* II.173.

8. Loisy published several articles under the pseudonym of Alfred Firmin in the *Revue du clergé français*. One of them, "Le développement chrétien d'après le Cardinal Newman" 7 (1898):5–20, was re-worked in *L'Évangile et l'Église*.

9. Ernest Dimnet (1866–1954), French priest, scholar and Newman interpreter.

10. Bracketed material published in *MW* II.173.

11. Reggie Balfour, assistant editor of the *Dublin Review*, sent a letter commenting on Bremond's bitter reply to *W*'s criticism to *La Verité français*. Under the heading "Traduttore—Traditore"; he published parallel columns of Newman's words and Bremond's translation, thus augmenting an already escalating hostility between Bremond and *W*.

12. Bremond wrote to *W* 13 August 1906 saying, "This means war, but you will give me the credit of not having sought it." There are 28 letters from Bremond to *W* in the *WWP* at *SAUL*. In a letter from Bremond to *W* 29 September 1904, Bremond says that Newman's work leads to "Loisy-ism." *W*, therefore, associated Bremond's interpretations with currents of thought he found to be dangerous to the church and to the future of Newman studies.

13. On 10 August 1906 Pope Pius X wrote a letter to the Archbishops and Bishops of France condemning the Law of Separation of Church and State in France, and forbidding the formation of the Associations for Public Worship provided by the law.

65

Boutre Vinon, Var.
27 August 1906

My dear Ward,

You should have underlined 'error' in your article and reply, for one naturally supposed your emphasis was on 'extraordinary'—the emphatic word of the phrase '*paroles extraordinaires*.'[1] To speak of a paraphrase as a man's 'words' is not fair when one quotes him in his own language; but when it is a rendering of a foreign tongue I think it is defensible if the paraphrase represents the substance of the original (as Bremond supposes in this case); not if it perverts it (as you suppose). I think you might cite the pith of one of Pascal's[2] thoughts as his 'words' just because everyone knows that a tolerable translation must always be more or less of a paraphrase and that liberalism is often misrepresentative.

As to my decision, it is quite irrevocable;[3] but I think if you knew all the circumstances you would be satisfied that it was the lesser evil. To accept suspension is my best chance of escaping excommunication—though as things are going, that may follow.

That the censorship would have been more or less nominal is not to the point. It would cost me little or nothing to have my correspondence supervised as it has been for twenty-five years. It is simply a question of principle. Is the church's authority over a priest so absolute that he has no private self left? Is he simply a 'minor' or an idiot or a slave? The monk freely, by his vow, becomes a 'minor' in canon law; he is incapable of a contract; he freely emasculates himself and as such he has no private life or private correspondence: his superior has a right to read every letter he sends *or receives*. But now, under Jesuit influence, the whole church is governed like the society; bishops are superiors, priests are religious. This is the very intoxication of authority and true respect for authority forbids us to take such claims seriously. Were I to yield, they would try the same trick on us all, priests first and then laymen. As regards *private* correspondence, the secular priest and layman are *exactly* on a footing. Would *you* submit your correspondence to censorship? Would the Duke of Norfolk?[4]

Having made the claim in my case they cannot retract it without loss of dignity and so the impasse is final. But they will think twice before they try the trick again. There is no doubt that the whole thing is a miserable intrigue on the part of Rudolf Meyer S J[5] and two or three of his fanatical colleagues of the Merry-del-Val set. The late general would never have played so low for all his intransigence, but he used to say that Meyer simply lost his reason when I was in question—and now Meyer has his fling. I can't pretend not to feel the privation most deeply; but against the great religious loss there is some moral gain in being dissociated from the Roman clerical world with all its paltriness, intrigue, delation, envy, hatred and malice. One feels cleaner and purer. Still I would fain hope for a day in which one might enlist again without sacrifice of principle; but what is there to hope for from organised ignorance?

Kindest regards to Mrs. Ward.

Ever yours faithfully,
G. TYRRELL

Notes to Letter 65

1. extraordinary words. Bremond introduced a paraphrase of Newman by saying they were "paroles extraordinaires." The whole argument between *W* and *T* on this was whether or not Bremond was pretending to quote Newman; the words which followed were clearly a paraphrase, but they were just as clearly marked off by quotation marks.

2. Blaise Pascal (1623–1662), French theologian and mathematician associated in his later life with the Jansenists.

3. As of February *T* was no longer able to exercise his priestly functions. He then began to look for a bishop who would accept him as a diocesean priest and had reason to believe that Archbishop Mercier of Malines might receive him. *T* wrote to Cardina Ferrata, Prefect of the Sacred Congregation of Bishops and Regulars asking him to allow Mercier to accept him. Ferrata agreed on the

condition that *T* promise not to publish anything on religious questions, even letters, without explicit approval (see *A&L* II.504). *T* believed this meant that his private correspondence would now be subject to censorship; in July he wrote an "open letter" to Ferrata categorically declining the condition and accepting his status as final (see Schultenover, Epilogue). *W*, apparently, knew nothing of the backstage intrigues in the matter and probably thought *T*'s decision hasty.

4. The Duke of Norfolk, *W*'s wife's uncle, was the first peer of the realm.

5. Rudolf Meyer, S.J. (1841–1912), an American Jesuit (from St. Louis) who was an assistant to the General of the Society of Jesus assigned to assist in the English-speaking provinces.

66

Storrington,[1] Sussex
6 November 1907

My dear Ward,

As you know I agree with those who deny that Newman was a potential modernist; and though I have been called, I have never of later years called myself a Newmanist.[2] Williams (whose competence as to John Henry Newman is far greater than my own) differs from me as his letter to the *Times* indicates.[3] But is it any use denying that whatever Pius X meant, Billot[4] and Janssens[5] have *de facto* slain not only 'modernism' but Newmanism: or that they deliberately intended to do so? To Gasquet's[6] preposterous letter I make the following notes: (1) He assumes that in refusing the Encyclical, Williams gives up his faith. Is the Encyclical *de fide*? (2) His raft metaphor is heretical. The raft is the condition of *getting* ashore, but not of *remaining* ashore. Reasonableness is the condition not merely of getting to the Church but of remaining in the Church. The *natural* assent of reason is (according to the Vatican council—Denzinger 1639) the presupposition of the assent of faith; it is the matter supernaturalised; it is a *conditio sine qua non*[7] of the *rationabile obsequium*.[8] The reasons that brought us to the Church may fail; but we must get others if we are to remain there. For the masses this 'reasonableness' is based on their usual sources of natural certainty—education, tradition etc. For thinkers, it is based on some process of reasoning. Our *faith* may rest on the authority of the Pope; but not the reasonableness of our faith, which however is its indisputable condition. The authority of the pope does not rest on the authority of the Pope. (3) The agreement of

Newman with the Encyclical is surely a matter to be settled by observation and not by oracle. Why does not 'the highest possible authority'[9] commit itself by giving its name? Will it say *openly* that 'no theory, no idea, no opinion' contained in *The Essay on Development* or in *The Grammar of Assent* is condemned by the Encyclical; and that Newman's attitude toward scholastic theology is still permissible? If so, I for one will withdraw all I have written against the Encyclical and confess my utter inability to comprehend its meaning. It is quite possible that in his dense ignorance the Pope did not know that his Encyclical had condemned Newman. But if he now refuses to say openly what he has apparently said secretly (for who else is the 'highest *possible* authority?') he is simply dishonest. I am not in a position to write; but I trust this ignoble shuffling will not pass unchallenged.

Yours faithfully,
G. Tyrrell

I go to Moorhurst tomorrow for two or three days.

Notes to Letter 66

1. Maude Petre's home where she built a small house for *T*; he often stayed there until his death in 1909. For more information about where he stayed and who he visited these last couple of years see Thomas Michael Loome, "Revelation and Experience," *Heythrop Journal* 12 (January 1971): 125f n.6.

2. *T* wrote a long letter to *The Times* (published in two parts, 30 September and 1 October 1907, pp. 4 and 5) in response to *Pascendi dominici gregis* (16 September 1907). His analysis of the encyclical was witty and bitter, accusing church officials of unrestrained authority in response to freedom of thought; the encyclical, he said, was surely not infallible and would not fool the "living heart of the Church—the intelligent, religious-minded, truth-loving minority." On 23 October he received word from Peter Amigo, bishop of Southwark, that he had been excommunicated because of his articles in *The Times*. He wrote to Mrs. Gibson (wife of William Gibson, later Lord Ashbourne) saying, "No one can be surprised. Let not Ward crow too much—ego hodie, tu ciras." He did not suppose *W* would really be excommunicated, but that the climate of authority was dangerous for everyone and that for all his caution and occasional self-righteousness, *W* ought not to feel too secure. Two other letters to the Gibsons have indications of *T*'s feelings about *W* at this time: to Mrs. Gibson (13 October), "Is it true that Ward says that if you read the Encyclical as it ought to be read, back before on to a looking-glass, it is really a very cautious approval of Newman and only a condemnation of Bremond and myself?" and to Mr. Gibson (28 October), "I believe Ward says that *evolution* but not *development* of doctrine is condemned,

and that we should distinguish between mod*erns* and moder*nists*; and between Newman*ites* and Newman*ists*, as is quite plain if you read between the lines and alter the punctuation." Copies of some letters from *T* to the Gibsons are in *WWP* at *SAUL*.

3. Willie Williams wrote to the editor of *The Times* 2 November 1907, p. 10e. Speaking for a number of liberal Catholics, he says that he differs from *T* on particular points, but agrees with him in his recent criticism of *Pascendi*. He and his colleagues, he says, "regard it as an unprecedented evil that, while one Pope had implied a direct approval of the writings of an English Catholic by making him a Cardinal, his successor should reverse the decision by condemning every characteristic proposition for which that writer made himself responsible."

4. Louis Billot (1846–1931), Jesuit theologian and Cardinal, professor of dogmatic theology at the Gregorian (1885–1910) and an ardent fighter against modernism and liberalism.

5. Henri Janssens (1855–1925), Benedictine theologian. From 1893 he was Rector and professor of dogma at the College of Saint Anselm in Rome and held several posts in the Curia, among which was as a Consultor for the Congregation of the Index.

6. Francis Aidan Gasquet (1846–1929), English Benedictine scholar and Cardinal. He wrote to *The Times* 5 November 1907, p. 8c, criticizing Williams in very patronizing language.

7. the necessary condition

8. reasonable service

9. On 4 November 1907, p. 10b, John Norris wrote from the Oratory in Birmingham to the editor of *The Times* that he was "enabled to state on information received today from the highest authority that 'the genuine doctrine and spirit of Newman's Catholic teaching are not hit by the Encyclical...' " In a letter 5 November (see note 6) Gasquet defended Newman on the basis of information *he* had received from "The highest authority."

67

Mulberry House, Storrington, Pulborough
19 May[1]

[My dear Ward,

You once (1900) told me about the destruction of Newman's letter to Lord Emly[2]—as a matter of confidence; and I treated it as such. You are evidently not the sole depository of that secret which has come to me since from nearly a dozen sources as a matter of notoriety—sometimes with the apocryphal embellishment that you yourself were the destroyer (which I have always contradicted). The serious point is that your work on Newman is being discounted in advance as vitiated by *suppressiones veri*.[3] It seems to me most important that you should make such a charge impossible by holding back nothing out of deference to the prevalant fanaticism. This might be done by an elaborate insistence on the fact that a man's final judgment is to be sought in his deliberate published utterances and not in private letters written in often passing moods. If even that were not enough to smooth the waters, it might be better to wait for the demise of Pius X—though he apparently is not of those 'whom the gods love.' There can never be a 'climb down' that would leave room in the Church for me, but there will surely be a détente that will give you and yours a breathing space before the next wave of fanaticism is ready to fall.

At all events, it is right that you should know the prejudice that awaits your book in the *Athenaeum* and elsewhere.

Yours faithfully,
G. TYRRELL][4]

Notes to Letter 67

1. Probably 1908; *T* moved to Storrington in August, but may have visited there earlier.
2. See *MW* II.344 for an explanation of the destroyed letter.
3. suppressions of the truth.
4. Bracketed material published in *MW* II.345–6.

68 Mulberry House, Storrington, Pulborough
20 May[1]

[Dear Ward,

My letter was dictated by a genuine interest in your *work* that overcame my reluctance to approach *you* again. There was no question of your 'falsifying facts' in my mind; but only of the omissions that must be made in every selection of correspondence. I felt it important that you should make it plain that your omissions were not influenced by the fear of Rome. Such a suspicion, just or unjust, would rob the work of its claim to finality.

As for your somewhat uncivil A-B-C-D theory, it shatters on the fact that my last informant, unfortunately dead, had his information from *you*.

When you say that I repeated a confidence in strict confidence and 'forget' the treason, you say the thing which is not; and you make me wonder whether this is a habit of your own. Indeed, the fact that you should reveal Lord Emly's secret to me, a comparative stranger on our second or third meeting and *à propos des bottes*[2] makes it hard to believe that you have not made the same 'strict confidence' to your friends at least five hundred times. I kept your confidence faithfully till I discovered that it was all over the shop and then I treated it as public property. Even had you not been a gossip yourself, you should remember that you were not the only witness to the *suppressio veri*.

You seem to have 'forgotten' how little you told me of the details of the crime. I did not know its author nor that you were 'consenting' to his deed. I cannot say that this latter item is very reassuring.

Yours truly,
G. TYRRELL][3]

Notes to Letter 68

1. Probably 1908.
2. about nothing, or irrelevantly
3. Bracketed material published in *MW* II.345–6.

APPENDIX A

"Who Are the Reactionaries?"[1]

In the April number of the *Nineteenth Century*, the late editor of the *Weekly Register*, after passing certain strictures on the spirit and method of the Society of Jesus in dealing with intellectual problems of modern times, proceeded to quote, in condemnation of the same, the words of 'an English Jesuit father,' whose views he declared to be altogether 'out of harmony with the spirit of the Society,' and presumably in perfect harmony with his own.

It would be ungracious in the extreme on the part of the said Jesuit were he not to credit Mr. Dell with a sincere desire of saying something entirely complimentary and amiable and with a complete, though scarcely credible, obliviousness as to the pain and embarrassment which such a remark must necessarily occasion to the person so lauded, and as to the awkward and invidious position in which it must place him in relation to others.

Yet it would hardly need a moment's reflection to see that, no man can feel particularly complimented by being publicly assured that he is altogether unsuited for his vocation and state of life, as a Jesuit 'absolutely out of harmony with the spirit of his order' would necessarily be. Even were it true, it is not the sort of truth one cares to be told, still less, to have told to the public. There are misfortunes, such as a mistaken marriage, a failure in ambition, a family disgrace, which no man is anxious to have flaunted about even were it for the sake of bringing discredit on the author of his mishap.

It is hard therefore on any supposition to acquit Mr. Dell of a certain criminal thoughtlessness in his impetuous desire to exalt the said Jesuit's reputation at the expense of that of his order; and perhaps chiefly with a view of depreciating the latter.

Odious as such a task is from every point of view, it becomes absolutely necessary for me to save myself from my friend; and to deal with matters more or less personal to myself and with which the public ought to have and has no concern whatever.

In the previous pages of his article Mr. Dell has been carefully delineating his own conception of the spirit of the Society of Jesus in relation to modern thought—a spirit, he believes, of narrow, unsympathetic, unaccommodating intolerance and obscurantism. Now it is with this particular spirit that he accuses me (mostly justly and truly) of being wholly out of harmony. It is therefore only those who are willing to accept Mr. Dell's estimates of the Jesuit spirit as just and true, who can agree with him in regarding me as a round man in a square hole, that is, as one absolutely 'out of harmony' with the body of which he is a member.

Frankly, it is precisely because I am a Jesuit, and because I am so keenly in sympathy with the creative principles[2] of the founder of the Jesuits, that I am absolutely out of harmony with that narrow unaccommodating spirit which Mr. Dell wrongly imagines to be the spirit of the Society. Doubtless it is an exceedingly difficult thing to gauge the precise essential spirit of any institution, especially if we try to gather it by way of some compendious induction from the conduct and utterances of its individual members here or there, in this period and crisis or in that—a difficulty which increases in proportion to the greater extension and duration of the said institution; and to the consequent variety of its manifestations. Who for example would venture to define the spirit of Catholicism from a study of the ideas and manners of the Catholics of some one country at some one period? Indeed, the basic and valid induction in this matter would be far too widespreading to come within the compass of any mortal mind; and therefore it is by another method, namely, by recourse to profession as distinct from realizations, that the truth is to be reached. We go to Christ for the spirit of Christianity. Not that Christians are not to some extent impregnated with that spirit so far as they are worthy of the name; but that in them it is manifested partially—*participative*, the schoolmen would say—and is with difficulty disentangled from much adulteration that is their own. A man is a good Christian and may sit down to meat in this Kingdom of God and feel at home there, however he fell short of the full spirit of Christ, provided he accept that ideal and strive towards it. And so, it seems to me, of any other body or institution, he is a lawful and true member who accepts its governing principles and strives to obey them according [to] his best intelligence and ability.

Now it is very obvious that as the genuine spirit of Christianity is the spirit of Christ, so the genuine spirit of the Society of Jesus is the spirit of the founder—Ignatius of Loyola. That spirit is notoriously a spirit of elasticity and accommodation—the antithesis in every respect of that which forms the theme of Mr. Dell's strictures. Indeed, is it not upon a perverse understanding of this fact that all the most popular calumnies and fables about the Society are founded? Is not the Jesuit of popular fiction (sacred or profane) before all else a wily, serpentine, self-accommodating monster of insidiousness? Is not his one solitary principle the all-importance of the end, the absolute indifference of the means? And the foundation is not far to seek. Standing on the threshold of a new order of things, Ignatius beheld the Church of his day imperiled by a timorous conservatism which saw the need of changes and accommodations, but had not the courage to make them. The man who dared to put the end (namely, God's greater glory) before every consideration of custom, precedent, tradition, before everything short of sacrifice of principle, and so saved the situation, was bound to incur obloquy not merely from the baulked adversaries of the Church, but still more from Churchmen whose methods had failed where his had succeeded. His accommodation and elasticity was described as unscrupulousness, and his fidelity to the end, as criminal indifference to the means.

I need not waste words to show that elasticity was the characteristic principle of the founder of the Jesuits and that his own idea was to subordinate ruthlessly every *morally indifferent* means to this one aim of God's greater glory in the salvation of souls.

It seems to me then, that any Jesuit who cordially accepts these governing ideas and strives to live by them according to his intelligence and ability (though doubtless there will [be] an inevitable diversity in the application of them) is absolutely in harmony with the spirit of his order. A wooden uniformity, as of toy soldiers, is popularly attributed to Jesuits, and there is therefore an unusual tendency to generalize rapidly from one to all when they are in case. If one Jesuit is seen to use a red handkerchief, the observer will most likely go about saying: 'The Jesuits are all bound by a strict vow to use red handkerchiefs,' and thus it is easy, by taking a representative of one extreme as the type of all, to make a representative of the other extreme appear abnormal as out of harmony with the whole. In matters theological, for example, the Society professes to represent no particular clique or school such as other orders very legitimately may and do represent. As the Jesuit is supposed to have no peculiar office, man or rite of his own, no habit distinct from the men of the ordinary clergy, so neither is his theology that of any one school, but simply such as is current for the time being in the Church at large. Hence there is room for a greater variety of opinions among his numbers than would be tolerable in an order bound to swear by some particular doctor or the other. The variety of opinion represented by classical Jesuit theologians is sufficient justification of this statement. No man therefore who holds any doctrinal opinion that is tolerated by the theology of the Church can be considered in any way out of harmony with the theology of the Society, since the latter profess to [be] identical with the former. The only true discord would be created by the attempt on the part of one member to deprive others of their legitimate liberty in this matter.

If this spirit of the Society of Jesus is truly what Mr. Dell represents it to be, many apologies are due to that much abused body on the part of popular sentiment which has so universally and persistently regarded it as the most subtle and versatile agency in the promotion of the Roman Catholic religion. If, in sullen defiance of the laws of vitality, the Society is but the uncompromising advocate of Chinese inflexibility, mainly bent on keeping out the inevitable tide of ecclesiastical progress with some ineffectual theological pitchfork, then let us hear no more of Jesuit wiles and guiles and let the protestant open his arms to welcome as his best ally in the destruction of Catholicism one whom he had unwittingly deemed his most implacable foe.

While, however, gladly disavowing for myself such a spirit as Mr. Dell attributes to the Society as a body, I would not for a moment be thought to be in sympathy with that diametrically opposite extreme of 'liberalism' which to some hasty minds seems the only conceivable alternative. Indeed, I have always looked upon the popular representatives of this school as the worst enemies of solid theological advances. In the Church like the state, life and progress is conditioned by the balance of the conservative and the progressive tendencies whereof now one, now the other tends to preponderate; but were either to prevail unchecked, death would result, from petrification in one case, in the other from disintegration.

Each class of mind, therefore, the progressive and the conservative, has got its own place and function in the evolution of dogma. Nor is it to be imagined as though any sane mind were altogether conservative or altogether progressive; rather each is characterized according to a certain prevalence of one tendency over the other. Now there are cases where the prevalence is so exaggerated that the mind is simply unbalanced and lopsided this way or that. Hence in each of the above classes there will always be a number of extremists who have no patience with, or tolerance for the opposite class, not recognizing its function and value. It is these extremists—constituting as it were, the tails of their respective classes—who bring their own cause into trouble and disrepute, making it, by their conduct and utterances, seem so ridiculous and impossible as to furnish a patent argument in favor of the opposite cause and to make even the extravagances of the opposition unassailable. Unfortunately, the crudest, loudest, most confident exponents of any cause are usually those who are newest in its service and least deeply imbued with an intelligent appreciation of its principles. Slow to hear, swift to speak, and swift to wrath they are just those who have to accentuate differences rather than agreements to widen the chasms of division rather than to bridge them over. They are the backbone of a sect or party as such, that is, they are its irreconcilable element, by which it is kept a sect or a party.

Hence it comes that those who profess to be the least reactionary in spirit and desire are the most reactionary in effect; and, in general the extremists on either side are the ultimate authors of their own grievances.

To say things that in themselves are true and undeniable, but to say them in such a way as to make them sound false; to place them in a misleading context; to entangle them with things untrue or disputable; to urge them at a wrong time or in an offensive way; to care little how much wheat is uprooted with the tares; in a word, to be narrow and illiberal even in one's very profession of liberality and tolerance—all this is characteristic of that school of the 'extreme left' whose spirit I dislike and distrust every bit as much as I do that which Mr. Dell considers to be the spirit of the Society of Jesus.

In this connection I thoroughly endorse what Newman has said:

> I will go on to say further, that, in spite of all that the most hostile critic may urge about the encroachments or securities of high ecclesiastics in times past, in the use of their power, I think that the event has shown after all, that they were mainly in the right, and that those whom they were hard upon were mainly in the wrong. I love, for instance, the name of Origen: I will not listen to the notion that so great a soul was lost; but I am quite sure that, in the contest between his doctrine and followers and the ecclesiastical power, his opponents were right and he was wrong. Yet who can speak with patience of his enemy and the enemy of St. John Chrysostom, that Theophilus, bishop of Alexandria? Who can admire or revere Pope Vigilius? And here another consideration presents itself to my thought. In reading ecclesiastical history, when I was an Anglican, it used to be forcibly brought home to me how the initial error of what afterwords became heresy was the urging forever some truth against the prohibition of authority at an unseasonable time. There is a time for everything, and many a man desires a reformation of an abuse, or the fuller development of a doctrine, or the adoption of a particular policy, but forgets to ask himself whether the right time for it is come; and, knowing, that there is no one who will be doing anything towards its accomplishments in his own lifetime unless he does it himself, he will not listen to the voice of authority, and he spoils a good work in his own century in order that another man, as yet unborn, may not have the opportunity of bringing it happily to purification in the next. He may seem to the world to be nothing else than a bold champion for the truth and a martyr to free opinion where he is just one of those persons whom the competent authority ought to silence; and though the case may not fall within that subject matter in which that authority is infallible, or the formal conditions of the exercise of that gift may be wanting, it is clearly the duty of authority to act vigor-

> ously in the case. Yet its act will go down to posterity as an instance of a tyrannical interference with private judgment, and of the silencing of a reformer, and of a base love of corruption or error; and it will show still less to advantage if the ruling power happens in its proceedings to evince any defect of prudence or consideration. And all those who take the part of that ruling authority will be considered as time servers or indifferent to the cause of uprightness and truth, while, on the other hand, the said authority may be accidently supported by a violent ultra party, which exalts opinions into dogmas and has it principally at heart to destroy every school of thought but its own.
>
> Such a state of things may be provoking or discouraging at the time, in the case of two classes of persons: of moderate men who wish to make differences in religious opinion as little as they fairly can be made; and of such as keenly perceive and are honestly eager to remedy existing evils—evils of which divines in this or that foreign country know nothing at all and which even at home, it is not every one who has the means of estimating.[3]

In the face of this it is strange and indeed somewhat irritating to find the advocates of the kind of extravagance here condemned sheltering themselves under shadows of Newmanian and other really great thinkers who could be broad because they were proportionally deep and bold because they were profoundly reverent. But this is the commonest and most obvious device, quite akin to that of the schoolboy who takes shelter behind his big brother when he wants to give 'cheek.' The latter, if wise, will throw him off and leave him to his just fate.

And now at the risk of repeating much that I have said in almost identical words, I think it well to quote what I have elsewhere published on the same theme, lest any one should imagine that, owing to the present electrical state of the ecclesiastical atmosphere or to other self-interested motives, I have taken up a new and safer position. One thing is certain that no man who desires to be perfectly sincere and independent can escape a double allowance of obloquy since he will be a target for the shifts of both one extreme and the other. If to shout with the larger crowd is consummate wisdom, to shout with neither is the abyss of folly—from a prudential point of view, and yet in the measure that one cares for truth one is found to desert the extremes for the more central positions.

In this connection I wrote in the *Weekly Register* (16 September 1899) as follows:

> One of the chief obstacles to unity in truth is the fact that every party, coterie, sect or school has its *peripsema*—its tail of camp followers, shorter or longer as the case may be, but ever tending to assume a larger proportion to the rest of the body as the party grows more multitudinous and in its desire for numerical strength becomes indifferent to qualitative excellence. Those who think are necessarily the few; the many either do not think, or, still worse, only think that they think; they follow blindly for some merely affective motive, or, at most, they try to understand something of the general gist of the movement, picking up phrases, catch-words, war-cries, which they interpret or misinterpret according to the particular character of their incapacity. It is the self-confident over-readiness of such to 'rush in' and push themselves forward on all occasions as the exponents and representatives of their cause, that brings discredit upon it and makes mutual understanding and reconciliation between conflicting parties so impossible. Indeed, it would sometimes seem that these 'tails' are the very *notae individuantes*, the sole differentiating principles by which parties are divided from one another, like the rays of a starfish; and that as we pass upwards from these noisy extremities of wriggling agitation we converge towards a silent centre of comparative agreement and tranquility. Towards this centre a man will be necessarily forced in the measure that he strives at any sacrifice to be perfectly honest and impartial . . . and, indeed, it cannot but be that he who would be perfectly fair and honest must be a name for being unfair and dishonest and must be, to some extent, 'hated of *all* men' and parties. For he will see and sympathize with whatever germ of justice each faction is built upon, and that so cordially and ungrudgingly as to make it a matter of aggrieved astonishment that he is equally ready to laugh at their extravagances, and by no means prepared to participate in their bigotries. This they will by no means tolerate; he who will go with them one mile must, forsooth, be compelled to go with them twain; and he who will give them his coat must give them his cloak also . . . If it were not for this inevitable tail-developing propensity, an association of those of one mind for the furtherance of a good cause would be a source of great strength and solace to the individuals so united, and of great profit to society at large. But no sooner is there a movement for, say, a wider and more intelligent interpretation of orthodox principles than it is at once joined by a rag-tag and

bob-tail of semi-educated novelty mongers athirst for that cheap notoriety which is purchased by recklessly destructive criticism, who make the cause ridiculous in the eyes of all sober-minded men, and thus play into the hands of the party which they are labouring to extinguish.

If, on the other hand, there is a constructive or conservative party labouring for the prevention or cure of such extravagances, its loudest-mouthed allies will be just those who have the least intelligent sympathy with the principles which justify its existence, and will in like manner verify the truth that 'a man's foes are those of his own household.'[4]

In conclusion I will add some quotations from what I wrote in the *Month* for May 1898:

> To require . . . that the Church should throw herself heartily and indiscriminately, with blind trust and confidence into the stream of modern progressive ideas, is the extravagance towards which a *soi disant* 'Liberal' school of Catholics gravitates in virtue of its principles, or the haziness of its principles . . . The church may neither identify herself with 'progress' nor isolate herself from it. Her attitude must always be the difficult and uncomfortable one of partial agreement and partial dissent. Indeed, it is altogether similar to that which faith must maintain with regard to the advance of science and knowledge. The *soi-disant* 'Liberal' is all agog for embracing the very latest results of science and history, and would see the Church decked out in the newest fashions of the day and chattering the shibboleths of the passing hour. He would have her 'smart' and 'up to date' and thus wipe away forever her eternal reproach of lagging behind the times. But in truth we must not shirk from the paradox that contemporary science and history is always wrong; not wholly wrong, nor void of all grounds for priding itself on advance; but mingling so much extravagance and excess with its reason, so much dross with its gold, as to make it invariably safe to hold back and wait. It is truth 'in solution' but not attainable apart and in its purity till it has long ceased to be a theme of discussion and excitement. Then it is that the Church will quietly adopt and assimilate what no longer admits of controversy. There is an antagonism between faith and false science or the extravagances of true science; and in like manner between the Church and false progress or the excesses and errors of a progress which mingles good and evil. Hence, an antagonism nearly always between the Church and

the fashion of the day. Her very offices of moulding, leavening, checking, correcting, all imply a certain resistance to be overcome, not without conflict.

This, however, is what the 'Liberal' will not abide for a moment. It is not that his faith in the Church is necessarily weak, but that his faith in the world and in modern progress is crude and strong. He knows well that the Church must eventually give her full sympathy to all that is true and good, and being convinced that most of what seems so must be so, he is impatient with the suicidal over-caution, the apathy, the lethargy of the Catholic body.

Rightly understood, there is a 'Liberalism' which combined in due proportion with 'Conservatism' is a necessary ingredient in the life of every society, and therefore in that of the Church. But the true Liberalism is really for the very few who are capable of thinking widely, deeply and temperately; whereas, for the great majority, who form the receptive and conservative element of society, and who have neither leisure, ability nor education, they must take their thought ready made from others. It is when Liberalism becomes 'popular' when it is affected by the half-educated, and is made the catch-word for party, that it becomes ridiculous, shallow, and irritating to any one who knows the patience and labour which must be expended—how often vainly!—in the formation of a correct all-round judgment touching most questions which the Church has to deal with . . . Indeed, nothing hinders the sane and healthy progressive movements of the Church more than the crude extravagances of the self-constituted *coryphaei* of advance, who contrive to disgust all men of judgment, and to drive their sympathies over to the opposite side. No doubt every party is frequently brought into disgrace by its camp-followers, who are always its loudest, most popular, and most incompetent exponents; but anything like a 'Liberal' movement is tenfold more liable to such a doom . . .

Taking the words in their literal sense, there is no sane man who would not claim to be at once liberal and conservative; but so far as they are party names, he is a wise man who declines to label or brand himself even in his own thought, and thereby really to sacrifice his liberty of mind by introducing into it an unnecessary bias.

We are of necessity members of the human family, of the Christian and Catholic church, and as such must in some sense wear a party badge and bear our share of the discredit brought upon the body by the sentiments and conduct of those with whom we are associated. But beyond what duty or greater good exacts of us, surely it is wisdom to swear neither by Paul nor by Apollos nor by Cephas but to be a Catholic unqualified even by the glorious but hopelessly perverted title of 'Liberal'—[5]

> Defamed by every charlatan
> And soil'd with all ignoble use.[6]

G. TYRRELL

Notes to Appendix A

1. See letter 21 note 2. *T* wrote this in response to a remark by Robert Dell, but defends the Jesuits in a way they did not and could not appreciate by stressing the fact that the Society of Jesus was not at that time as tolerant or flexible as the founder intended it to be.

2. *T* believed that the true spirit of the Jesuits was one of toleration and creativity. Even while he was having severe problems with the order, he welcomed the opportunity to write an introduction to the life of Ignatius (see *The Testament of Ignatius Loyala* (London, 1900) with Preface dated 31 July 1899 (1–23), and epilogue dated 8 December 1899 (197–206), both by *T*).

3. *Apologia*, pp. 259–60.

4. "Zoophily Again" a review of La Marquise de Rambures, *L'Eglise et la pitié envers les animau textes originaux* (Paris, 1899) in the *Weekly Register* 16 September 1899, 381–3.

5. " 'Liberal' Catholicism," *Month* 91 (May 1898):449–57; reprinted in *FM* I.68–84. This article is one of *T*'s most important pre-"modernist" statements.

6. Quoted from Tennyson's *In Memoriam*, cxi, stanza 6.

APPENDIX B

Text of the Joint Pastoral Letter[1]

THE CHURCH AND LIBERAL CATHOLICISM. JOINT PASTORAL LETTER

By the Cardinal Archbishop and the Bishops of the Province of Westminster.

The Cardinal Archbishop and Bishops of the Province of Westminster, to the Clergy, Secular and Regular, and to the Faithful of the said Province.

HEALTH AND BENEDICTION

Rev. and dear Brethren and dear Children in Jesus Christ,—The thought of the great and unmerited mercies, so generously poured out by God upon our Fathers and upon ourselves during the Century that is ending, fills us with confidence and courage as we enter upon the work of a new Century. Among these blessings none have been more consolatory than the peaceful growth and expansion of the Catholic Faith in England. But though the storms of persecution have blown over, other dangers of a more insidious character—such as various forms of rationalism and human pride—at present confront the Church in England as elsewhere. We must look these in the face and deal with them patiently but firmly, under the guidance of the great Prince of Pastors.

SOURCE OF EVILS AFFLICTING SOCIETY

1. The evils that afflict modern society formed the subject of the first Encyclical addressed by his Holiness Leo XIII. to the Catholic world.

If we look for the source of these evils we shall observe that the Holy Father shows it to consist, either in the habit of belittling and despising, or of utterly rejecting, the authority of the Church, which presides in the name of God over the welfare of mankind, and is the divinely-appointed guardian of those principles of eternal truth and justice, on which all human authority ultimately rests.

It is with profound sorrow and regret, dear children in Jesus Christ, that we admit that some of the false maxims, referred to by the Holy Father as afflicting the world at large, have taken a deep root in England. For 300 years no religious tribunal, capable of teaching with unerring certainty, or of binding the conscience in the name of God, has been recognised by the English people. The result has been to substitute the principle of private judgment for the principle of obedience to religious authority, and to persuade the people that they are the ultimate judge of what is true and proper in conduct and religion.

It has become a dominant principle in England that all power and authority in civic, political, and religious matters are ultimately vested in the people. The people govern; to the people appeal is made, as to a final tribunal, for guidance on questions, often involving the gravest interests.

LOYALTY TAINTED BY FALSE PRINCIPLES

2. It can hardly be necessary to point out how insidiously a small minority, such as that of Catholics in England, may become affected by an overwhelming majority that continually acts upon a theory so flattering to human pride as the supremacy of the people in religion as in politics. We need not, therefore, wonder if there be occasionally found among our own flock some whose loyalty to the Church is tainted by false principles, insensibly imbibed by too close a contact with the world; or if there be others, who have come into the Church without having altogether shaken off the critical spirit of private judgment, in which they had been brought up.

MEANING OF TERM "LIBERAL CATHOLIC"

3. A small number of men suffice to infect and unsettle the minds of many, not only by license in private speech; but, if they are literary, by use of the press. They take leave to discuss theol-

ogy and the government of the Church with the same freedom of speech and opinions that they are accustomed to use in launching new theories on social science, political economy, art, literature, or any other subject. Being wanting in filial docility and reverence they freely dispose of doctrine, practice, and discipline upon their own responsibility and without the least reference to the mind of the Church or to her ministers. This is to be liberal, indeed—with the rights and the property of another—with the sacred prerogatives of Christ and His Church. It is the exercise of liberality of this counterfeit sort that characterises what is known as "the liberal Catholic." He is like to one who, having received a gracious invitation from his Sovereign to reside in the royal palace, should take advantage of his position to destroy, or dispose of, the royal furniture according to his own caprice or that of friends outside, and to make even structural alterations, without any kind of warrant or authority for so doing.

Or to go back to the lessons of history; it was against the action of liberal Catholics that St. Thomas of Canterbury vindicated the liberties of the Church in his day; and it is against liberal Catholics that the rights and liberties of the Church have to be defended again in our own time. The Catholic clergy and laity of England will always need to be strong in the spirit of St. Thomas of Canterbury, if they are always to resist successfully the restless encroachments of liberalism upon the sphere of religion.

Where this strange habit of mind exists among us, we believe that it is generally traceable to ignorance of the true character of the Church of Christ, and of the position and duty of her individual members, or to ignorance of the continuity and indefectibility of Catholic belief. It is a habit of mind to be found, we trust, in very few English Catholics. But the thought of the possibility of it spreading, if unnoticed, has stirred our pastoral vigilance to sound a note of warning, and to set forth at some length certain doctrines that may be needed for the guidance of the faithful.

I.

What is meant by the Teaching Church.

1. God has not abandoned mankind to the guidance of private judgment in the affairs of salvation, but has guaranteed to

them the presence and authority of a Divine Teacher, who shall remain on earth until the end of time.

It is obviously of extreme importance to possess precise and accurate knowledge as to where this Divine Teacher is to be found, and as to the manner in which He makes known His Will. Vague impressions on such a subject lead inevitably to doubts and errors, whereas honour and obedience are readily rendered to an authority whose claims are clear and definite.

Now God Himself is the Divine Teacher of whom we speak. When our Lord Jesus Christ was upon earth, God spoke through the lips of His Sacred Humanity. After He had ascended into Heaven the Divine Teacher spoke through the mouth of Peter and the Apostles; and He now teaches and will continue to teach through their legitimate successors, "until the consummation of the world" (Matthew xxviii., 20).

The doctrine of the abiding presence of the Divine Teacher upon earth is proved by the most abundant testimony of Catholic Tradition, and by the brief Gospel summary, (which we shall now have refer to) of the words spoken by Our Lord Himself. The purpose of His Mission He stated thus: "I am come that they may have life, and may have it more abundantly" (John x., 10). And as clearly He expressed the purpose for which He sent His Apostles and the power with which He invested them. "All power is given to Me in heaven and on earth: going therefore, teach ye all nations," and He defined the subject matter of their teaching thus:—"teaching them to observe all things whatsoever I have commanded you" (Matthew xxvii., 18–20).

The object, then, of their mission is to continue His teaching: and the power with which He endowed them for that purpose, is the same as that, which in its fulness He had Himself received from the Father: "All power is given to Me, going therefore teach." And elsewhere He had said, "He that heareth you heareth Me, and he that despiseth you despiseth Me" (Luke x., 16). They are to teach, to be believed, and to be obeyed. They are sent to all men without exception, "Go ye into the whole world and preach the Gospel to every creature. He that believeth and is baptised shall be saved, and he that believeth not shall be condemned" (Mark xvi., 15–16).

To enable them to fulfill their difficult and superhuman task they were to receive the Spirit of Truth, whom I "will send to you" (John xvi., 7).

"And when He, the Spirit of Truth is come, He will teach you all truth" (John xvi., 13),—and this not transiently, but continuously, because He shall so come, "that He may abide with you for ever." And as though to prepare His Apostles for the antagonism they were to meet from the world, the Lord warned them that "the Spirit of Truth," whom they were to receive, "the world cannot receive, because it seeth Him not, nor knoweth Him: but yet shall know Him, because He shall abide with you, and shall be in you" (John xiv., 17).

"He shall teach you all things, and bring all things to your mind, whatsoever I have said to you" (John xiv., 26). "He shall give testimony of Me: and ye shall give testimony, because ye are with Me from the beginning" (John xv., 26–27). In other words, the Holy Ghost was to abide in the teaching Church, in order to perpetuate Christ's teaching and ministry to the end of time. Here then we have the abiding presence of the Divine Teacher promised by Christ to the Church. That Divine Teacher claims unreserved allegiance, love and obedience, whether He speak through the Sacred Humanity, or through the Vicar of Christ and the Bishops, who are the successors of the Apostles and "Ambassadors for Christ" (2 Corinthians v., 20).

Before their death the Apostles handed on their ministry to others, by imparting to them also the Holy Ghost, and ordaining them "Bishops to rule the Church of God" (Acts xx., 28). They did more; they imposed upon them the obligation of selecting suitable persons to carry on their office: "Thou, therefore, my son, be strong in the grace which is in Christ Jesus; and the things which thou hast heard of me by many witnesses, the same commend to faithful men, who shall be fit to teach others also" (2 Tim. ii., 1–2).

Two orders of persons, therefore, constitute, by the design of Christ, the visible Church. The small body of chosen men, assisted by the Holy Ghost, who represent the authority of Jesus Christ; and the large body of the faithful taught, guided and guarded by the Divine Teacher, speaking through the audible voice of the smaller body. Theologians call the one the *Ecclesia docens*, the other the *Ecclesia discens*.

THE "ECCLESIA DOCENS"

2. The *Ecclesia docens* consisted, in the beginning, of Peter and the Apostles, and afterwards of the Pope, successor of St. Peter

and of the Bishops of the Catholic world in communion with him. These descending in a regular succession with the powers originally communicated by Christ, have always discharged the office, imposed by Him, of teaching without interruption the doctrine confided to them—teaching it without loss or damage to its integrity, and of building up in the Faith, to the image of Christ, that multitude of souls who, as docile disciples, obey the word and will of God, as made known to them by their pastors.

The task imposed upon the Shepherds was a heavy one—to take charge and render an account of the flock. Consider how peremptory was the injunction given by St. Paul to the Bishop Timothy. "I charge thee before God and Jesus Christ, who shall judge the living and the dead, by His coming and His Kingdom; Preach the word; be instant in season and out of season; reprove, entreat, rebuke in all patience and doctrine. For there shall come a time when they will not endure sound doctrine; but, according to their own desires, they will heap up to themselves teachers having itching ears, and will indeed turn away their hearing from the truth, but will be turned unto fables." And, lest the Bishop might be deterred from action by the perversity of his flock, the Apostle turns to him again, to stir him up to a becoming state of vigilance and fear, and reminds him that nothing less than the zeal and labour of a true Evangelist will enable him to fulfil the essential duties of his ministry: "Be thou vigilant; labour in all things; do the work of an Evangelist; fulfil thy ministry" (2 Tim. iv., 1–5).

Such is the apostolic ideal of a Bishop's duty. It is clear that the obligations laid upon Bishops have been imposed by no less an authority than that of God Himself. It is He who has placed the Sovereign Pontiff with his prerogatives, and the Episcopate in union with him, in supreme command of the flock: "Take heed to yourselves and to the whole flock, wherein the Holy Ghost hath placed you Bishops to rule the Church of God, which He hath purchased with His own Blood" (Acts xx., 28).

It is not, therefore, because specialists in divinity, philosophy or the natural sciences have been consulted, or have lent their assistance, that the Church proclaims the doctrine contained in the deposit of faith, confided to her guardianship. It is not because fewer or more schools of thought are represented in the Senate of the Church, in her Councils, or in her Hierarchy, that declarations of doctrine are drawn up and promulgated. Nor can it be conceived for a moment that the fluctuating opinions and fashions of the hour, which flit over the surface of the public mind, like shadows over a landscape, could ever be used by the Church of God as a rule by which to fix the cardinal points of revealed truth, or to draw the lines of immutable dogma.

The *Ecclesia docens* is fully conscious of her Divine mission, and needs no dictation from without, as to the course she should pursue, in the guardianship of truth and the condemnation of error. Her governing rule and law is the rule and the law that brought her into existence, namely, the Authority of God, who has commissioned her "to teach all nations all those things that He has revealed."

THE "ECCLESIA DISCENS"

3. The *Ecclesia discens*, on the other hand, consists not only of the laity, but also of Ecclesiastics, and even Bishops in their individual and private capacity. When these submit their mind and their will to the Church in matters of religion, their submission is given in reality to the Divine Teacher. They are simply disciples, but they are the disciples of Christ and of His Spirit. As disciples they have no right to legislate, to command or to teach in the Church, be they ever so learned. They are disciples taught and directed without error, in the way of salvation. The mind of the Church on this subject is illustrated by the law which forbids the faithful to publish anything on religion, without the "Imprimatur" of the *Ecclesia docens.* All, even the most learned among clergy and laity, are subject to this law, which is without exception. The Church indeed may encourage even the faithful laity to write, and lecture upon matters relating to religion, when she sees that they are fit to serve her in these ways; not, however, in their own right, but in strict subordination to her authority. What they teach must be her doctrine, not their own; and unless they loyally propagate her doctrine, her spirit, her mind, she regards them as workers of iniquity. "He that gathereth not with Me scattereth" (Matt. xii., 30).

Nor should this jealous guardianship of the Church over her teaching and pastoral office create surprise or difficulty to the mind of modern society. The civil governments of the world act upon a similar principle. They are wont to confide the highest branches of the public service only to men of proved capacity, and they do not hesitate rigidly to exclude all other persons therefrom, however well-intentioned they may be.

The conduct of the Church, in the various measures she adopts for the preservation of the doctrines of faith, is guided by the assistance of the Holy Ghost. This Divine Spirit can admit of no religious teaching other than His own. And here we may remark incidentally, that while He maintains within the Church the sanctity of truth, He at the same time inculcates another great virtue, specially distinctive of the Life of Jesus Christ, the virtue of humility;—a virtue acquired with extreme difficulty by man whose bane has been pride from the beginning. Now to be docile and obedient to teachers is to practise Christian humility—the very foundation of faith and holiness of life.

Some there are whose pride chafes under the restrictions imposed by religion. Not content with the vast fields of profane science and speculation open to them, and with the civil government of the world, which is theirs, they itch to have their hand in the government of the Church and in her teaching: or if this cannot be, they vainly strive to enforce their views by appeals to the press and to public opinion. This restlessness and independence of the Gospel have shown themselves more or less in all times. In his own day St. Paul noted disloyalty and disobedience to the *Ecclesia docens*, and expressed "his wonder" at converts being "so soon removed unto another Gospel, which is not another, only there are some that trouble you, and would pervert the Gospel of Christ." But against any one "that troubles you" the Apostle does not hesitate to say, "Let him be anathema" (Gal. i., 6–8).

MODERN THEORIES OF "ANOTHER GOSPEL."

4. What this "other Gospel" is to-day may be learnt by the bare enumeration of some of the theories advanced in the name of science, criticism and modern progress.

For instance—that in the past, the Episcopate or *Ecclesia docens*, was not competent to define doctrinal truths with accuracy, because recent discoveries were then unknown; that the dogmas of Catholic faith are not immutable but tentative efforts after truth, to be reformed under the inspiration of modern science; that the Church's teaching should be limited to the articles or definitions of Catholic faith; that it is permissible to reject her other decisions; to set aside her censures; to criticise her devotions; to belittle her authority, and especially that of the Roman Congregations; to distrust her ability in dealing with intellectual and scientific objections; to place her character as nearly as possible on the level of that of a human institution— that the constitution as well as the teaching of the Church ought to be brought into harmony with, what is styled, modern thought and the progress of the world; that the government of the Church should be largely shared by the laity, as a right; and that men of science and broadminded culture should employ themselves in devising means to bring this about: that the distinctions of Shepherd and Sheep should be blended by entitling the more learned among the laity to rank no longer as disciples, but as teachers and masters in Israel; that the growth of popular interest in ecclesiastical affairs and the spread of education render it right and expedient to appeal from ecclesiastical authority to public opinion; and that it is permissable to the faithful to correct abuses and scandals by recourse to the people and to the powers of the world, rather than to the Authorities of the Church; that as the Pontiff has been deprived of his temporal power, so ecclesiastical property should be held and administered no longer by Ecclesiastics, but by laymen with business capacity; that Catholics are free to read and discuss matter, however dangerous to faith or morals, if they are inclined to do so; that they may retain the name of Catholic and receive the Sacraments, while disbelieving one, or more of the truths of Faith; and that they are in these respects subjects to no ecclesiastical authority, or Episcopal correction.

One or other of these and such like errors, which are attacks, more or less thinly veiled, upon the rights and liberties of the Church, is to be met with among ill-instructed and liberal Catholics. They are opinions generated in the national atmosphere of free thought and public criticism, of which we have spoken. It would not be possible to discuss them all within the limits of a Letter—nor is it in the least necessary to do so—though we shall say a word about two or three of them. The best antidote to all such poisonous opinions is to be found in a clear and intelligent belief in the abiding presence within the Church of the Divine Teacher.

II.

What conformity of mind with the mind of the Church is required.

THE ASSENT OF FAITH

1. From the words of Scripture referred to above it is clear that Jesus Christ constituted His Church a living authoritative and perpetual Teacher of His doctrine; that He invested her with His own power; that He informed and invigorated her with the Spirit of Truth; and that He declared that the doctrines proclaimed by her were to be received as though proclaimed by His own voice. Hence arises the obligation upon everyone to think as the Church thinks, in order to think aright; and therefore to yield a firm assent to whatever she presents for acceptance.

Two kinds of assent may be given by the mind, in the matters on which we are speaking. One is the "assent of Faith," in the exercise of the virtue called Divine Faith. It is given when the subject matter is a truth revealed by God, or else closely connected with the deposit of Revelation; and, as such, is either defined, or universally held by the Church. In both cases, the assent rests ultimately on the authority of God, revealing either the truth itself or the infallibility of the Church that teaches it.

No one, calling himself a Catholic, can doubt the obligation of giving a firm assent to all revealed doctrines that are defined or universally held by the Church as of "Catholic Faith;" and this under pain of heresy and of being cut off from the Church and salvation. Upon this elementary doctrine we need do no more in this place than refer to the Third Session of the Ecumenical Council of the Vatican.

But it may be well to insist, with the same Council, on the further truth, namely, that Catholics are found to give their assent also to the decisions of the Church concerning matters appertaining to or affecting revelation, though these matters be not found, strictly speaking, within the deposit of Faith.

Such matters are, for instance, the interpretation of Scripture; the canonisation of Saints; the matter and form of the Sacraments in a given case, in which a dogmatic fact is under consideration; other facts which are called dogmatic; and the condemnation of false doctrines by the Holy See.

RELIGIOUS ASSENT ELICITED BY RELIGIOUS OBEDIENCE

2. The second kind of assent is that elicited by virtue of "religious obedience." It is given to that teaching of the Church which does not fall under the head of revealed truth nor even under the endowment of her infallibility, but under the exercise of her ordinary authority, to feed, teach, and govern the flock of Christ.

To think as the Church thinks, to be of one mind with her, to obey her voice, is not a matter of duty in those cases only when the subject matter is one of divine revelation or is connected therewith. It is an obligation also, whenever the subject matter of the Church's teaching falls within the range of her authority. And that range, as we have said, comprises all that is necessary for feeding, teaching, and governing the flock.

Under this ordinary authority, or *magisterium*, come the Pastoral Letters of Bishops, diocesan and provincial decrees, and (though standing respectively on higher ground, as being of a superior order and covering the whole Church), many Acts of the Supreme Pontiff, and all the decisions of the Roman Congregations. It is by virtue of ordinary ecclesiastical authority, not of infallibility, that the larger number of the hortative, directive, and preceptive acts of the Church are issued.

As points of discipline may be decreed at one time and modified or set aside at another, so may novel theories and opinions, advanced even by learned men, be at one time censured by the Roman Congregations, and at a later time tolerated and even accepted. For instance, the Holy Office in a case of a disputed text of Scripture or any similar point, after careful consideration—customary in matters of this importance—may declare, that the arguments brought forward do not warrant the conclusion claimed for them by certain students. Such a decision is not immutable, and does not prevent Catholic students continuing their research, and respectfully laying before the Holy See any fresh or more convincing arguments they may discover against the authenticity of the text. And thus it becomes possible that, in time, the tribunals of the Holy See may decide in the sense which the earlier students had suggested, but could not at first establish by satisfactory arguments as a safe conclusion.

Meanwhile the Church exercises her authority, as she judges

best, so that no child of hers "shall add to" or, "shall take away from the words of the Book," of which she is the sole Guardian. In such a case loyal Catholics should accept her decision, by virtue of "religious obedience," as the one to be followed for the present. But while they gratefully accept such guidance in the matter that concerns religion, they will be careful to distinguish between this guidance and the Church's definitions of faith.

It stands to reason that if individuals had the right, in virtue of their own private reason or opinions, to withhold the "religious assent" demanded of them in virtue of "religious obedience," their assent would never be "religious," for it cannot be religious assent unless based upon the principle of obedience to a religious authority. Unless so based, conformity of mind with the mind of the Church would simply be the result of private judgment and a mere coincidence. Conformity of this kind might even cover doctrines which the Church teaches as Articles of Faith; and may be found in persons who have never entered the Church. Indeed such accidental conformity is compatible with a total absence of all faith. Such assent would then stand on no higher ground than that of a coincidence of private opinion with the teaching of the Church.

Speaking of the assent which the children of the Church owe to her guidance, Pope Pius IX. declared, in his Apostolic Letter of December 2, 1862, that:

> The Church, in virtue of the power entrusted to her by her Divine Founder, has not only the right but a special duty not to tolerate—has even the duty to brand and condemn—any kind of error, in the interests of the soundness of Faith and of the salvation of souls. And it is the duty of every philosopher who wishes to be a son of the Church, and of every Catholic school of philosophy, never to advance anything in opposition to the Church's teaching, and to retract any statements which have drawn on them the censure of the Church. The opinion which teaches the contrary we declare to be altogether erroneous and in the highest degree harmful to the very Faith of the Church and to her authority.

Here, it is to be observed, that the Pope speaks not only of the body of the faithful, but expressly, and in a special manner, of those who are learned.—But still more explicit are the following weighty words used by his Holiness Leo XIII., happily reigning:

> In settling how far the limits of obedience extend, let no one imagine that the authority of the sacred pastors, and above all of the Roman Pontiff, need be obeyed only in so far as it is concerned with dogmas, the obstinate denial of which entails the guilt of heresy. Again, it is not enough even to give a frank and firm assent to doctrines which are put forward in the ordinary and universal teaching of the Church as divinely revealed, although they have never been solemnly defined. Another point still must be reckoned among the duties of Christian men, and that is, they must be willing to be ruled and governed by the authority and direction of their Bishops, and, in the first place, of the Apostolic See" (*Sapientiae Christianae*, January 10, 1890).

Such has always been the firm persuasion and the loyal practice of Catholic England. Let it suffice to recall the teaching of the First Provincial Synod of Westminster, held in the year 1852:

> Look unto the rock, whence ye are hewn. Look unto Abraham your father" (Is. li., 1). It is right that we, who have received our faith, our priesthood, and the true religion immediately from the Apostolic See, should beyond others be bound to it by the bonds of love and veneration. Wherefore, the foundation of true and orthodox faith, we rest on the same basis on which Our Lord and Saviour Jesus Christ was pleased to place it, namely, on the immovable Chair of Peter, the Holy Roman Church, the mistress and mother of the whole world. Whatever has been defined by her we, on that account, hold to be certain and sure; her traditions, rites, pious uses and all apostolic constitutions regarding discipline, with our whole heart we welcome and venerate. Finally, with all sincerity we profess obedience and reverence to the Supreme Pontiff, as the Vicar of Christ, and cling to him in the closest bonds of Catholic communion (*Decree VII*).

THE ATTITUDE OF THE LIBERAL CATHOLIC

3. Far removed from this spirit of faith, from this conformity of mind with the mind of the Church, is another spirit which has begun to manifest itself amongst us. It is a spirit which strips itself of all the instincts of faith and religious obedience, till scarcely any sentiment survives beyond a desire to avoid actual heresy. In place of those noble Christian instincts, which consti-

tute the franchise of the Catholic soul, reposing trustfully in the care and guidance of a Divine Teacher, the intellect becomes a victim to fears and apprehensions. There are cases in which theories, criticisms and assertions, advanced in the name of intellect or science, seem to exercise an almost irresistible control over the mind, while it often happens that those who were loudest in claiming liberty and independence of thought in religious matters, become themselves slaves to human respect, trembling with fear in the presence of the bitter criticisms and worthless theories, which are often launched against the Church by her enemies.

It is not so much that the liberal Catholic has formed independently for himself a scientific opinion, as that he has practically surrendered his own independence, by taking for granted, and as venerable and true, the halting and disputable judgments of some man of letters or of science, which may represent no more than the wave of some popular feeling or the views of some fashionable or dogmatising school. The bold assertions of men of science are received with awe and bated breath; the criticisms of an intellectual group of *savants* are quoted as though they were rules for a good life, while the mind of the Church and her guidance are barely spoken of with ordinary patience. The liberal Catholic appears to be nervously apprehensive lest the Church should in some way commit herself and err. He doubts her wisdom, her patience, her ability in dealing with mankind. And he flatters himself that his own opinions are the outcome of a strong-minded, impartial and philosophical spirit.

It is from germs such as these that the most noxious liberalism has infected the Catholic Church in other lands. It is from seeds such as these that schisms and heresies arise, take shape and form. It is from the spread of such opinions by persons who have won a position in literature or in science, that the faithful begin to lose their holy dread of erroneous doctrines and false principles. Thus faith becomes tainted, moral virtue becomes relaxed, and, in process of time, liberalism in religion invades the whole mind until, like their leaders, many of the faithful are thought to be alive, and they are dead.

From what has been said it will be seen that it is always a characteristic of a faithful and docile disciple of Christ to conform his mind and judgment in matters of religion to the mind and judgment of the Divine Teacher. This should become a moral habit moving the will, whose wish and inclination is so often the father of the thought and belief of the mind. In all matters of faith, whether positively defined or only felt to be the general mind, or the approved sentiment, of the Church, the ground on which a Catholic stands is plain and solid—the authority of God speaking to him through His Church. He knows that the spirit of our Lord Jesus Christ and the spirit of the Church, His Bride, are one and the same. By the Divine Teacher, through the voice of His Church, we are ruled and directed unto salvation. One and the same is the Lord and the Teacher, who gave the Ten Commandments to Moses on Mount Sinai, and who now instructs and rules the hierarchy of the Church unto the well-being and sanctification of the faithful.

ESSENTIAL CONDITION FOR THE RECEPTION OF CATHOLICS

4. And here we cannot refrain from pointing out to the clergy the absolute necessity of thoroughly instructing converts on the ground and motive of faith before receiving them into the Church. Unless they believe that they have found in the Catholic Church the Divine Teacher, they must not be admitted into her pale, no matter how many of the articles of Catholic faith they may assent to. In other words, they must believe in the authority and infallibility of the Divine Teacher in matters of faith and morals as an essential and fundamental condition for reception into the Church. All the articles of Catholic faith, all the verities of religion must be accepted on the authority and claim of the Teacher, not on the taste, will, or judgment of the individual. Our Lord when upon the earth exacted this kind of submission from His disciples; and if men would be His disciples now, they must submit in like manner to the authority of the Divine Teacher, speaking in the Church. When this fundamental has been thoroughly grasped, there will be no logical or reasonable difficulty in accepting whatever doctrines the Church teaches.

THE RIGHT ATTITUDE TOWARDS DEVOTIONAL PRACTICES

5. Before concluding this portion of our subject, we must say a word on the devotional practices of the Church.

It is a "reasonable service," to use the Apostle's phrase, to obey on being commanded. And it is "reasonable" instinct or inclination of the mind to approve the rites, customs and devotions practised in the Church, even where there is no precept. Numberless are the forms of Catholic piety. There are special devotions to each of the three Divine Persons of the Trinity, to the name of Jesus, to His Infancy and to His Passion, to the Sacred Heart, the Precious Blood, the Five Bleeding Wounds: to each of His Mysteries: to His Immaculate Mother: to His Foster-Father, To S. Peter His Vicar, and to His Apostles and Saints. There are pilgrimages to shrines, indulgences, jubilees, relics, images, medals and scapulars, chants, hymns, vocal prayers, processions and many other practices of devotion and penance, blessed and approved, and some of them instituted by the Church.

The range of devotional acts is wide and long,—reaching from the sublime elevation of the soul and its seraphic communion with God on the heights of Thabor or of Calvary,—from the perfect and permanent consecration of mind, will, life and person to God's love and service,—through an infinite variety of national vibrations of feeling and public manifestations of faith and piety, down to the simple and spontaneous expression of a personal devotion. Provided there be nothing inconsistent with the doctrines of faith, provided religious dignity and the proprieties of person, time and place be decorously observed, these various manifestations of religious sentiment are not alien to the mind of the Church, and they are not to be despised and condemned as out of harmony with modern thought; nor is the expression of feeling and temper of one nation to be censured, because not in accord with that of another.

Man's religious life is like his person, which is not simply a skeleton, but is built up in form and rounded figure, and endowed with subtle feelings and with the graces of feature, colour and complexion. His religious life is not as bare fibre of a tree without foliage to adorn it, to protect its fruit and to assist the essential functions of nutrition. But in man the external growth of religious practices corresponds and co-operates with his inner life, helping, protecting and embellishing it in manifold ways.

God in His wisdom has constituted all organic life upon earth complex, with interdependent parts; and most of all is this true of men's intellectual, moral and physical being. In addition to what is essential, he is enriched with a thousand accidental gifts and properties; there are internal and hidden as well as external and visible functions; and no form of beauty worthy of contemplation, no integrity of life worthy of admiration, can ever be attained, without the contribution of each and every part to the perfection and beauty of the whole.

It is therefore "reasonable" to praise the Church for large-minded and affectionate care of her disciples, when in addition to the great acts of Religion and the Sacraments, she opens out so wide a field of devotional exercises, to be used according to the taste and attraction of her children, who are of all races and tribes. These devotions are calculated to contribute in their place and measure to the perfection of Christian life, which, in its simplest expression, consists in the knowledge of God and in the knowledge of oneself—in the love of God and in the love of our neighbour for God's sake.

III.

The Theory of Development and the Deposit of Faith.

ERRORS CURRENT IN ENGLAND

1. One of the errors current in England is the belief that the Catholic Church of to-day is not the same as the primitive Church—that she has departed from the original doctrines of Christianity. And another error is that the Church possessed more authority at one time than at another—that she possessed a Divine claim to obedience in the early centuries, which she does not possess in the present day.

We, on the other hand, hold that the Church as the Divine Teacher is identical with herself in every age. The Divine Teacher speaks through His chosen organs, the Pope and the Bishops, in union with him. He speaks with the same wisdom, the same authority, the same infallibility to-day as during the infancy of the Church in the first three centuries of persecution or in the subsequent centuries of General Councils. The Church is continuous and indefectible in her existence and constitution; so also in her doctrine. But her continuity and indefectibility is that of a living organic being, animated by the Holy Ghost. It is not the changeless continuity of the dead letter of a book, or the indefectibility of a lifeless statue.

THE TRUE THEORY OF DEVELOPMENT

2. Living beings are never stationary, they grow while they maintain their identity. The Church also grows. She has a progress, an evolution of her own. Not only do the faithful grow in the faith, but faith itself grows in its own form and character, or as a tree in its own unmistakable properties. Such development implies no essential change. Essential change is—not development, progress, or evolution but—the destruction of what was, and substitution for it of something else. As St. Vincent of Lerins wrote fifteen centuries ago:

> It is the property of progress that a thing be developed in itself: it is the property of change that a thing be altered from what it was into something else (*Commonitorium* n. 23).

It was thus that a Father of the Church in the fifth century understood the unity of doctrine, which constitutes the internal and substantial continuity of the Church—a unity always fixed and determinate in its principles and in harmony with its original, in the deposit of truth; but, at the same time, progressive in the inferences, definitions and applications to which the original doctrine is rightly and logically extended.

Answering the question "Whether there shall be no progress of religion in the Church of Christ?" St. Vincent of Lerins replies: "Certainly, let there be progress and as much as may be, . . . but so that it be really a progress in the faith, not an alteration of it" (Id. Ibid.).

Then he explains what this true progress or development really consists in, and continues:

> The Church of Christ, being a vigilant careful Guardian of the doctrines committed to her, makes no change in these at any time, subtracts nothing, adds nothing, does not curtail what is essential nor tack on what is not needed. She does not let slip what is her own, she does not pilfer what is another's; her whole endeavour, her one aim by her treatment of all questions, at once faithful and wise, is to bring out into clearness

> what was once vague and incomplete, to strengthen and secure what is already developed and distinct, to keep watch and ward over doctrine already established and defined (Ibid.).

In other words, the doctrines of faith have not been cast into the world to be torn to pieces, or to be discussed by mankind generally, and elaborated at pleasure into a system of philosophy. They have been entrusted, as a Divine deposit, to the teaching Church and to her alone—to guard faithfully, and to develop and explain, with divine and infallible authority.

Truths, therefore, at one time held implicitly, by degrees become explicitly realised and defined, as one or other of those truths becomes a more special object of attention on the part of theologians or of the Holy See, in the face of those who are hostile to her. It is difficult, therefore, to understand the intellectual state of those friends of knowledge and progress, who argue that the modern Church is unfaithful to the primitive Church, because it teaches some truths explicitly, which were formerly held implicitly—unless they are prepared to defend the paradoxical position that implicit knowledge is in itself preferable to knowledge that is explict and clearly defined.

TEACHING OFFICE OF THE CHURCH NEEDED TO MEET PRESENT DANGERS

3. The words of Leo XIII., in his recent letter to Cardinal Gibbons, may be quoted here for the benefit of those "who would limit the exercise of the power of the Church, so that each one of the faithful may act more freely in pursuance of his own natural bent or capacity, as men do in civil society." The Holy Father points out the wisdom and providence of God in the definition of the Vatican Council, "whereby the authority and teaching office of the Apostolic See was affirmed, in order the more effectually to guard the minds of Catholics from the dangers of the present times. The license which is commonly confounded with liberty—the passion for criticising and finding fault with everything—the habit of throwing into print whatever men think or feel—have so confused and darkened men's minds that the Church's Office as a Teacher has now become more than ever useful and necessary, to save Christians from being drawn away from conscience or duty."

WELCOME TO EVERY INCREASE OF KNOWLEDGE

4. And then, he adds: "Nothing can be further from our thoughts than to reject indiscriminately the intellectual gains and progress of our own day. On the contrary, we gladly welcome as an addition to the heritage of knowledge and as a widening of the borders of the world's prosperity, every victory of research in the pursuit of truth, every effort of man for the attainment of good. But if all this progress is to bear lasting fruit and to continue to go forward, assuredly it must not set at defiance the authority and the wisdom of the Church."

And here we may re-echo the noble desire, expressed by the Vatican Council, in the Dogmatic Constitution *de Fide Catholica*, for the continued progress and development of all knowledge, of all science, within their own proper sphere.

A FALSE THEORY OF DEVELOPMENT

5. Very different from this is the theory of progress or development excogitated in recent times, and approved by certain writers on the continent, and even in England. They make the progress of Christian doctrine to consist in real change. They argue that certain truths of revelation may become obsolete and die out; that having served their time, higher truths will supplant them, in accordance with some real or fancied progress of natural science. They even suggest that higher perceptions in natural science will reduce mysteries to the level of natural phenomena; and that the development of Christian doctrine really means the reception into the deposit of faith of a number of extraneous truths, which will, in course of time, bring the Church into perfect conformity with modern ideas.

There are even Catholics who imagine that they can save their orthodoxy by holding the creeds and definitions of faith, not according to the Church's constant understanding of them, but according to their own. They profess to believe that the Church's teaching may receive new light to illuminate it, so that the traditional sense, given by the Church to her formularies, shall give way to other meanings partially or wholly different. Against errors of this kind the Church, in the Vatican Council, has launched her formal anathemas:

> If anyone shall say that it may ever be possible, with the progress of science, for a sense to be given to the doctrines proposed by the Church, other than that which the Church has understood and understands, let him be anathema (*De Fide et Ratione*, IV. Canones, n. 3).

CATHOLIC TRUTH NOT TO BE MINIMISED OR SUPPRESSED

6. We are well aware that one cause of this error, which is to be found in England as elsewhere, is the mistaken belief that the way to commend the Catholic religion to non-Catholics is to pare down supernatural doctrines of Faith, and to hold out a hope and a prospect that the dogmas, they object to, may by degrees be explained away, or brought into conformity with their opinions. But it is not lawful to tamper with divine Truth, or to treat the deposit of Faith as though it were a human treasury, to be dealt with and disposed of at the will of man.

Leo XIII. has recently spoken as follows. He says that—

> There are persons who think, that in order the more easily to bring over to Catholic doctrine those who dissent from it, the Church ought to adapt herself somewhat to our advanced civilisation, and, relaxing her ancient rigour, to show some indulgence to modern theories and methods. Many think that this is to be understood not only with regard to the rule of life, but also to the doctrines in which the deposit of faith is contained. For they contend that it is opportune,—in order to work in a more attractive way upon the wills of those who are not in accord with us,—to pass over certain heads of doctrine, as of lesser moment, or so to soften them that they may not convey the same meaning which the Church has invariably held.
>
> Now, few words are needed to show how reprehensible is the plan that is thus conceived, if we only consider the character and origin of the doctrine, which the Church hands down to us. On that point the Vatican Council says: "The doctrine of faith which God has revealed is not proposed like a theory of philosophy, which is to be elaborated by the human understanding, but as a divine deposit delivered to the Spouse of Christ to be faithfully and infallibly declared. . . . That sense

of the sacred dogmas is to be faithfully kept which Holy Mother Church has once declared, and is not to be departed from under the specious pretext of a more profound understanding" (*Constit. de Fide Cath.*, C. iv). Nor is the suppression to be considered altogether free from blame, which designedly omits certain principles of Catholic doctrine and buries them, as it were, in oblivion. For one and the same is the Author and Mother of all the truths that Christian teaching comprises—*the Only Begotten Son, who is in the bosom of the Father* (Jo. i. 18). . . . Far be it then from any one to bate, or for any reason whatever, to pass over one tittle of the doctrine delivered from above; whoever would do so, would rather wish to detach Catholics from the Church, than to bring over to her those who are outside her pale. As for those who are wandering far away from the Fold of Christ, let them retrace their steps. Nothing could more rejoice our heart. Let them retrace their steps, one and all, along no other path than that which Christ Himself has traced out.

ROMAN DECISIONS NO OBSTACLE TO PROGRESS

7. If it be a pernicious error to say that science and progress can read a new meaning into the Creeds and Definitions of faith, it is a no less pernicious and revolutionary error to assert that decrees emanating from the Holy See are an encumbrance on the field of science and an obstacle in the path of progress.

But even should it happen—and the Roman Congregations do not claim infallibility—that the decree of a Roman Congregation were issued under a misunderstanding, it would be well to remember how frequently miscarriages of justice take place in our own civil and criminal courts; yet that their authority is always strictly upheld, while their erroneous judgments can be rectified only by a legal tribunal.

SERVICES OF THE ROMAN CONGREGATIONS TO SCIENCE

8. But if these be days in which fullest liberty is claimed for science and literature to teach and write as they please, why not gladly accord the same liberty to the Church to define the truths of religion and to point out errors and dangers to the Faith?

Indeed, ought not the impartial observer to acknowledge that careful definitions of truth and condemnations of error in matters of religion, far from inflicting an injury upon science, are calculated to render the greatest service to the cause of truth and progress? In a state of society in which truths, and half-truths, and errors without number, are confounded together,—in which there are at least as many teachers of error as of truth—no more signal benefit could be conferred upon searchers after the true and the good than the occasional promulgation by the Holy See of calm and well-weighed judgments concerning truth and error. In cases in which the decisions of the Holy See, or of her tribunals, have hit the dangerous speculations and rash assertions of science, it has been often admitted, by learned and scientific thinkers, that such decisions have been an important contribution to the cause of truth. They often compel students to pause and to retrace their steps, to weigh further evidence, and above all things to avoid the danger of regarding their hypotheses as established laws or well-ascertained facts.

But whatever incidental advantages may accrue from the action of the Holy See and the Roman Congregations, the primary and essential end they have in view is the protection of faith and morals. Let these be impugned, denied, misrepresented or exposed to loss by false, rash or scandalous theories or assertions, and the Church will step in to warn her faithful disciples against danger.

THE CONGREGATION OF THE INDEX

9. It has been a fashion to decry the Roman Congregations by persons who have little or no knowledge of their careful and elaborate methods, of their system of sifting and testing evidence, and of the pains taken by the Holy See to summon experts, even from distant parts of the Church, to take part in their proceedings.

Take, for instance, the Congregation of the Index of prohibited books, of which so much has been said of late. It is governed by a code of rules and instructions drawn up by Clement VIII., revised by Alexander VII., Benedict XIV., and recently by his Holiness Leo XIII. in his Constitution *Officiorum*. No work is condemned without a previous rigorous examination of its contents; no Catholic writer of eminence is censured without being allowed opportunity for defence, either personally or by proxy. The considerateness of the Holy See is further illustrated by the way in which she grants special facilities for dispensation in regard to one or other rule of the Index, thus making it just as easy for Catholics in this country to be guided by the authoratative direction of the Congregation as for Catholics elsewhere.

WRITINGS TO BE AVOIDED BY ALL

10. But no dispensation from rules of the Index can leave Catholics at liberty to read whatever they please. By the natural law a man is bound to avoid reading anything that he knows may undermine his faith, his religion, or his morality; and this law of nature is emphasised by the highest sanctions in the law of grace. Divine faith is a supernatural gift which may be lost through our own fault. It may be forfeited—indirectly by neglect of prayer and the Sacraments, and by the deadening effect upon the mind of an immoral life; and directly by habitual indulgence in thoughts and speculations against faith. Temptations against faith are generated and wonderfully strengthened and disseminated by sneering and profane conversation and carping criticisms, in which mind stimulates mind in an unholy rivalry of unbelief. "The tongue is a fire—a world of iniquiry—an unquiet evil, full of deadly poison" (James iii, 5).

HOW RATIONALISM IS IMBIBED

11. But indiscriminate reading is, perhaps, the most insidious form under which the poison of rationalism and unbelief is injected into the soul. Without attracting attention men, and women too, take up books or magazines that lie about, and, as it were casually, turn to the cleverly written and highly spiced articles against their faith, which they find therein. Their minds have no tincture of philosophical or theological training; they possess no antidote to the poisonous draught. But they read on without excuse or necessity, allured by fashion, curiosity, or a desire to taste of forbidden fruit. A common result eventually produced by indulgence of this sort is, either distrust of the

Church, doubts of revelation and of the existence of God Himself, ending in secret or open unbelief; or a general loosening of the spiritual ties and bonds that hold the religious structure of life together. Hence loss of the instincts of faith and a liberal Catholicism, in which semi-rationalism has secured a permanent lodgment. Feeding the mind and imaginations upon arguments and pictures against the virtue of faith must end as fatally to the soul as feeding them upon lascivious suggestions and forbidden images. Faith and Chastity are equally gifts of God, that need careful guardianship; for they that love the danger shall perish in it. To say that it is impossible to get away from the literature of the day is only to say that in the choice of what to read and what to avoid, the exercise of a wise discretion and of a strong will are absolutely necessary. To read, without necessity, matter calculated to create doubt or to sap faith, is a sin against religion and the first commandment.

APPEAL TO CATHOLIC LOYALTY

12. Finally, dear Children in Christ, to sum up the argument and instruction contained in this Pastoral Letter. There is but one fitting attitude for a Catholic towards the Church, namely, that of unswerving loyalty. Mark the loyalty which men of the world exhibit towards societies they join for the pursuit of some common object; mark their hearty allegiance to a temporal Sovereign, their deep patriotism for the land of their birth. But the claims to loyalty of institutions, that must perish with time, are not to be compared with those of the Church of God. The Church stands forth, on the one hand, as the Spouse of Christ, dyed with His Blood, animated by His Spirit, while on the other, she walks the earth as a defenceless lamb in the midst of wolves, exposed and abandoned like Christ Himself, to the hatred of persecutors. The noblest and most generous sentiments, of which the human breast is capable, fall short of the homage and fidelity that are due to this our incomparable Mother, who has borne us, and who still carries us at her breasts.

Remember also that, while we are pilgrims, in exile, upon earth, we must live in the midst of mysteries. Mysteries of the natural order are all around us, so also mysteries of the supernatural order. Men reconcile themselves to the former: they rebel against the latter. Be it not so with you. "This is the victory which overcometh the world, our faith" (John v., 4). This Catholic faith, if pure and simple, is "mighty to God upon the pulling down . . . every height that exalteth itself against the knowledge of God, bringing into captivity every understanding unto the obedience of Christ" (II. Cor. x., 5).

Remember, too, that you are messengers for God to those who in this country are called to the knowledge of the faith.

Beginning a new Century, each one may well ask himself, What must be characteristic of my service, if I am to glorify God? Is greater self-restraint, a more docile spirit, demanded of me, that I may save my own soul and help to win back my neighbour to the Fold? Surely, it is needful, that we should be all of one mind with the Church, and that we should all bear common witness to the Faith, in order to glorify God and our Lord Jesus Christ. In return for this we are promised the divine gifts of hope, of joy, and of peace, such as the world cannot give. This is the teaching of the great Apostle of the Gentiles, who has written: "Let every one of you please his neighbour unto good, to edification, for Christ did not please Himself. . . . Now the God of patience and of comfort grant you to be of one mind, one towards another, according to Jesus Christ; that with one mind and one mouth you may glorify God and the Father of Our Lord Jesus Christ. Now the God of hope fill you with all joy and peace in believing, that you may abound in hope and in the peace of the Holy Ghost."

"I have written to you, brethren, more boldly in some sort, as it were putting you in mind; because of the grace which is given to me from God that I should be a minister of Christ Jesus" (Rom. xv.).

And now, Rev. Brethren and dear Children in Christ, that we are entering upon the Twentieth Century, we pray most earnestly to the Faithful Virgin, the Glorious Mother of God, to intercede for the children of her Dowry; to Blessed Peter, to show himself once more throughout this realm of England, so loyal and faithful to his See during a thousand years. And we pray thus, that Mary and Peter, Thomas of Canterbury, and all the other Saints of God may unite with us in imploring Our Lord Jesus Christ to come again, and reign in the mind and heart of the people of this country, and lead us all, in His own good time, into life everlasting. Amen.

Given at Westminster, this 29th day of December, being the Feast of the glorious Martyr, St. Thomas of Canterbury, to be read, on consecutive Sundays, to the faithful in all the Churches of the Province of Westminster.

✠ HERBERT CARDINAL VAUGHAN, Archbishop of Westminster.
✠ WILLIAM, Bishop of Plymouth.
✠ JOHN CUTHBERT, Bishop of Newport.
✠ EDWARD, Bishop of Nottingham.
✠ EDWARD, Bishop of Birmingham.
✠ RICHARD, Bishop of Middlesborough.
✠ ARTHUR, Bishop of Northampton.
✠ THOMAS, Bishop of Hexham and Newcastle.
✠ WILLIAM, Bishop of Leeds.
✠ JOHN, Bishop of Salford.
✠ WILLIAM, Bishop of Clifton.
✠ THOMAS, Bishop of Liverpool.
✠ FRANCIS, Bishop of Menevia.
✠ FRANCIS, Bishop of Southwark.
✠ SAMUEL, Bishop of Shrewsbury.
✠ JOHN BAPTIST, Bishop of Portsmouth.

Notes to Appendix B

1. See letters 31–36.

APPENDIX C

Letters Relating to "Semper Eadem."[1]

5 January 1903,

My dear Father Gerard,[2] *Pax Christi,*

I have sent an article on Ward's book to Griffin and told him to let you have the slips *quam primum.* Much as I sympathise with Ward's aims I have long felt that in his desire for conciliation he is muddling things up that must be kept apart. I feel that if the conservative theologians fail to grasp the progressive standpoint, the progressives equally fail in a comprehensive understanding of the distinctive essence of Catholic as opposed to Liberal theology. It will conduce the truth in the long run to clear up the state of the question as much as possible instead of attempting a premature solution. Hence in my article (though I do not overtly attack his position, but rather assume that he means what I mean) I break the bone that I regard as ill-set; and though I leave a loop-hole for a more satisfactory solution, I do not—for obvious reasons—attempt that solution myself. If questions are put clearly enough they will often answer themselves. I am *afraid* the article will be a sixteen pager, and will much regret if the close connection of its argument must be broken. Needless to say there is nothing that can offend and much that will delight the simplicity of the Slaters and Humphrys, and for this reason if it—or part of it—could appear in January it might act as a breakwater against possible misunderstandings of and attacks on *Lex Orandi.* Those who see the devil in the latter will see an exorcism in the former. While the discerning will see that there is a perfect unity of position throughout. I must apologize for the number of gift copies (twenty-four) of *Lex Orandi*; one's friends multiply. But I think nearly all of the gifts have a distinct advertisement value.

Yours faithfully,
G. TYRRELL

Richmond York
8 January 1904 [[COPY]]

Dear Mr. Devas[3]

Your letter gratified me so far as it indicated that I had succeeded in my intention of bringing out into sharp contrast the difference between the liberal and the Catholic senses of 'theological development.' While I am *quite* with Ward in realising the immense difficulties entailed by the supposition that we are bound finally to the categories and thought forms of past ages, I cannot see clearly any *via media* between the two extremes though I hope such may be found. In Newman's Oxford Sermon on 'The Theory of Development' he seems to me to be still dominated by the protestant conception of revelation as a vision of supernatural realities *accorded to each believer*; and not as a record of such a vision granted to a past age and handed on by tradition through the symbolism of language. That was in 1843. In 1845 in his *Essay on Development* he seems to me to have come 'round to the exact position of 'Catholic theology' as I have stated it. He differs from the usual presentment of it only in tone and in virtue of a more liberal education; but I see no difference of principle, no room for such a development as the sermon of 1843 would have tolerated. Alterations and interpretations of doctrines are judged finally in 1845 not by an appeal to a *present vision* of revealed realities (virtually an appeal to experience) but by the infallible utterances of external authority which, as it were, supplement the indeterminateness of the primitive revelation and thus save it from being merely an archeological document or monument like the bricks of Babylon.

As to the evolution of monotheism my remark was no doubt too sweeping and ill considered, for I am no specialist but a mere layman in comparative religion. I was thinking vaguely of J. E.

Harrison's *Prolegomena to Greek Religion*[4] which I had just read, and also of Robertson Smith's,[5] Wellhausen's[6] and Montefiore's[7] treatment of Semitic religion—not to say, of Loisy's *Religion d'Israel.*[8] Still my statement does not refer so much to the progress of peoples and races as to that of the human mind in its endeavors to formulate the object of its religious sentiment and need. Unification of chaos is the term of all constructive mental labor; hence in theology monotheism seems to be the inevitable issue of speculation—Polytheism, henotheism, monotheism. Historically this *a priori* order may be disturbed by a thousand contingencies as regards both races and individuals. Also, I hold it to be of faith, rather than of reason or experience that Providence is leading things steadily *upwards* and that which seems the longest way round may be the shortest way home. Reason suggests endless oscillations up and down, not even of things *as a whole* but of different parts of that whole, making a more or less constant sum-total of ups and downs and no substantial progress whatever—yet this dreary future does not exclude the eternal difference between up and down, between constructive and destructive; growth and decay; between God and non-God. Hence even if we can imagine that creation began with an 'up' this would not alter the fact that the Power which works in nature and in the soul of man makes upwards and not downwards and that (apart from miraculous intervention and revelation) polytheism is the natural antecedent of monotheism—as the germ is of the organism. But this is not a bit the sort of 'development of doctrine' of which Newman speaks in 1845; for the germ is lost in the organism whereas the deposit of faith persists unchanged amid all its theological accretions and explications—or rather that is the theological *theory* of the matter; for such a persistence is psychologically impossible. Creeds and symbols, or dead things, may persist for centuries; but the mind-forms for which they stand are ever growing into something else.

Yours ever faithfully,
G. TYRRELL

Notes to Appendix C

1. See letters 46–57.
2. John Gerard S.J. was then editor of the *Month.*

3. Charles Devas (1848–1906), economist and distinguished convert to Roman Catholicism; a friend of *W*'s and *T*'s; he later advised *W* not to respond to *T*'s review.

4. Jane Ellen Harrison (1850–1928), *Prolegomena to Greek Religion* (Cambridge, 1903).

5. William Robertson Smith (1846–1894), Scottish theologian and Semitic scholar who was in the center of the storm provided by the higher criticism of the Bible.

6. Julius Wellhausen (1844–1918), biblical critic devoted to the principles of higher criticism.

7. Claude Joseph Goldsmid Montefiore (1858–1938), scholar of Judaica and the origins of religion.

8. Loisy's *Religion d'Israel* (Paris, 1901). In October, 1900, Loisy published an article on the origins of Israel's religion in the *Révue de clergé français*, under the pseudonym, Firmin (his mother's maiden name and his own middle name). The article was condemned by Cardinal Richard of Paris and the publication of further articles forbidden.

APPENDIX D

Letters to Mrs. Wilfrid Ward

Moorhurst
Friday Eve[1]

Dear Mrs. Ward,

I must not let your kindness hurt you. In his present delicate position it would do Mr. Ward no good and possibly much harm to receive me as his guest.

With the Gibsons[2] it is, of course, quite different.

Ever yours faithfully,
G. TYRRELL

Pension Bellevie, Freiburg, i.B.
11 April 1906

Dear Mrs. Ward,

If I don't write now I may have to delay till my impressions of your book[3] get blurred; for at Paris there will be much to do and write *à propos* of the troubles of my friends there. As a description and contrast of two lines of Liberalism—I use the word with all due reserve for lack of a better—and even of *the* two lines, I think it is quite excellent and very useful. But to me it suggests the inadequacy of both, and the need of another path hardly now trodden by any but trodden by saints in the past. I am not thinking of Piero Maironi[4] but of a greater Liberal whose way was neither Sutcliffe's nor Paul's. I am not quite sure whether you wished to suggest that, or whether you wished to approve the Sutcliffe method without reserve. There is a pagan disobedience and a Christian disobedience; the latter a stern duty at times. Paul displays the former, but I wish Sutcliffe had recognised the claims of the latter. As an unqualified principle of edification has been the source of infinite scandal; or as unqualified asceticism ends in licentiousness, so unqualified obedience ends in tyranny followed by rebellion and anarchy. No one dares to deny it; yet no one dares to say it. It is not disobedience but the motive and spirit of pagan disobedience that wants reproof. But then much of our obedience is as pagan in spirit and motive, and as reprehensible. The book will be much read and criticised; indeed it could not have appeared at a better moment for the publishers' interest. There will be and is great guessing as to who is who, for the public will not be baulked of its scandal or believe in 'creation out of nothing.' And then of course there is the human interest of the story; though I suppose it is too subordinate to commend the book to those not very interested in the Church. I shall be curious to see the reviews. As to Bremond's book I think it is useful as a plough is useful to the soil. It raises questions and challenges conclusions and suggests view-points, all of which, whether accepted or not, will help to save Newman's portrait from being too quickly stereotyped and copied blindly by author after author.[5] As you say, it is too soon to sum him up. But writers will never wait; and the best antidote is a variety of conflicting summings-up that keep the question open. Out of the variety the unity will be evolved. Certainly I have no Newman of my own; or else a very eclectic production, and I am not capable of forming a verdict on the whole Newman or the whole Newmanism—only on bits. I hear Turinaz is insistent for the condemnation of the *Essay on Development*. If he got it it would hardly be more surprising than the condemnation of Laberthonnière's *Essai*. *Anything* is possible in the present panic with the power in such nervous, ill-instructed hands.

As to myself I am very satisfied that I am as I am; above all that at the last moment the responsibility of so drastic a step was taken out of my hands. My chief annoyance now is that my loyalty to my many Jesuit friends is interpreted as loyalty to Jesuitism and the Society; and I am supposed to be longing to return. That was a clever turn that I did not foresee. I like Germans individually and distributively; but I have strong opinions about the Kaiser and Germanism; and there might arise circumstances where my friendship to Germans might have to cede to my profound antipathy to Germanism. However they have other things to talk about now, so I hope soon to be forgotten and left in peace.

With many thanks and best wishes.

Ever yours faithfully,
G. TYRRELL.

18 April 1906

To Mrs. Ward:

I did not like 'parts' of your book, I liked it *all*—as a novel; and I *think* better than any of your books. Only the circumstances gave it an unintended 'actuality' and my poor brain just now is very *borné* and preoccupied with ecclesiasticism—the most harrowing of interests. When I am free of the mire and more aloof I hope my more humane and literary interest will revive; and I will re-read you in the atmosphere for which your book was intended. As far as I have deciphered Ward's letter of the 16th—it usually takes several readings broken by rests for unconscious cerebration—I am in agreement. It is quite true that I read his article 'standing and with girded loins' ready for flight from Freiburg and very determined to use my German stamps before leaving. Hence I read quicker and wrote sooner than usual. I will give his message to Laberthonnière today. Not only was no warning given (as was legally due) to the three condemned,[6] but even their ordinaries learnt the news first from the papers. Hence much indignation here at the Archbishop's palace. Brunetière's anger sent him to bed; Violett burned with a protest to Rome. If they begin condemning books with *Imprimaturs*, no honorable man will ask a bishop to incur such a risk; nor will his misguide the public by a dubious hall mark.

Ever yours,
GT

Notes to Appendix D

1. It is not clear what date this letter written, though likely sometime after *T*'s trouble with the Jesuits (after February 1906) and perhaps even after his excommunication (October 1907).

2. See letter 7 note 4; the Gibsons were neighbors of the Wards at one time and good friends, but entirely on the other side of every religious and political issue (see *MW* II.121–4).

3. See letter 61 note 2; Mrs. Ward published *Out of Due Time* in 1906, and many people thought it was inspired by contemporary problems within the church; she declared, however, that the main character was modeled on Félecité de Lamennais. See *MW* II.239–53.

4. Main character in *Il Santo*, a novel by Antonio Fogazzaro (1842–1911) which was placed on the Index in 1905 for its "liberalism."

5. See letters 63–6.

6. In April 1906 a book of each of three authors was placed on the Index: Lucien Laberthonnière's *Essai de philosophie religieuse* (Paris, 1903) see letter 61, note 3; Ferdinand Brunetière's *La science et la religion* (Paris, 1896); and Paul Marie Viollet's *L'Infaillibilité du Pape et le Syllabus* (Besançon, 1904).

APPENDIX E

Letters to Maria Longworth Storer[1]

31 Farm Street
5 April 1900

Dear Madame Storer,

Just a line to thank you very cordially for your kind notice of *External Religion*.[2] I need not say how completely I am in agreement with the substance of your article,[3] were it not for such little evidences from time to time, of a healthier underground of Catholic-minded Catholicism, one would often feel very hopeless in the face of the strong reactionary party which at present holds all the ecclesiastical power in its tight grip. While this continues we must expect the scandals and apostasies that result from the attempt to oppose an excessive liberalism by an excessive conservatism. Doubtless Dr. Mivart's[4] views demanded his excommunication; but had he not in past years been irritated by senseless and ignorant criticism, he could have easily been kept within the lines. Now, of course, the upshot of the whole affair will be to prove the wrong people abundantly right. 'See' they will say 'what roving views about inspiration and about hell always lead to!'

Let me also thank you for the volumes of Archbishop Ireland's discourses[5] which you and Mr. Storer were good enough to send me a few weeks ago, and which are full of stimulating thought: three or four such men could do much to counteract the lethargic *intransigence* of the majority.

Ever yours faithfully,
G. Tyrrell

31 Farm Street
9 March 1900

Dear Mrs. Storer,

It was immensely kind of you to send such encouraging words; for as you may divine, one who attempts anything like a new departure in method is bound to encounter a great deal of opposition even from good and wise people and at times to be shaken in one's self confidence. But I cannot help feeling that in taking a wider and more sympathetic line I meet the wants of a fairly large and increasing number of Catholics who need a little more breathing space than their forefathers; and for this reason I think I should be let alone as I am willing to let others alone who differ from me.

At present the tension between the old and young, between those who would yield nothing to modernism and can see no good will and those who would yield everything and can see no evil in it, is very acute and dangerous; but such crises are nothing new in the Church's story and are as natural as the periodic sloughing of a snake's skin. We who are more in sympathy with the Catholicism of the next generation than with that of the last are as much factors in the process of growth as the others; for growth means sameness and variety, and the guardians of both interests should tolerate one another seeing the truth is divided between them. I am not at Oxford but only go there at times to give lectures on Sundays. I have great hopes that eventually we shall get much good from Oxford, but at present it is hard to accommodate ourselves after three centuries of isolation and barbarianism.

Ever yours faithfully,
G. Tyrrell SJ

Boutre, Vinon, Var,
3 October 1906

My dear Mrs. Bellamy Storer,

Indeed I remember our correspondence quite well. The kindness of your letter has touched me most profoundly and all I can do is tell you in all simplicity how things stand with me at present, without any attempt to make out that I have been ideally prudent, or theologically infallible; or that there is not heaps to be said on the other side. It was the fact that my sympathies with all those to whom the Jesuits are most opposed had become more and more pronounced and active that made me feel that the position had become a dishonest one for me; especially as I was always getting the English Jesuits into trouble with Rome. I asked for release in February 1904; but was persuaded to wait. Again more strongly last August twelvemonth. Then in deference to my personal Jesuit friends I withdrew the request and left the matter to the General's honor, giving him all my reasons against the Society, yet offering to lay aside my pen if he, in conscience, decided to keep me. Then it was that declining to decide on that ground he took the occasion to dismiss me on account of the insufficiency of my apology for the extracts published in the *Corrière*.[6] The letter to Cardinal Ferrata[7] which I am sending you will explain subsequent events. I am quite sure that under the present Pope and his colleagues representations could only do harm. Were I set right to-day, there would be some new difficulty to-morrow. No bishop, as they are now, would have the courage to give me an *Imprimatur* for my books for which he might receive a reprimand from Rome. For the sake of others it is necessary to stand out against the condition imposed on me; else they would try the same game with the rest of us. Besides the principle is a wrong one. A priest is not a child or an idiot or a minor in law. Meanwhile I have on or about one hundred pounds a year which is enough to live on and to save me from the danger of living to write for pay which is fatal to the quality and sincerity of one's work. I cannot deny that to be deprived of mass and the sacraments is very grievous; but God seems to stand closer in one's trouble; and I think the authors of the outrage are far more to be pitied.

I am fairly sure to be in Paris about the 16th or 17th in which case I should very much like to pay a visit to Versailles. In that case I will send a post card from Aix with the date of my arrival in Paris and the address of my hotel or pension.

I am afraid you have had a great deal of anxiety and pain over Mr. Roosevelt's diplomacies. If we are not embittered by such things we may feel that our Christianity has got roots.

With sincere gratitude for your kind sympathy,

Ever yours faithfully,

G. TYRRELL

23 rue Emeric-David,
Aix en Provence,
11 October 1906

Dear Mrs. Storer,

I cannot thank you enough for your most kind and sympathetic letter. I only hope I did not give you the idea that I am more of a martyr and confessor than I really am. Naturally my letter to Cardinal Ferrata is more or less a bit of special pleading and magnifies my grievance as much as is consistent with perfect truth. Still in some way I stand outside it all as a spectator of my own conflict, and far from being bitter or intolerant find myself only too wanting in that sort of anger which I think a better man would feel in my place. I am perfectly sensible that the clerical mentality of Rome is the result of causes as impersonal as the law of gravitation and almost as necessary. I am as puzzled how to deal with it as if it were some strange epidemic, but I cannot feel 'angry' or 'bitter' against the influenza even though it has struck me down and ruined my constitution. It seems to me that when evils come to a certain pass, they are beyond all human control and that the best we can do is to help them to work themselves out. Have not the tactics of the present Pontificate done more for a living, social, intelligent Catholicism than the feeble half-hearted little 'liberalisings' of Leo XIII? What a complete demonstration they have afforded of the weakness and obsoleteness of mediaeval methods! The root-evil however is hard to cure—I mean, that profound mendacity which is of the very warp and woof of the Roman ecclesiastical mind. One sees more and more the wisdom of the old protestant Anglo-Saxon 'prejudice' against lying. It *may* be only a 'venial' sin, but it indicates a rot at the soul's root like an ill weed on a worthless soil. I have heard from two French archbishops the story of the 'bogus' unanimity against the Separation Law[8]; and one of them said that it had shaken his whole faith to its very foundations. But then again there is no *person* to be angry with but only a vile and ancient tradition of government by fraud and intrigue. You could not persuade Merry del Val that such crookednesses are wrong in the great game of God's cause, though in private life he is probably as honourable as need be. The only remedy is the slow steady spread of knowledge forcing its way even to the darkest corners of seminaries and convents. There the resistance is greatest, but at last it must yield.

And now it is true I should thank you for your most generous and liberal offer of financial help, which I rather defer than decline to accept. I had already thought of an American trip to see my many warm friends over there; but on reflection I felt that this was not the time or occasion. It might look too like a beating-up of adherents and sympathisers or an attempt to make a little faction against authorities. Also, I know how my American friends would forget all prudence and go out of their way to identify themselves with me, and how much harm they might thereby do themselves to no purpose. My great difficulty has been to prevent some of my clerical friends from committing ecclesiastical suicide for my sake and so drowning two instead of one. If the storm should subside and I should ever become comparatively respectable enough to attempt such a tour without harm to others I will not hesitate to ask you to help me should I be in straits at the time. At present I am going to spend the winter as a paying guest with some friends in England and shall probably go about very little, if at all, so that I have no reason to anticipate pecuniary pressure.

There is just a chance after all that I may be able to get to Paris on Thursday (18) evening, in which case, if I am not too train-sick, I would try to see you at Versailles on Friday. I am ashamed of all these changes of plan, but the blame rests with an expected letter that does not arrive and upsets everything by its delay.

With sincere sympathy,

Ever dear Mrs. Storer,

Yours faithfully,

G. TYRRELL.

P.S. I send three copies of the letter.[9] I marked it 'confidential' because if either the letter or the fact of its existence got into the Press, it would give my opponents a technical card against me. So far they are quite wrong from the canon-law point of view. But the *publication* of my correspondence with a Sacred Congregation would put me in the wrong. Otherwise I don't want to make a mystery.

Notes to Appendix E

1. Maria Longworth Storer (b. 1849) was the wife of Bellamy Storer (1847–1922), who was United States Minister to Belgium, then to Spain (after the Spanish-American War) and finally Ambassador to Vienna. They were friends to many different high-ranking people both in the United States and abroad, and were converts to Roman Catholicism. Mrs. Storer, especially, used the rank and power of her husband's office to try to have Archbishop John Ireland made a Cardinal. For more on the relationship between the Storers and Archbishop Ireland see James H. Moynihan, *The Life of Archbishop John Ireland* (New York, 1953). I have not been able to determine why these letters are with the Ward papers.

2. *External Religion: Its Use and Abuse* (London, 1899) see letter 4 note 7).

3. She apparently wrote an article on "Americanism" (see Moynihan, p. 345), but I have been unable to locate it; perhaps it was not published. She did publish poetry later in her life.

4. See letter 7 note 8.

5. Probably some of Ireland's celebrated works, *The Church and the Age* (Baltimore, 1893), and *The Church and Modern Society* (Chicago, 1897), though there is also a "Discourse" for the Columbian Exposition of 1892.

6. See letter 60 note 5.

7. Domenico Ferrata (1847–1914), Prefect for the Congregation of Religious. Open Letter to Cardinal Ferrata (dated 4 July 1906) see letter 65 note 3; he had one hundred and fifty copies printed, but distributed only a few, yet he sent one to the Cardinal numbered 67 (see Schultenover, Epilogue).

8. See letter 64 note 12.

9. His letter to Cardinal Ferrata (see note 7).

Bibliography

I. Specialized Bibliographies

Note: Since most of the works of both Tyrrell and Ward were consulted for the preparation of this book, and since virtually complete bibliographies have been prepared on the writings of both men, the reader is here referred to those bibliographies rather than to a re-listing of works by Tyrrell and Ward.

A. *General*

Burke, Ronald and Gilmore, George. *Current Research in Roman Catholic Modernism.* Mobile: Spring Hill College Press, 1980.

—pp. 34–102 contain an updating of Loome's bibliographic work on primary and secondary sources in England, Germany, Italy and France.

Loome, Thomas Michael. *Liberal Catholicism, Reform Catholicism, Modernism: A Contribution to a New Orientation in Modernist Research.* Tübinger Theologischen Studien, volume 14. Mainz: Matthias Grünewald, 1979.

—pp. 199–359 contain an impressive and helpful list of specialized bibliographies and a catalogue of unpublished sources.

B. *Published Writings of Tyrrell and Ward*

Loome, Thomas Michael. "A Bibliography of the Published Writings of George Tyrrell, 1861–1909." *The Heythrop Journal* 10 (1969):280–314;

———"A Bibliography of the Printed Works of George Tyrrell: Supplement." *The Heythrop Journal* 11 (1970): 161–9.

Weaver, Mary Jo. "A Bibliography of the Published Works of Wilfrid Ward." *The Heythrop Journal* 20 (1979):399–420.

II. Secondary Sources: A Select Bibliography

Abercrombie, Nigel. *The Life and Work of Edmund Bishop*, with a Foreword by David Knowles. London: Longmans, Green and Co., Ltd., 1959.

Altholz, Josef L. *The Liberal Catholic Movement in England.* London: Burns and Oates, 1962.

Barmann, Lawrence F. *Baron Friedrich von Hügel and the Modernist Crisis in England.* Cambridge: The University Press, 1972.

———. "The Heresy of Orthodoxy." *Theology* 71 (1968): 456–62.

———. "Newman and the Theory of Doctrinal Development." *American Ecclesiastical Review* 143 (1960):121–9.

Barry, William F. *Memories and Opinions.* London: G. P. Putnam's Sons, 1926.

———. *Newman.* New York: C. Scribner's, 1904.

Bedoyère, Michael de la. *The Life of Baron von Hügel.* London: J. M. Dent and Sons, Ltd., 1951.

Bella, Julius I. "George Tyrrell's Dogmas." *Church History* 8 (1939):316–41.

Blondel, Maurice. *The Letter on Apologetics and History and Dogma*, translated by Alexander Dru and Illtyd Trethowan. London: Harvill Press, 1964.

Boudens, Robrecht. "George Tyrrell and Cardinal Mercier: A Contribution to the History of Modernism." *Église et Théologie* 1 (1970):313–51.

Braybrooke, Neville. "Wilfrid Ward and Wilfrid Meynell." *The Dublin Review* 228 (1954):46–52.

Bremond, Henri. "La methode apologetique du P. Tyrrell." *Demain* 1 (1906):2–4.

———. *The Mystery of Newman*, translated by H. C. Corrance with a Preface by George Tyrrell. London: Williams and Novak, 1907.

———, ed. *Newman. Le développement du dogme chrétien.* Paris: Bloud, 1906.

Brickel, A. G. "Wilfrid Ward's Life Work." *America* 18 (1917):191–2.

Burke, Ronald. "An Orthodox Modernist with a Modern View of Truth." *The Journal of Religion* 57 (1977):24–43.

Burtchaell, James Tunstead. "The Biblical Question and the English Liberal Catholics." *The Review of Politics* 31 (1969): 108–20.

———. *Catholic Theories of Biblical Inspiration Since 1810: a Review and Critique*. Cambridge: The University Press, 1969.

Caird, Edward. *The Evolution of Religion*. 2 vols. Glasgow: J. MacLehose & Sons, 1893.

Chadwick, Owen. *From Bossuet to Newman: The Idea of Doctrinal Development*. Cambridge: The University Press, 1957.

Chesterton, G. K. "An Appreciation of Wilfrid Ward." *The Dublin Review* 159 (1916):23–32.

Clifford, Cornelius. "Modernism Father George Tyrrell, and Miss M. D. Petre." *The Review of Religion* 3 (1938): 156–65.

Clutton, K. M. "The Death of George Tyrrell." *Modern Churchman* 22 (1932–3):678–86.

Corrance, Henry C., review of Tyrrell's *Christianity at the Cross-Roads. Revue Moderniste Internationale* 1 (1910):35–8.

———. "Modernism." *The Hibbert Journal* 6 (1908): 930–4.

———. "A Vindication of Modernism." *The Nineteenth Century* 43 (1908):311–26.

Cuthbert, Fr. "Apologist of the Catholic Church." *The Dublin Review* 159 (1916):1–22.

Daly, Gabriel, O.S.A. "Some Reflections on the Character of George Tyrrell." *The Heythrop Journal* 10 (1969):256–74.

———. "Tyrrell's 'Medievalism'." *The Month* 230 (1969):15–22.

David, Anne Louis. *Georges Tyrrell: Lettres a Henri Bremond*. Paris: Aubrier, 1971.

Dean, H. S. "Mr. Wilfrid Ward." *The Month* 127 (1916): 461–7.

Dell, Robert. "The Crisis in the Catholic Church." *The Fortnightly Review* 82 (1904):846–60.

———. "George Tyrrell." *The Cornhill Magazine* 27 (1909): 665–75.

———. "A Liberal Catholic View of the Case of Dr. Mivart." *The Nineteenth Century* 47 (1900):669–84.

Dru, Alexander. "From the 'Action française' to the Second Vatican Council." *The Downside Review* 81 (1963):226–45.

———. "The Importance of Maurice Blondel." *The Downside Review* 80 (1962):118–29.

———. "Modernism and the Present Position of the Church." *The Downside Review* 82 (1964):103–10.

Fawkes, Alfred. "Baron Friedrich von Hügel." *The Modern Churchman* 14 (1925):662–6.

———. "Father George Tyrrell." *The Nation* (1909): 601–2.

———. "Modernism: A Retrospect and a Prospect." *The Hibbert Journal* 8 (1909):67–82.

———. "Recent Theories of Development in Theology." *Edinburgh Review* 198 (1903):52–81.

———. *Studies in Modernism.* London: Smith, Elder and Co., 1913.

Gardner, Percy. "M. Alfred Loisy's Type of Catholicism." *The Hibbert Journal* 3 (1904):126–38.

Gerard, John. "The Papal Encyclical: From a Catholic's Point of View." *The Hibbert Journal* 6 (1908):256–63.

Gibson, William. *The Abbé de Lamennais and the Liberal Catholic Movement in France.* London: Longmans, Green and Co., 1896.

Gilley, Sheridan. "Wilfrid Ward and his Life of Newman." *Journal of Ecclesiastical History* 29 (1978):177–93.

Goetz, Joseph. *Analogy and Symbol: A Study in the Theology of George Tyrrell* King's College, Cambridge, 1969 (unpublished dissertation).

———. "Father Tyrrell and the Catholic Crisis." *New Blackfriars* 50 (1969):589–98.

Goodier, Alban, S.J. Review of May's *Father Tyrrell and the Modernist Movement. The Dublin Review* 193 (1932):288–93.

Gore, Charles, ed. *Lux Mundi: a Series of Studies in the Religion of the Incarnation.* From the 5th English edition. New York: J. W. Lovell Co., 1889.

Gruber, Jacob W. *A Conscience in Conflict. The Life of St.*

George Jackson Mivart. New York: Columbia University Press, 1960.

Hanbury, Michael. "The Lesson of Wilfrid Ward." *Pax* 28 (1938):35–40.

———. "Von Hügel and Tyrrell." *The Month* 32 (1964): 323–6.

Hartrett, Thomas P. "A Modernist Ecclesiology: The Relationship of Church and Doctrine in the Writings of George Tyrrell." *Dunwoodie Review* 11 (1971):125–69.

Healey, Charles J., S.J. "Aspects of Tyrrell's Spirituality." *The Downside Review* 97 (1977):133–48.

———. "Tyrrell on the Church." *The Downside Review* 91 (1973):35–50.

Heaney, John J., S.J. "The Enigma of the Later von Hügel." *The Heythrop Journal* 6 (1965):145–59.

———. *The Modernist Crisis: von Hügel*, Washington, D.C.: Corpus Books, 1968.

———. "Von Hügel: The Search for Balance." *Continuum* 3 (1965):178–86.

Himmelfarb, Gertrude. *Victorian Minds. Essays on Nineteenth Century Intellectuals*. New York: Alfred J. Knopf, 1968.

Hogarth, Henry. *Henri Bremond: The Life and Work of a Devout Humanist*. London: S.P.C.K., 1950.

Holland, Bernard, ed. *Baron Friedrich von Hügel: Selected Letters, 1896–1924*, with a memoir by the editor. London: J. M. Dent and Sons, Ltd., 1928.

Holmes, J. Derek. "Cardinal Raphael Merry del Val—An Uncompromising Ultramontane: Gleanings from his Correspondence with England." *Catholic Historical Review* 60 (1974):55–64.

———. *More Roman than Rome: English Catholicism in the Nineteenth Century*. Shepherdstown: Patmos Press, 1978.

———. "Notes on Liberal Catholicism and Catholic Modernism." *Irish Theological Quarterly* 38 (1971):348–57.

———. *The Triumph of the Holy See. A Short History of the Papacy in the Nineteenth Century*. Shepherdstown: Patmos Press, 1978.

———, and Murray, Robert. *Newman—On the Inspiration of Scripture*. London: Geoffrey Chapman, 1967.

Houtin, Albert. *La Crise de Clergé*. Paris: Emile Nourry, 1907.

———. *Histoire du Modernisme Catholique.* Paris: Chez l'Auteur, 1913.

———. *The Life of a Priest: My Own Experience, 1867–1912,* translated by Winifred Stephens Whale. London: Watts and Co., 1927.

———. *La Question biblique chez les catholiques de France au XIXe siècle.* Paris: Alphonse Picard et Fils, 1902.

Hügel, Friedrich von. "The Death-Bed of Father Tyrrell." *The Tablet* 114 (1909):182.

———. "Eudoxe Irenée Mignot." *The Contemporary Review* 113 (1918):519–26.

———. "Father Tyrrell." *The Tablet* 120 (1912):866–7.

———. "Father Tyrrell: Some Memorials of the Last Twelve Years of His Life." *The Hibbert Journal* 8 (1910):233–52.

———. "The Late Father Tyrrell and the Faith." *The Tablet* 114 (1909):738.

Hughes, Philip. "The Coming Century." *English Catholics 1850–1950,* edited by George Andrew Beck. London: Burns, Oates; 1950.

Inge, W. R. "The Meaning of Modernism." *The Quarterly Review* 210 (1909):571–603.

Kelly, Edward E. "Newman More Ecumenically Read." *Journal of Ecumenical Studies* 5 (1968):365–70.

———. "Newman, Wilfrid Ward and the Modernist Crisis." *Thought* 48 (1973):509–19.

Laberthonnière, Lucien. "La question de méthode en apologetique." *Annales de philosophie chrétienne* 2 (1906): 500–15.

Lacey, T. A. *Harnack and Loisy,* with an Introduction by Lord Halifax. London: Longmans, Green and Co., 1904.

Lash, Nicholas L. A. "Can a Methodologist Keep the Faith?" *Irish Theological Quarterly* 38 (1971):91–102.

———. "Development of Doctrine: Smokescreen or Explanation?" *New Blackfriars* 52 (1971):101–8.

———. "Faith and History: Some Reflections on Newman's 'Essay on the Development of Christian Doctrine'." *Irish Theological Quarterly* 38 (1971):224–41.

———. "Modernism, Aggiornamento and the Night Battle." *Bishops and Writers: Aspects of the Evolution of Modern Catholicism,* edited by Adrian Hastings. Wheathampstead: A. Clarke, 1977.

———. *Newman on Development: The Search for an Explanation in History.* Shepherdstown: Patmos Press, 1975.

Laubacher, James A. "*Dogma and the Development of Dogma in the Writings of George Tyrrell, 1861–1909.*" Louvain, 1939.

Lease, Gary. "Merry del Val and Tyrrell's Condemnation." *Annual Papers of the Roman Catholic Modernism Group in the American Academy of Religion*: 1979, 25–63.

Lebreton, Jules, S.J. "Origine et développement du Christianisme d'après F. Heiler et George Tyrrell." *Recherches de science religieuse* 28 (1938):482–96.

Lilley, A. L. "L'Affaire Loisy." *The Commonwealth* 8 (1903): 73–6.

———. "Modernism." *Encyclopaedia of Religion and Ethics* 8, edited by James Hastings. Edinburgh: T. and T. Clark, 1916. Pp. 763–8.

———. *Modernism: A Record and Review.* London: Sir Isaac Pitman and Sons, Ltd., 1908.

———, ed. *The Programme of Modernism.* London: T. Fisher Unwin, 1908.

———. "A Real Catholicism." *The Interpreter* 6 (1910): 264–77.

———. "The Religion of George Tyrrell." *The Commonwealth* 14 (1909):361–4.

———. "Roman Catholic Modernism." *The Modern Churchman* 17 (1927):333–44.

———. "A Roman Catholic Protest Against the Recent Vatican Policy." *The Commonwealth* 11 (1906):216–20.

———, trans. *What We Want: An Open Letter to Pius X.* London: John Murray, 1907.

Loisy, Alfred Firmin. *Autour d'un Petit Livre.* Paris: A. Picard, 1903.

———. *Choses Passées.* Paris: Émile Nourry, 1913.

———. "La Définition de la Religion." *Revue du clergé français* 18 (1899): 193–209.

———. "Le Développement Chrétien d'après le Cardinal Newman." *Revue de clergé français* 17 (1898):5–20.

———. *L'Évangile et l'Église.* Paris: A. Picard et Fils, 1902.

———. *George Tyrrell et Henri Bremond.* Paris: Émile Nourry, 1936.

———. "L'Idée de la Révélation." *Revue du clergé français* 21 (1900):250–71.

———. *Mémoires pour servir a l'histoire religieuse de notre temps*, 3 vols. Paris: Émile Nourry, 1930–1.

———. "Les Preuves et l'Economie de la Révélation." *Revue du clergé français* 22 (1900): 126–53.

———. "La Théorie Individualiste de la Religion." *Revue du clergé français* 17 (1899): 202–15.

Loome, Thomas Michael. "The Enigma of Baron Friedrich von Hügel—as Modernist." *The Downside Review* 91 (1973): 13–34, 123–40, 204–30.

———. "The Meanings of Modernism." *The Tablet* 225 (1971): 544–7.

———. " 'Revelation as Experience': An Unpublished Lecture of George Tyrrell, edited with notes and historical introduction." *The Heythrop Journal* 12 (1971): 117–49.

———. "Tyrrell's Letters to André Raffalovich." *The Month* 229 (1970): 95–101, 138–49.

Lunn, Arnold. *Roman Converts.* London: Chapman & Hall, 1925.

Maignen, C. *Études sur l'Americanisme. Le Père Hecker est-il un saint?* Rome: Desclée, Lefebvre et Cie; Paris: V. Retaux, 1899.

Major, H. D. A. "George Tyrrell." *Great Christians*, edited by R. S. Forman. London: I. Nicholson and Watson, 1934.

———. "In Memoriam—Alfred Fawkes." *Modern Churchman* 20 (1930): 437–41.

Marlé, René. *Au coeur de la crise moderniste.* Paris: Aubrier, 1960.

May, J. Lewis. *Father Tyrrell and the Modernist Movement.* London: Burns, Oates and Washbourne, Ltd., 1938.

Merry del Val, Rafael. *Memories of Pope Pius X.* Forewords by Cardinal Hinsley and Cardinal Hayes. London: Burns, Oates and Washbourne, Ltd., 1939.

Misner, Paul. "Newman's Concept of Revelation and the Development of Doctrine." *The Heythrop Journal* 11 (1970): 32–47.

Mivart, St. George Jackson. "The Catholic Church and Biblical Criticism." *The Nineteenth Century* 22 (1887): 31–51.

———. "The Continuity of Catholicism." *The Nineteenth Century* 47 (1900): 51–72.

———. "Happiness in Hell." *The Nineteenth Century* 32 (1892): 899–919.

———. "The Happiness in Hell: A Rejoinder." *The Nineteenth Century* 33 (1893):320–38.

———. "The Index and My Articles on Hell." *The Nineteenth Century* 34 (1893):979–90.

———. "Last Words on the Happiness in Hell." *The Nineteenth Century* 33 (1893):637–51.

———. "The Roman Catholic Church and the Dreyfus Case," *The Times* (17 Oct. 1899):13–14.

———. "Roman Congregations and Modern Thought." *North American Review* 170 (1900):562–74.

———. "Some Recent Catholic Apologists." *The Fortnightly Review* 67 (1900):24–44.

———. "What Church Has 'Continuity'?" *The Nineteenth Century* 46 (1899):203–12.

Moyes, James. "Modernism and the Papal Encyclical." *The Nineteenth Century* 62 (1907):865–78.

Murphy, J. "Dr. Mivart on Faith and Science." *The Dublin Review* 19 (1888):400–11.

Newman, John Henry Cardinal. *Apologia pro Vita Sua: being a History of his Religious Opinions.* London: Longmans, Green & Co., 1885.

———. *An Essay on the Development of Christian Doctrine.* London: J. Toovey, 1845.

———. *Fifteen Sermons Preached before the University of Oxford.* London: J. Rivingtons, 1872.

———. *Lectures on the Present Position of Catholics in England.* London: Burns & Lambert, 1851.

———. *Loss and Gain. The Story of a Convert.* London: J. Burns, 1848.

———. *Parochial and Plain Sermons.* 8 vols. London: Rivingtons, 1868.

———. *The Via Media of the Anglican Church. Illustrated in Lectures, Letters, and Tracts Written Between 1830 and 1841.* 2 vols. London: B. M. Pickering, 1877.

Newsom, G. E. "George Tyrrell." *The Church Quarterly Review* 69 (1909):114–45.

O'Connor, Francis M., S.J. "The Concept of Revelation in the Writings of George Tyrrell." Unpublished dissertation, Paris, 1963.

———. "George Tyrrell and Dogma." *The Downside Review* 85 (1965):13–34, 160–82.

———. "Tyrrell: The Nature of Revelation." *Continuum* 3 (1965):168–77.

———. "Tyrrell's Cross-Roads." *The Heythrop Journal* 5 (1965):188–91.

O'Dwyer, Bishop Edward Thomas. *Cardinal Newman and the Encyclical "Pascendi Dominici Gregis"*. London: Longmans, Green & Co., 1908.

Osborne, Charles E. "Father George Tyrrell." *T.P.'s Weekly* 7 (1909):213.

———. "Father Tyrrell: Some Impressions by an Anglican Friend." *The Church Times* 62 (1909):121.

———. "George Tyrrell. A Friend's Impressions." *The Hibbert Journal* 8 (1910):253–63.

———. *The Life of Father Dolling*. London: E. Arnold, 1903.

Petre, M. D. "The Advantages and Disadvantages of Authority in Religion." *The Hibbert Journal* 12 (1914): 295–305.

———. "Alfred Fawkes." *Modern Churchman* 20 (1930): 542–3.

———. "Alfred Loisy (1857–1940)." *Theology* 41 (1940): 132–40.

———. *Alfred Loisy: His Religious Significance*. Cambridge: The University Press, 1944.

———. *Autobiography and Life of George Tyrrell*. 2 vols. London: Edward Arnold, 1912.

———. *Catholicism and Independence: Being Studies in Spiritual Liberty*. London: Longmans, Green and Co., 1907.

———. "Friedrich von Hügel, Personal Thoughts and Reminiscences." *The Hibbert Journal* 24 (1925):77–87.

———. "George Tyrrell and Friedrich von Hügel in Their Relation to Catholic Modernism." *The Modern Churchman* 17 (1927):143–54.

———. *George Tyrrell's Letters*. London: T. Fisher Unwin, 1920.

———. *Modernism: Its Failures and Its Fruits*. London: T. C. and E. C. Jack, Ltd., 1918.

———. *My Way of Faith*. London: J. M. Dent and Sons, Ltd., 1937.

———. "New Wine in Old Bottles." Review of May's *Father Tyrrell and the Modernist Movement*. *Modern Churchman* 22 (1932):212–8.

———. "A Religious Movement of the First Years of Our Century." *Horizon* 6 (1942):328–40.

———. *The Soul's Orbit, or Man's Journey to God.* London: Longmans, Green and Co., 1904.

———. "Still At It: The Impasse of Modern Christology." *The Hibbert Journal* 20 (1922):401–10.

———. "Von Hügel and the Great Quest." *Modern Churchman* 21 (1931):475–83.

———. *Von Hügel and Tyrrell: The Story of a Friendship.* London: J. M. Dent and Sons, Ltd., 1937.

Pittenger, W. Norman. "Modernism." *Theology* 68 (1965): 53–60.

Pole, Dom Fabian. "A Great Liaison Officer of the Catholic Church." *The Downside Review* 53 (1935):153–63.

Poulat, Émile. *Histoire, dogme et critique dans la crise moderniste.* Paris: Casterman, 1962.

———, ed. A. Houtin and F. Sartiaux. *Alfred Loisy: sa vie et son oeuvre.* Paris: Editions du Centre National de la Researche Scientifique, 1960.

Ratté, John. *Three Modernists: Alfred Loisy, George Tyrrell, William L. Sullivan.* London: Sheed and Ward, 1968.

Reardon, Bernard M. G. "Liberal Protestantism and Roman Catholic Modernism." *The Modern Churchman* 13 (1969): 72–86.

———. "The Modernist Movement in Retrospect." *The Ampleforth Journal* 75 (1970):213–21.

———, ed. "Newman and the Catholic Modernist Movement." *Church Quarterly* 4 (1971):50–60.

———. *Roman Catholic Modernism.* London: Adam and Charles Black, 1970.

Rivière, Jean. "Modernisme." *Dictionnaire de théologie catholique.* Vol. 10. (1929):2009–47.

———. *Le Modernisme dans l'Église.* Paris: Librarie Letouzey et Ané, 1929.

Rollmann, Hans. "Baron Friedrich von Hügel's *Mystical Element of Religion.* Reviewed by Himself." *The Downside Review* 97 (1979):304–7.

———. "Holtzman, von Hügel, and Modernism, I, II." *The Downside Review* 97 (1979):128–43; 221–44.

———. "Troeltsch, von Hügel, and Modernism." *The Downside Review* 96 (1978):35–60.

Root, John D. "English Catholic Modernism and Science: The Case of George Tyrrell." *The Heythrop Journal* 18 (1977):271–88.

———. "George Tyrrell and the Synthetic Society." *The Downside Review* 98 (1980):42–59.

Sabatier, Auguste. *The Vitality of Christian Dogmas and Their Power of Evolution.* Trans. Mrs. Emmanuel Christen. London: Macmillan, 1898.

Sabatier, Paul. "Modernism." *The Contemporary Review* 93 (1908):300–7.

———. *Modernism: The Fowett Lectures, 1908.* Trans. C. A. Miles. London: T. Fisher Unwin, 1908.

———. *Les Modernistes.* Paris: Fishbacher, 1909.

———. "De la situation religieuse de l'Église catholique romaine en France, à l'heure actuelle." *The Hibbert Journal* 9 (1910):1–14.

Schoenl, William J. "English Liberal Catholicism in the Early 1890's" *The Clergy Review* 62 (1977):92–105.

———. "George Tyrrell and the English Liberal Catholic Crisis, 1900–1901." *The Downside Review* 92 (1974): 171–84.

Schultenover, David G. *George Tyrrell: In Search of Catholicism.* Shepherdstown: Patmos Press, 1981.

Smith, Sydney F., S.J. "The 'Edinburgh Review' on Cardinal Newman." *The Month* 119 (1912):561–78.

———. "What is 'Modernism'?" *The Month* 111 (1908):284–301.

Smith, Warren Sylvester. "George Tyrrell and the Modernist." *The Christian Century* 80 (1963):490–2.

Stewart, Herbert Leslie. *Modernism, Past and Present.* London: John Murray, 1932.

———. "Wilfrid Ward." *The Hibbert Journal* 18 (1919):61–73.

———. "Wilfrid Ward's Reconciling Attitude." *Constructive Quarterly* 8 (1920):182–92.

Swidler, Leonard. "Liberal Catholicism—A Lesson from the Past." *Cross Currents* 21 (1971):25–37.

Thureau-Dangin, Paul. *The English Catholic Revival in the 19th Century.* 2 vols. New York: E. P. Dutton, 1899.

Trevor, Meriol. *Newman: Light in Winter.* New York: Doubleday, 1969.

———. *Newman: The Pillar of the Cloud.* New York: Doubleday, 1969.

———. *Prophets and Guardians: Renewal and Tradition in the Church.* London: Hollis and Carter, 1969.

———. "Who Were the Modernists?" *New Blackfriars* 49 (1968):600–8.

Vaughan, Herbert Cardinal. "The Church and Liberal Catholicism: Joint Pastoral." *The Tablet* 97 (1901):8–12, 50–2.

Vidler, Alec R. *The Modernist Movement in the Roman Church.* Cambridge: The University Press, 1934.

———. Review of M. D. Petre's *Alfred Loisy. The Journal of Theological Studies* 45 (1944):234–7.

———. *A Variety of Catholic Modernists.* Cambridge: The University Press, 1971.

Ward, Josephine. "Introductory Study." *Last Lectures by Wilfrid Ward.* London: Longsman, Green and Co., 1918.

Ward, Maisie. *Insurrection versus Resurrection.* London: Sheed and Ward, 1937.

———. "W. G. Ward and Wilfrid Ward." *The Dublin Review* 198 (1936):235–52.

———. "Wilfrid Ward and Tennyson." *Commonweal* 21 (1934):87–8.

———. *The Wilfrid Wards and the Transition.* London: Sheed and Ward, 1934.

———. *Young Mr. Newman.* London: Sheed and Ward, 1948.

Weaver, Mary Jo. "George Tyrrell and the Joint Pastoral Letter." *The Downside Review* 99 (1981).

———. "Wilfrid Ward, George Tyrrell and the Meanings of Modernism." *The Downside Review* 96 (1978):21–34.

———. "A Working Catalogue of the Ward Family Papers." *Recusant History* 15 (1979):43–71.

Webb, Clement C. J. *Religious Thought in the Oxford Movement.* New York: Macmillan, 1928.

Wells, David F. "George Tyrrell: Precursor of Process Theology." *Scottish Journal of Theology* 26 (1973):71–84.

———. "The Pope as Antichrist: The Substance of George Tyrrell's Polemic." *Harvard Theological Review* 65 (1972): 271–83.

Wetmore, Louis. "Wilfrid Philip Ward, Victorian." *America* 15 (1916):35–7.
Williams, W. J. *Newman, Pascal, Loisy and the Catholic Church.* London: Francis Griffiths, 1906.

Index

A Note on the Type

The text of this book was set by phototypesetting in Baskerville, a modern rendering of the typeface cut by John Baskerville in the 17th century. Baskerville approached the creation of a new letterform from an entirely different point of view from that of previous designers of his day. Upon the introduction of his types, the printing world suddenly lost interest in "old style" faces such as Caslon. Without previous experience in type designing, he startled the world by becoming the father of "modern" roman type.

This book was composed and printed by York Composition Company and bound by the Maple Press Company of York, Pennsylvania.

Book design by Howard N. King